"In VOICES FROM THE COSMOS, Drs. Scott Jones and Angela Smith provide detailed transcripts of remote viewing/telepathic interviews with members of 18 extraterrestrial (ET) races, including the Large Grays, Nordics, Small Grays, Annunaki and others. These interviews provide answers to some of the perennial ET questions such as: "Who are they? Where are they from? What, if anything, is their agenda? Are they friendly or unfriendly? Do they have an interest and stake in sound human development processes on Earth?" etc.

Also addressed in the book is the ET link with the Outer Space Security and Development Treaty. This treaty bans all space-based weapons and at their request, Cosmic Cultures are identified as Parties to the treaty. Crafted by Jones, Dr. Carol Rosin, Astronaut Edgar Mitchell, and other colleagues, it is clear the ETs are concerned with keeping space a weapon-free zone. It is a safe assumption that the ETs can easily verify the Treaty is being honored. Their request to be included in the Treaty is a very positive sign that other cooperative ventures are in our future.

The authors are joined by the ETs in a call for a pre-disclosure dialogue on the anticipated consequences of established contact, and a detailed plan of how this can be accomplished is provided. Academe at all levels must play a leading role.

The book is a must read for UFOLOGISTS, Exopolitics analysts and all other planetary citizens, both new and experienced with the subject."

—Bill Wickersham, Ed.D., Adjunct Professor of Peace Studies,
University of Missouri – Columbia

"As cosmic knowledge, reality and truth unfolds a host of human beliefs and assumptions will be challenged. In over fifty-years of working with ET experiencers, I have concluded that the contact event can result in a number of positive outcomes. I consider this book to be one of those positive outcomes. Drs. Jones and Smith have drawn from a lifetime of contact and moved into a rich, largely unexplored area of research. Direct communication and dialogue with sentient life in the cosmos that is complex, ancient, and apparently waiting for the opportunity to tell their stories. Followers of this field and those who are ready to join this enlightened community will be fascinated by what the little Grays say about what most earth authors call abductions and the purpose of them. These "take and return" operations are to produce a hybrid race of pioneers that explores and settles throughout multiple universes.

These two authors are uncommon in their contributions that come from both heart and mind. Their combined experience supports critical assessment of the Planetary Plight and the activities of military and government leaders. This is presented with courage, competence and compassion. The huge bonus of this book is the unfiltered voices from the cosmos. Listen to them – they are willing to share."

—R. Leo Sprinkle, Ph.D., Professor Emeritus,
Counseling Services, University of Wyoming

VOICES FROM THE COSMOS

C. B. Scott Jones Ph.D.
& Angela T. Smith Ph.D.

"There are as many other races as stars in the sky."
—Large Gray

Headline Books, Inc.
Terra Alta, WV

Voices From The Cosmos

by C. B. Scott Jones Ph.D. and Angela T. Smith Ph.D.

To order additional copies of this book or for book publishing information, or to contact the authors:

Headline Books, Inc.
P.O. Box 52
Terra Alta, WV 26764
www.headlinebooks.com
800-570-5951

ISBN 13: 9780938467960

Library of Congress Control Number: 2014936897

PRINTED IN THE UNITED STATES OF AMERICA

Contents

Dedication

C. B. Scott Jones & Angela T. Smith

The subject of this book has been carefully and deliberately ignored by academe in the United States and throughout the world. We will discuss this in one of our chapters and how that situation must be changed. Among the few academics that recognized how important the subject is, none stood taller than John E. Mack M.D., professor at Harvard Medical School. John and Scott met before John knew anything about humans interacting with ETs. Their first connection was over the message that the Cold War sent. The global policies of the US and the USSR were being manipulated to assure continuing war economies with unpredictable military risks. When Scott learned that John was involved with individuals reporting ET contact, a visit to Cambridge was made and subsequently Scott recommended to Lawrence Rockefeller that John's work should be financially supported. This resulted in his first book on the subject in 1994, *Abduction: Human Encounters with Aliens.* John was later invited to be a speaker at the May 1995 *When Cosmic Cultures Meet* conference in Washington, D.C. It was not known at the time that he was under vicious attack by the Dean of Harvard Medical School, Daniel C. Tosteson. The committee that Tosteson appointed to confidentially investigate John's clinical care was not deemed to be disciplinary and therefore John was not protected by the normal university rules of procedure. John was not told of the nature of the complaints against him until eight months after the investigation started. The plan was to intimidate him, to stop his work on a subject fearful to his detractors. When the work of the committee became known, other Harvard faculty became concerned because no charges of professional misconduct or ethical violations were involved. The Rockefeller support of Mack at this time was most important. After fourteen months of this attack, the Dean "reaffirmed Dr. Mack's academic freedom to study what he wishes and to state his opinions without impediments." Harvard's other tenured professors sighed in relief, and the non-tenured professors continued to trudge down the status quo road.

When John came to the May 1995 conference he was exhausted but gave a reasonable presentation. While the proceedings of the conference were being edited prior to being published, John called Scott and asked if he could replace the talk he gave in Washington, D.C. with one he had subsequently given after he had regained his normal drive and energy. This was agreed to and a paper full of insights was published that showed John's personal transformation. This was abundantly shown in his next and last book, *Passport to the Cosmos: Human Transformation and Alien Encounters.*

John has given us some pithy quotes addressing his discoveries. Two of our favorites are: "The alien abduction phenomenon appears to be kind of spiritual outreach program from the cosmos for the spiritually impaired," You will remember that one when you read later in this book what the interviewed ETs say about abductions. And finally, "UFOs are outreach to the consciousness-impaired." John was comfortable with the reality that consciousness was non-local, and wondrously shared throughout the cosmos.

For all good reasons we dedicate this book to John E. Mack who somewhere we are sure is delighted that the envelope of understanding is still being expanded, and to academics such as Bill Wickersham at the University of Missouri who, still in harness, has survived much and with true grit points a bright light to the future.

Foreword

C. B. Scott Jones

This book is about communicating: verbal and non-verbal communications. There will be nothing new presented about the physical and mental "mechanics" of communication, but some details may be new to many even though they are ancient in practice and clearly important to survival. Long before the beginning of written communications and the advent of technologically supported communication, indigenous cultures were communicating well beyond the limits of sight and sound. The evidence of this is robust in that some remaining indigenous cultures still practice this art and credit the learning to their ancestors.

We open with this snippet of information because the majority of what is ahead for the reader was obtained by communicating in this ancient way. Current labels for this form of communication include telepathy for the exchange of thoughts and ideas, remote viewing for exchange of graphic material and events; and the very efficient modality of loaning your voice for someone communicating from a distance. This, of course, is known as channeling. Both authors have used these human technologies in their personal and professional lives. It has served them well. These skills are resident in every conscious being and Smith has taught many to become remote viewers. However, it is as much as remembering as learning anew.

The importance of the information garnered by these techniques is a decision for each reader to make. We ask you to answer that for multiple levels. The first answer we ask you to seek is personal. What does this information mean to YOU? The second level is what does this information mean for the world, our planet, and all life on it?

It should not surprise you that the authors' focus and concerns are about what these communications, this information means to Earth and all life supported by our beautiful blue orb. That concern and hope will surface throughout the pages ahead.

Chapter One
Introduction
C. B. Scott Jones

Hip deep into the Information Age, there is no shortage of ways to move information around the world, and even into deep space. The prime mover of this information is business. The success of global marketing strategies is dependent upon effective global communications. Rivaling business investment in communications is the world's military investment in communication infrastructure.

The plethora of personal communication devices is staggering. Equally so are the number of hours spend texting to "keep in touch."The World Wide Web has become a depository of stale and irrelevant information. It is a "digital dump" that appears to live forever because there is no flushing mechanism.

But not everything can be found on the World Wide Web. Critical attention is given to protect investment and proprietary business secrets. Every country is seriously concerned about keeping its own secrets and finding out the secrets of others. This is an ancient game.

And there is a very interesting category of information that has been of high interest to a few, and of extreme importance to a much smaller group to keep out of all forms of communications. With confidence we can say that those who do not want any discussion about this subject are the masters of global finances. For them it is a simple issue. A global dialogue about this subject will directly threaten their power and profit.

For the few who are very much in favor of a global dialogue about this subject, the issue is also simple but not with an agenda of gaining power and profit. The agenda is to show the world's population that there is a non-violent way to change the status quo that egregiously favors the few to a new situation that brings full relief to a planet in peril and a population enduring great hardships. This is not a fantasy. It will be a test of the power of truth, of the knowledge that we are not alone, and have never been alone!

In following chapters the flower of this book will be in full bloom when you read the transcripts of communications with a spectrum of cosmic cultures. The most recent estimates of the number of planets in our galaxy that are in what astronomers call the "Goldilocks Zone," a region just right for life as we know it, is about 20 billion. What you will read in our modest sample on this issue suggests another number. We find the metaphor they use to answer that question to be a gentle wakeup call: "How many grains of sand are there?" Obviously, the assumption that the "Goldilocks Zone" is relevant to life in the Cosmos deserves more thought.

Food for that thought is ahead when you hear from, for example, the Orbs who are present throughout the Universe and appear as balls of light. By the natural laws of the Universe they are sentient, have a mission, and enjoy communicating with Humans. As they will tell you, and this is confirmed by other Cosmic Cultures, communicating is their mission. They are not shy and are easily photographed. The reason for this jump ahead information about one friendly and useful cosmic entity is to shift the subject to challenges encountered when talking about the unknown, and what we have tried to do to add to the subject list new things that are timely and important to talk about. That effort is a bumpy road, and Fyodor Dostoyevsky nailed it years ago when he observed that change is "what people fear the most."

Plan C and its Antecedences

The first really significant effort to try to start a dialogue about Earth/Extraterrestrial relationships developed when Mr. Lawrence Rockefeller asked me to develop a strategy to engage the Clinton administration to request a review of the policy they inherited from previous administrations concerning saying anything about UFOs and ETs. The objective was to encourage President Clinton to change the policy that appeared to be one of secrecy, denial and disinformation. Historically, although it was never referred to by that name, this was Plan A: a direct approach to the White House through the President's Science Advisor, Dr. John Gibbons.

Shortly after 07:30 on April 14, 1993, in the first meeting in the Executive Office Building west of the White House, Gibbon's opening statement was that he knew nothing about the subject.

This was an astonishing comment and known to be less than the truth for two reasons. The first was that I had known Gibbons for six years when I was Special Assistant to Senator Claiborne Pell and Gibbons was the director of the Office of Technology Assessment, a Congressional Think Tank. Senator Pell was one of six Senators on the advisory group of the OTA and I prepared Pell for all OTA meetings. I developed a close relationship with OTA staff members and learned from them that when Gibbons was with the Congressional Research Service (CRS) at the Library of Congress, he supervised Marcia Smith who was Director Science and Technology Division of the CRS. In that capacity Smith had produced both unclassified and classified reports on UFO phenomena and extraterrestrial intelligence.

The second reason was more current and relevant. Gibbons had sufficient time and direct access to the CIA to receive a briefing on the subject. However, the CIA failed to deliver it in time for the meeting, and Gibbons was in an embarrassing position. Mr. Rockefeller responded to Gibbons with what can be labeled as a spontaneous Plan B when he told Gibbons that he had considered taking out a full- page ad in all of the nation's largest newspapers urging citizens to write and phone the White House requesting the President to tell the truth about UFOs. Gibbons was stunned and quickly responded that this would not be necessary, that he was ready to work with us, and he asked what Mr. Rockefeller wanted.

We had anticipated being asked this question, and a short shopping list that included the famous Roswell incident was in hand. While Roswell was not the first on the list, Rockefeller turned to me and simply said "Roswell". He had decided to go for the gold and in a euphoric blunder I agreed with him. Before I could comment, Gibbons recovered and said the Secretary of the Air Force was a personal friend and he was confident that she would direct a thorough search for all documents about Roswell and make them available to the public.

The resulting "Final Report on Roswell" was a sad effort to explain how some highly classified projects of that era could have been misinterpreted as an otherworldly event. The forward to the report proudly stated that the Secretary of the Air Force had waved all security restrictions related to the Roswell incident. The lesson we learned was that the gatekeepers of knowledge about the significance of Earth/ET contact will never allow the relatively insignificant Roswell event to be used as a crowbar to leverage the truth.

In retrospect, there was one idea on our short list of requests for the White House to do that could have made a difference. President Clinton and his Chief of Staff, John Podesta, were both publicly known to be personally interested in the subject of extraterrestrial life. The plan was to have Podesta in one of his public speeches make a comment that he found the subject to be most interesting and intellectually challenging. This would be staged before a scheduled Clinton press conference. A friendly reporter would be primed to ask the President if he agreed with what his Chief of Staff had said. He would respond that he completely agreed and hoped that some university would take up the challenge to do a White Paper on what we know about the subject and to look into the future when there is no doubt about contact, and what that will mean to the world. That would have provided a modest level of political cover that we subsequently learned was absolutely necessary to get the academic community into the game.

The formal Plan C has gone through several evolutions and is global in scope. In summary it involved inviting major universities around the world to research and write a White Paper that assessed the challenges and opportunities that formal disclosure of Earth/Extraterrestrial contact would present to their country and culture. It was to be a view of an accepted future without need to argue if or when that future would occur. Early in discussing this concept with academic friends at U.S. universities the point was repeatedly made that some evidence of the potential reality of such a future would be necessary before anyone would agree that the effort was worthwhile to undertake. Some used the lack of success of the SETI program to detect any electronic signal from a putative ET source as a reason not to worry too much about contact. This was effectively countered by the suggestion that when a qualifying signal was received it would not likely contain any information about who sent it and what it meant. At that point there would be a scramble to consider a future that Plan C anticipated. A few remembered the sarcastic comment from Senator Richard Bryan (R-NV) when the NASA SETI program was defunded, "This hopefully will be the end of Martian hunting season at the taxpayer's expense." SETI has survived by virtue of private funding and they do have a protocol for informing certain groups if they receive a signal believed to come from extraterrestrial sources.

To meet the need of relevance of the proposed White Paper, several short paragraphs were added to the invitation letter sent to universities that noted the oral histories and creation stories of indigenous cultures, the sacred literature of India – including the Mahabharata and the Ramayana, and the archeological evidence from Sumer. For the modern era the extraordinary number of global sighting by qualified observers of aerial craft that do not match publicly known flying objects was presented. An offer was made to discuss this subject in detail if an invitation to visit the university was made.

During the period August 2008 – November 2008, twenty-six of the world's premier universities were contacted by mail and Email inviting them to participate in PEACE Inc's Sustainable Peace and Development (SPD) program and Plan C. Each was offered $100,000 to research and write a White Paper on the consequences to their country and culture of disclosure of extraterrestrial contact with Earth. Only two, the University of Queensland, and the University of Melbourne in Australia, responded to this correspondence, both indicating that they would not participate. . A five-page outline of the White Paper was prepared and sent in a follow up letter one month after the first letter was sent. The last three of these pages provided evidential information that the U.S. government was seriously concerned about what UFOs represented.

Personal visits were made to the University of Missouri in Columbia, and the University of Texas – Pan America (Edinburg, Texas), where meetings were held with administrators at the Dean level and a few faculty members. Neither of these two universities was willing to become involved with Plan C. The University of Missouri did adopt the Sustainable Peace and Development (SPD) program. Two Deans provided helpful feedback. Fear of the consequences flowing from involvement with the ET subject was the controlling issue. One Dean observed, "Without political cover, we would lose funding from all of our traditional sources if we touched that third-rail."

Fear of consequence trumped the vision of any possible positive outcome from doing the work. A change in Plan C was made to try a direct approach to the students. The Annual Graduate Student Essay Challenge on Consequences of Disclosure and Contact was added to the website and sent to the original twenty-six universities requesting them to disseminate to the Department level.

Requirements: From an accredited university, certification from an academic department head that a minimum of ten graduate students will participate in the essay challenge; that the essays will meet the university's academic standards for graduate work and will receive earned academic credit. All traditional academic departments, e.g., sociology, history, economics, history, political science, philosophy, psychology, biology, and anthropology, are eligible.

Annually, at each participating university, a prize of $1,000 will be awarded to one student writing the winning 4-5 thousand-word essay on the following subject: "**Sociological** Consequences in **Vietnam** of Disclosure of Earth/Extraterrestrial Contact." (The example given illustrates a specific academic department in a specific country. The academic discipline and the country in bold font are obviously variables.)

Each academic department will judge the essays done in its discipline, ranking each entry. All entries will be sent to P.E.A.C.E. Inc where a committee of Exopolitics professionals will grade the top four essays for all departments. One winner will be selected based upon the skill of using exopolitical data in research.

The winning essay will be judged a second time in competition with other winning essays from other universities. A second $1,000 prize will be awarded in that competition.

Entries may be submitted in any language, but must also be translated into English.

There was no response. This idea can be improved upon by opening it up to undergraduate students.

Lessons learned from the failure of direct approach to academe, administration, faculty and students, suggested that a strategy designed to engage elite groups might result in the creation of political cover that would make it safe for academe to get involved, and to provide a cultural sensitive foundation for a global dialogue.

The Cosmic Humanity Briefing

To implement this new strategy, Neil Freer and I created a three-part presentation designed to provide the evidence of ancient contact, modern era contact and dialogue on meaning and needful action. In April 2011, I had the first opportunity to present this briefing at three venues in India. The briefing is designed to be presented by two persons over a two-day period. However, Freer could not make the trip to India, and the presentation had to be edited to fit three different time periods scheduled at the three venues.

Personal contacts in India were recruited to assist in arranging briefing venues in Pune and New Delhi, India. The first presentation was at the Maharashtra Institute of Technology (MIT) at Pune. The senior scientist at the Centre for Biofield Sciences, Dr. R.N. Shukla, Ph.D., D.Sc., D.LIT. was my formal host. He had invited ten of his personal scientist friends for the presentation. One of these was Dr. Deglurkar, who is Vice Chancellor, Deccan College. He insisted after the successful MIT presentation that I accompany him to his school to make a second presentation. Dr. Deglurkar called ahead and we were met by some of his senior staff when we drove up to the Deccan College library.

The full title of the college is Deccan College Post Graduate and Research Institute (DCPRI). The school is the third oldest educational institution in India, dating from 1821 when it was established as the Hindoo College. In 1864 it was renamed Deccan College. In its current status it offers postgraduate instruction in Ancient India History, Culture and Archaeology, Linguistics, Medieval and Maratha History, Sociology-Anthropology, and Sanskrit Studies. Students have produced over 500 Ph.D. dissertations in these studies. In recognition of the excellence achieved by the Institute both in teaching and research, in 1990 it was awarded the status of a Deemed University.

After a short Library tour we were guided to a conference room where tea was served and the Vice Chancellor introduced me and asked me to tell his staff the purpose of my visit to India and Deccan College. I briefly addressed the issues of Earth's ancient contact with the Anunnaki and its home planet Nibiru, the challenge of the return of Nibiru (Planet X) sometime during this century, and the alien/human nexus. I ended by asking them to search the library's holding on Indian Astrology to see if references to the Moon and any of the planets carried a suggestion that in addition to their importance in astrology, there might be reference to some of them being Extraterrestrial bases, and if Nibiru and the Anunnaki were cited in any of their ancient manuscripts. This request was made to see if we could surface any new documentary links to the extensive Sumerian documentation.

A small party was then driven to a building housing the Department of Archeology where Professor Vasant Shivram Shinde met us. In addition to his thirty-years teaching archeology and conducting fieldwork in digs around India, Shinde is also the Joint Director of Deccan College, number three in college administration.

In his outer office he showed me a two-inch thick bound report of excavations at Madina (Late Harappan-PGW site in Rohtak District, Haryana) 2007-2008. Dr. Shinde is an expert on the ancient Harappan Culture of India. He has written that the Dhola Veera Harappan site in Kutch, Gujarat is much more important than Mohenjo-daro. It is an entire city made in stone instead of mud bricks, It has an 18-metre fortification wall and it has unparalleled water management techniques. The area was as arid as it is today, but there were two large streams that were prone to flash floods. The city was divided into three parts, with each having its own tanks and water from these floods were diverted into the tanks with underground pipes. Shinde has directed excavations at this site. He has also directed excavations at Farmana (Rohtak District) in 2007-2009, where a discovery of one of the largest Harappan cemeteries, with around 70 burials has been located.

Mohenjo-daro is mentioned in Sumer archeological research as an outpost of the Anunnaki settlement in Mesopotamia. I provided Dr. Shinde with copies of Zecharia Sitchin's books and he has become a valuable supporter of getting the global dialogue started about the ancient and modern ET/Earth relationship.

Deccan College was an obvious candidate to research and write a White Paper about the impact to India of acknowledging the ET/Earth relationship. For months it appeared that this would happen, but Dr. Deglurkar quietly withdrew his support of the idea without giving a reason. When we questioned our ET sources about this, they indicated that the government in India had vetoed the project. If this was the case, that decision was made in New Delhi after a very successful presentation was made at the India International Centre.

New Delhi and a Tad of Mystery

I was met at the airport by Come Carpentier de Gourdon who had coordinated an excellent New Delhi program for me. The centerpiece of this was an afternoon talk at the India International Centre. The IIC is a very prestigious institution in New Delhi. John D. Rockefeller III, brother of Laurance Rockefeller, provided early and critical funding support for its creation

As a speaker at the IIC, I was invited to become a temporary member of the club and therefore qualified to stay in its hostel and use its dining facilities. It also enabled me to host meetings arranged by Come and my second New Delhi resource person, Manmohan Sharma. Sharma is the Executive Secretary of the Indian Association of Parliamentarians on Population and Development (IAPPD). Sharma's government contacts are outstanding. Come and Manmohan worked effectively together and I had a full plate at Delhi as the result of their collaboration.

The IIC is the premier venue in New Delhi for intellectual stimulation. Come was asked by his IIC staff contact to change the proffered title of my presentation to something with more intrigue. The suggested title change was more than intriguing; it was a bait and switch move that required a bit of rewrite and removal of some material to keep the presentation within one hour. The negotiated new title of my talk was: **Cosmic Implications of Paranormal Research and Interests in the US Military and Intelligence Community**. Since the IIC program schedule is sent to all embassies, I thought that perhaps a couple of U.S. Men in Black would show up. I checked the audience very carefully, and everyone appeared completely innocent of Black Ops affiliation.

An outstanding number of questions came from the audience following the presentation. After more than an hour of them we had to firmly close it down. I have entertained the thought that the suggested title change came from the fertile mind of an Indian counter-intelligence officer to see if it would smoke out anyone from the New Delhi diplomatic community that they had not identified with intelligence responsibilities.

Perhaps the most important government contact was a Member of the Rajya Sabha (India's Parliament Council of States). Professor P.J. Kurien, MP, Congress Party Member from Kerala. He is a very senior Member of Parliament, having served six five-year terms in the Lok Sabha (House of the People), and now in his second six-year term of the Rajya Sabha. Accompanied by two of his Rajya Sabha colleagues he came to the IIC to meet. Over tea I briefed that group on the purpose of the visit to India. Because Kurien is a senior member of the Rajya Sabha Defense Committee, I detailed some of the U.S. military/ET contact experiences. He became very interested when I related the accounts of UFOs hovering low over U.S. ICBM sites and concomitant loss of operational control of a number of ICBMs in underground silos. This is part of an understanding that some ET groups are most concerned about nuclear weapons. I gave Kurien a copy of the Outer Space Security and Development Treaty, indicating that a copy of the treaty would also be given to the Minister of External Affairs and Ambassadors to India from China, Pakistan and the Russian Federation. We agreed to keep in touch. Subsequently I send him a copy of Robert Salas's book *Faded Giant*, that details the 1967 Malmstrom AFB Missile/UFO Incident, and asked him to push the Indian government to adopt the treaty what will ban all space-based weapons.

By special courier I sent a copy of the Space Treaty and a special gift to the Chinese, Pakistan and Russian Federation ambassadors to India. Previous to this I had requested a separate meeting with each of them, and gave a personal invitation to my IIC presentation. There had been no response to these communications. That was not unexpected. The gift was a one and a half inch square, three-quarter inch thick bronze cuboid. One side had a reproduction of a Harappa seal in deep relief. On the opposite side was the word PEACE above the P.E.A.C.E. Inc. logo, also in deep relief. I sent a follow-up email letter to each of them, explaining the bronze gift. The Harappa seal represents the continuing mystery of our alien origin that will be resolved with disclosure when extraordinary opportunities will develop provided certain conditions are met. The other side of the bronze cuboid is a reminder that solutions to potential Earth-ending issues will only be recognized through a lens of peace, and achieved by too long delayed and difficult decisions that all countries must make, particularly the current nuclear powers. All classes of weapons of mass destruction are a curse upon civilization. They are a denial of what it means to be civilized. The Visiting Other have made it very clear that support for Earth that they can provide will only be available to a peaceful, nuclear weapons free planet.

Manmohan had arranged for a meeting with Scientist Shantanu Bhatawdekar, Officer on Special Duty at the Indian Space Research Organization, Department of Space. Bhatawdekar's office was decorated with a number of photographs provided by India's successful moon orbiting satellite. Our conversation about this achievement was certainly guarded on his part. My suggestions that India may have learned much more from this accomplishment than they had made public were comfortably deflected. I did not expect him to confirm what our ET sources have told us about the presence of ET facilities on the avert side of the moon.

Of all nations, India's cultural heritage is most sympathetic to an ancient reality of extraterrestrial contact with Earth. However, India is an important player in the modern world and its government plays its political and diplomatic cards with care. When a White Paper is written that assesses India's public response to affirmed knowledge of Earth/ET contact in the current era, it will most likely be one of excitement and pride that they knew this all the time.

The Treaty: a New Strategy with an Essential Partnership

Much has been learned over the years by the failure of various iterations of Plan C to accomplish its objective: start a global dialogue about a future when there is no ambiguity about Earth/ET contact. The importance of the dialogue has been a repeated input from ET sources for years. The message has been consistent. The dialogue is an essential part of the process of disclosure. Increased sightings are also part of the process. The dialogue itself will surface other essential parts of the process, particularly involving violence on Earth and obvious political and economic decisions that must be made. Knowledge of helpful technologies from ETs will not exceed that already seeded in the minds of thousands on Earth. "Listen and act on the messages you have already received."

What new does the Outer Space Security and Development Treaty bring to the table? The value added came in a simple, quiet thought when drafting for the Treaty was well along. "Would you consider adding Cosmic Culture to the Treaty?" My response was a quick "yes," and that I would recommend that to the Treaty team. Carol Rosin is the team leader with years of experience with space treaties when she founded the Institute for Security and Cooperation in Space. Other members brought relevant experiences and skills to the team. Commander Will Miller, USN Retired was an advisor to the White House, U.S. Space Command, and the Department of Defense; Apollo Astronaut Captain Dr. Edgar Mitchell, USN Retired, and founder of the Institute of Noetic Science; Aerospace Executive and engineer Abe Kriger with Boeing for 37 years, joint U.S./Russian space programs; Honorable Paul Heller, former Minister of Defense, Canada; and myself. The team response to this idea from the ETs was immediately positive. All of the Team members realized that this request for ET inclusion was a very important as it quickly addressed the issue of verification when the Treaty became law. The language in the Treaty about the inclusion of Cosmic Cultures is straightforward. In the opening paragraphs:

"This Treaty invites Nation States to become Signatories to this Treaty and invites all parties, including Nation States, Indigenous Nations and Cosmic Cultures, to commit to plan and assist in the orderly development and implementation of a framework and procedures that will assure and verify that space is and will remain a neutral realm from which all classes of space-based weapons are banned in perpetuity."

This is followed by these entries in "The Parties to this Treaty" section:

"Acknowledge that we are not alone in the universe, that there are Cosmic Cultures that will be important allies for our security and development, and that our national and international policies must reflect this reality,"

"Acknowledge that from the beginning of nuclear weapon testing, extraterrestrial craft have demonstrated a capability to selectively shut down communications and/or the power of participating units, and have appeared over ICBM fields in several countries causing non-destructive failure of dozens of ICBMs – taking them out of operational control for days"

"Realize that the demonstrated capability of extraterrestrial cultures from the multiverse to neutralize any missile or nuclear capability is in itself not a threat message, but does serve notice of our limited understanding of physics and the clearly dangerous consequences of continuing to use destructive technologies."

"Affirm that the possibility of reclaiming a peaceful future for humankind and a safe environment on Earth is intimately linked with curbing violence toward each other and Earth, and with preparing to survive as Gaea heals herself, and that counsel and support from Cosmic Civilizations thousands of years our senior would be exceedingly helpful."

"Are inspired by the great prospect of Earth taking its rightful place in the Cosmos and the citizens of off-Earth realms sharing the fruits of their cultures with humankind."

"Understand that this space Treaty is now verifiable and enforceable via applying monitoring, observation, and information sharing techniques existing and forthcoming"

"Realize we are one interconnected and interdependent human species, and we are determined to live in peace with all our neighbors on Earth and in the universes,"

The above seven declarations in the Treaty are those that make a direct references to Cosmic Cultures and their enduring role in our lives, now and in the future. The other fourteen declarations also address the importance of the Treaty but without making reference to Cosmic Cultures.

When this Treaty becomes international and space law, Earth will have stepped back from a perilous future. It will do more. The process of getting it into the corpus of international law will also be a pathway to create the political cover needed for academe to play a leading role in starting the essential dialogue about disclosure. The plan is simple, but dependent upon invitation to meet with Heads of States in order to formally present the Treaty and to get it signed.

The strategy to secure invitations to meet with Heads of States involves establishing partnerships with individuals, businesses and organizations that share the vision that the Treaty will accomplish and who already have the necessary international contacts.

The first order of business is to get the Treaty signed into law. In that undertaking the existence and role of the Cosmic Community in the Treaty will be most obvious. We fully anticipate that advisors to the Head of States and the Head of States themselves will have questions about how the Cosmic Cultures became involved. This will open the door to more than the Treaty/ET link.

But Wait – There is More!

To the degree that Heads of State show interest in learning more about the current Earth/ET nexus, we will move into the ET request to start a global dialogue about the challenges and opportunities of that relationship. We will ask the Head of State to identify one or more university in his/her country who he/she thinks would be qualified to research and write a White Paper about the short term and long term impact on his/her country and culture of recognizing contact. The response to that question could provide the ultimate political cover for one or more White paper being created.

When Head of State approval is given for the White paper, we will meet with the identified university or universities and establish a working relationship with the designated leader of that program and provide support with presentations and documentation to assist the effort. We will suggest the four month delivery time, and link them with universities in other countries involved in the White Paper program for their country.

We have been given additional information about future communications between Earth and the Cosmic Community that we will share first with interested Heads of States. The background is that approximately 5,000 years ago Cosmic Cultures placed communication devices in four different Earth locations. Each of them is destined to be activated at a different future time period. Activation will be essentially determined by the level on consciousness on Earth. I was directed to the location of the first of these locations where the device will be activated. A protocol has been given about how the system will work when Earth is qualified to use it. Explicitly, when the Outer Space Security and Development Treaty becomes law, the White Paper supported global dialogue is underway, and other economic and political policy decisions are made that move Earth away from current levels of violence, the odds of activating the communication device with be increased.

The messages are clear. We are responsible for our own survival. Unconditional help is in the wings when we prove we deserve and can handle it. Cosmic Cultures have seeded the minds of thousands on Earth with knowledge about technologies capable of ameliorating every potential civilization- ending problem we are enduring. In that sense, the technologies are "free."

If the status quo keeps them from being developed and made available throughout the world to bring relief where needed and when needed, it is very likely that the Earth experiment will end. I have no idea if Earth will be missed, but I have been assured that greed and lust for power has resulted in the demise of many civilizations throughout the Cosmos. Earth is not an exceptional planet and our failing struggle to survive our sophomore era is not exceptional.

In the chapters to follow you will hear from some of the cosmic voices. The search for them is part of a respected pattern of human conduct. The urge to discover is a powerful part of the human consensus trance, and more than one group is involved in making contact with life in the cosmos.

Chapter 2

Vision And Discovery

Angela T. Smith

According to Allen Tough, Ph.D., and Scarlett Wang, Ph.D. (2006):

"The desire for communication with extraterrestrial intelligence seems to be normal, natural, and widespread. Several individuals and groups have tried to communicate with extraterrestrial intelligence in recent decades. A successful effort could have a profound impact on humanity's future."

Tough and Wang organized a group of 100 scientists who have similar goals to ours titled Invitation to Extraterrestrial Intelligence (ieti.org). Further in their writing, Tough and Wang noted that:

"Humans of all ages have a strong desire to communicate with others. Listening, talking, reading, and writing are normal, natural human activities. Most human communication is with other humans. But people also experience some form of two-way communication with their cats and dogs and horses. Many people wish they could experience communication with a benign alien intelligence that developed somewhere else in the universe.

Many reports of UFO sightings and abductions include communication with the alien beings, often through mental telepathy. Although such reports may well result from wishful thinking and other quirks of the human mind, their frequency does suggest a widespread human interest in aliens. Finally we should note that many people pray; that is, they communicate (one-way) with God, Yahweh, Allah, the Creator and Ruler of the Universe, or some other supernatural being or force. Some report a response (two-way communication). It is clear, then, that the desire for dialogue or other communication with a superior or alien intelligence is a common, normal, and natural human desire."

Putting our Goals into Perspective

There is an amazing graphic on the Internet that depicts the size of our Earth in relation to the rest of the Universe. You may have seen it. In relation to Venus, Mars, Mercury and Pluto, Earth is the largest planet: twice as big as Venus, around eight times bigger than Mars and much, much bigger than either Mercury or Pluto.

This relationship, to planets smaller than Earth, gives a false sense of our place in the Universe. Next compare Earth to Uranus, Neptune, Saturn and Jupiter and you can begin to see that the Earth is a marble in comparison to a basketball, putting our position in the Universe in greater perspective.

Now comparing all of those planets to our Sun reveals that the Earth is but a blip in comparison! And when taken to the next step our sun is dwarfed by Sirius, and the even more massive Pollux and Arcturus. Further out into the solar system our Sun becomes the equivalent of a pixel on a page compared with Rigel, Aldebaran and the even more massive Betelgeuse and Antares. Our tiny world, Earth, appears insignificant within this massive solar system and its giants.

Humanity and the Need for Exploration

Living on this tiny blip of Earth is a magnificent people: Humans. Over the millennia we have been explorers, discoverers, and innovators. We have explored our own world from the deepest ocean trenches to the highest Tibetan peaks. We have made discoveries ranging from the tiniest physics particles to our greatest galactic companions. Humans are sending probes out in the farthest reaches of our nearest universal neighborhoods and exploring inward to the deepest levels of the human psyche. To understand where we are going, it is important to understand where humans have been as explorers.

Over the past few thousand years the Earth and its seas have been the focus of intense exploration: the Phoenicians, the Egyptians, and the Vikings all initiated brave land and sea expeditions. The Chinese were one of the earliest, premier countries of exploration and had a huge impact on western civilization. Famous explorers can be found in every century: Alexander the Great in the late 1200s, John Cabot and Christopher Columbus in the 1400s, Francisco Pizarro in the 1500s, Abel Tasman in the 1600s, James Cook in the 1700s, and Lewis and Clark, and David Livingstone in the 1800s.

Robert Peary discovered the North Pole of the Earth and Robert Falcon Scott discovered the South Pole, both in the 1900s. Also Sir Edmund Hillary and Sherpa Tenzing Norgay climbed the highest peak on Earth in the 1900s. Humans reached out to space exploration in the mid-1900s with the first Moon landing by the crew of Apollo 11. Exploration of the seas, air, and space is continuing with oceanic and deep-space explorations.

The Four Focuses of Exploration

Traditionally, such land and sea explorations were championed and supported by European royalty such as King Henry VIII of England, and King Ferdinand and Queen Isabella of Spain and later, in the 20th century by the European and American governments. There was a vested, economic interest in who could find new routes first and who would come home with new discoveries and riches. Another motive during this and later era's was the desire to spread Christian beliefs and practices.

Expeditions focused on several layers of inquiry: the First being a mapping of the new territories, the Second; active exploration, the Third; initiating contact with indigenous peoples and lastly trading and sometimes assimilation. Our human quest to map and explore the galaxies (focuses One/Two) has already begun and active exploration is already in place.

The Third Focus: that of initiating contact and communicating with our universal neighbors has not yet been formally initiated. Or if it has, it has not been publicly announced. With any contact it is important to find the most appropriate forms of communication.

Anecdotal evidence has indicated that races living outside of the Earth do not communicate in the traditional, verbal manner. There is anecdotal evidence that communication is non-verbal and constitutes mind-to-mind contact. While being very controversial, this type of communication has a long history and research background that has been found suggestive of a real occurrence taking place.

Currently, this form of non-verbal communication takes two forms: spontaneous; where individuals feel that they have received communication from other non-Earth races and purposeful; with proficient individuals initiating two-way communication.

The Fourth focus: that of off-world trading is a vague area. There are rumors of such communication going on since the end of the last World War, focused on exchanges of information and technology with off-world civilizations.

Earth Ambassadors

As with early seafaring and land explorers, this new wave of explorers can be seen as ambassadors who can act as both receivers and senders of information: an exchange that could benefit both sides. There is a long history of civilian ambassadors being used in contacting and communicating with local citizens of other countries on Earth. There is a place for human civilian ambassadors to contact and communicate with off-planet races. It is audacious of us to assume that civilization exists on Earth alone. It is reasonable to assume that intelligent life exists elsewhere in the universe and that humans can communicate with this intelligence. Governmental and private organizations, such as SETI, have been operating for decades with ever-increasing complex and expensive technology. The human mind is a simple technology; it is a cheap technology, and one that has great potential for exploration, discovery, and contact.

It appears that there is an increased energy between the building level of ET/ Earth communication and, to some this has been seen as a push/pull situation. Both fear and compassion can be motivators in this dynamic. These ideas should be part of our dialogue as we communicate. There may be a rich mixture of fear and compassion involved. The potential failure of Earth civilizations to survive may be more important to ETs than we realize and should be part of the dialogue.

The Purpose of our Journey

What has been the purpose of our journey of exploration? It is aptly summarized by Tough and Wang: "When humankind does finally achieve communication with another culture, the new perspective and new knowledge that we gain will be valuable, deep, exciting, pervasive, and high-impact." We are walking the same path as the early seafaring and land explorers as we seek answers from some of our universal neighbors. It is an exciting journey of discovery!

Dr. Tough constructed a list of potential questions that humans should be asking of our neighbors and some things that our neighbors might like to know about us. It was an ambitious list and it was based on over 100 answers received by a group called Invitation to ETI from 224 people in 12 countries. The resulting 10 clusters of questions were designed to ask ETI what knowledge they would like to share with humans and how the dialogue should proceed.

Our journey of discovery could follow along the same charted path. This group has similar goals to ours: "that the information given and received should not be used for destructive or harmful purposes but to increase our understanding of the universe, to build a better world for future generations and to enhance our sense of meaning and purpose."

Conclusion

The original Exobiology Project, that began in 2006 and took nearly a year to complete, charted unknown waters and mapped new lands and civilizations that, until now, have remained un-contacted through purposeful interaction. Our human society has explored and mapped these locales and we are now talking to the local people in those charted lands. This is an important step in our understanding of the universe outside of our Earth and our dialogue will continue.

The Invitation to Extraterrestrial Intelligence (ETI) team appears to have dissolved following the passing of Dr. Allen Tough but their work is still available at: http://www.ieti.org/index.html

Chapter 3

The Flat Earth Society

C. B. Scott Jones

Consensus about the spherical shape of Earth is profoundly overwhelming. The contrary view that the Earth is flat is so marginally supported that the term "Flat Earther" is safely used to describe someone who is not only incorrect about a subject, but implicitly stupid as well.

An example of this came from President Barack Obama in June 2013, during a major speech on energy policy. He mocked skeptics of climate change as 'flat-Earth believers.' The President said he lacked "patience for anyone who denies that this problem is real. We don't have time for a meeting of the Flat-Earth Society. Sticking your head in the sand might make you feel safer, but it's not going to protect you from the coming storm."

This mini dustup inspired a reporter to contact the president of the Flat Earth Society in the United States. He commented intelligently about his agreement that there was an important anthropogenic input to climate change. He responded to Obama's dig at the Flat Earth Society by saying that it didn't surprise him, and that he didn't take it personally.

There are a number of reasons why "contrary" positions on facts are held and defended. Religious orthodoxy is an important one. Embarrassment about lack of knowledge can result in someone huffing and bluffing instead of simply admitting he does not know. Governments have security and diplomatic reason to walk and talk around the truth and reality.

Having just mentioned President Obama, the following example is appropriate to this discussion and central to the purpose of this book. The situation was the result of the commendable policy of the Obama administration to demonstrate openness and transparency with the "We the People" program. The rules are simple. Any citizen can petition the White House to respond to a question of interest. If that petition was supported by a reasonably sized number of other citizens enrolled in the program, the government would respond.

It didn't take long for a number of petitions to appear that requested the White House to address the extraterrestrial issue. When one of these reached the required number of supporting votes, the White House had to make an important decision: how not to tell the truth. None of us following this intriguing drama had any expectation that the White House would use this vehicle to make the disclosure announcement. How the White House handled it is indeed interesting. The date of the following online response from the White House was November 7, 2011. This was eighteen years after Lawrence Rockefeller and I met with President Clinton's Science Advisor, head of the White House Office of Science & Technology Policy (OSTP) as discussed in Chapter 1.

A brief assessment follows this 2011 White House response:

"OFFICIAL WHITE HOUSE RESPONSE TO: formally acknowledge an extraterrestrial presence engaging the human race - Disclosure.

Searching for ET, But No Evidence Yet

By Phil Larson

Thank you for signing the petition asking the Obama Administration to acknowledge an extraterrestrial presence here on Earth.

The U.S. government has no evidence that any life exists outside our planet, or that an extraterrestrial presence has contacted or engaged any member of the human race. In addition, there is no credible information to suggest that any evidence is being hidden from the public's eye.

However, that doesn't mean the subject of life outside our planet isn't being discussed or explored. In fact, there are a number of projects working toward the goal of understanding if life can or does exist off Earth. Here are a few examples:

SETI, The Search for Extraterrestrial Intelligence, was originally stood up with help from NASA, but has since been moved to other sources of private funding. SETI's main purpose is to act as a giant ear on behalf of the human race, pointing an array of ground-based telescopes towards space to listen for any signal from another world.

Kepler is a NASA spacecraft in orbit that's main goal is to search for Earth-like planets. Such a planet would be located in the "Goldilocks" zone of a distant solar system—not too hot and not too cold—and could potentially be habitable by life as we know it. The Kepler mission is specifically designed to survey our region of the Milky Way galaxy to discover Earth-sized, rocky planets in or near the habitable zone of the star (sun) they orbit.

The Mars Science Laboratory, Curiosity, is an automobile-sized rover that NASA is launching soon (Curiosity was launched on November 26, 2011, and successfully landed on Mars August 8, 2012.) The rover's onboard laboratory will study rocks, soils, and other geology in an effort to detect the chemical building blocks of life (e.g., forms of carbon) on Mars and will assess what the Martian environment was like in the past to see if it could have harbored life.

A last point: Many scientists and mathematicians have looked with a statistical mindset at the question of whether life likely exists beyond Earth and have come to the conclusion that the odds are pretty high that somewhere among the trillions and trillions of stars in the universe there is a planet other than ours that is home to life.

Many have also noted, however, that the odds of us making contact with any of them—especially any intelligent ones—are extremely small, given the distances involved.

But that's all statistics and speculation. The fact is we have no credible evidence of extraterrestrial presence here on Earth."

Phil Larson works on space policy and communications at the White House Office of Science & Technology Policy

The first obvious point to observe is that the official government of the United States is still sitting on a festering issue about which its hands are tied. It is accurate to say but currently difficult to explain and prove that this subject is not controlled by the U.S. or any other country. There are serious consequences from this. The worst is that the power and profit that accrues to the global financial community from suppressing the truth about ET/Earth contact has resulted in the corruption underlying more than a decade of perpetual war and savaging of the environment and Earth resources, and the inevitable consequences of placing profit before public interest. A saving grace of this boycott of reality protects us from sudden disclosure that would only exacerbate the existing problems and create others. The "other" news is that pre-disclosure mature global dialogue about what disclosure will mean is both essential and possible. Fundamentally, the problem is political and economic, and not about technology.

Following the dialogue, an expected building global consensus about the opportunities following disclosure will be the leverage needed for the "not so secret" government to shift to their Plan B that ultimately will be just as profitable as their current strategy. The added features are that the odds for Earth's survival will greatly increase, as will the quality of life of all the world's citizens.

But wait a minute, the White House told a flat-out lie in a program designed to show transparency and openness. Yes, that is correct and it cannot be excused by noting that all governments lie. Keep reading. The next section addresses a more important subject than denial about contact.

Here There be Dragons

In this context, dragons are a metaphor for danger, and danger avoidance is obviously significant. What follows is an assessment of danger identification. This is important because the specifically alleged danger is highlighted by two quite opposite agendas.

The first of these has been decades of drumbeats about the alleged threat presented to Earth by extraterrestrials. Another voice can be heard that represents a completely different vision and reality. This book is part of the voice. Please listen carefully. One voice is true. The other is false and dangerously so.

The warning "Here there be Dragons" can be traced back to ancient seafaring times when nautical charts were woefully lacking in details and accuracy. When this phrase was scripted on a chart it meant "sailor beware." As more adventurous captains returned with new information about distances to land masses, and detailed navigational data, the "dragon" alert warnings began to disappear from charts. What previously was unknown and therefore a potential hazard became known. Experienced based knowledge was the key. Certainly some of what was learned by experience was correctly determined to be a hazard to the ships and crews of the time.

Fear of the unknown is not exceptional in the human condition. And manipulation of fear by religions, parents, bullies, banks, governments, con artists (it is a very long list!) is a sad reality of life on Earth. When a Fear Card is played, it is important to discover who is behind the move in addition to accurately assess the reality of threat upon which the fear is based.

No U.S. president played the fear card with greater skill than Ronald Reagan. For years he repeatedly asked a clever question that introduced the alien threat theme. The absolutely best example of this was on September 21, 1987 in Reagan's speech to the United Nations General Assembly:

"Can we and all nations not live in peace? In our obsession with antagonisms of the moment, we often forget how much unites all the members of humanity. Perhaps we need some outside, universal threat to make us recognize this common bond. I occasionally think how quickly our differences worldwide would vanish if we were facing an alien threat from outside this world. And yet, I ask you, is not an alien force already among us? What could be more alien to the universal aspirations of our peoples than war and the threat of war?"

This articulation is very sophisticated. The alien threat is presented at the front end, and he finishes by co-opting the UN reason for existence, ending war, but that, of course would happen after we came together and defeated an alien attack on Earth.

It is no insult to Reagan's intelligence to suggest that this speech was given to him to read for that particular occasion. He gets to wave the flag of Peace on Earth while making the case for spending billions for his hopeless Star Wars dream. Of course, the real dream was the profit of the military-industrial –congress complex, and the Reagan administration's booming increases of the military budget was a dream come true.

We cannot end this section without noting something very historically important from the Reagan Cold War period. The Cold War, 1947-1991, between the USSR and the US followed the end of World War II. It was marked with cycles of peek tension as each side responded to what they perceived to be an unacceptable change in the balance of power. For example, the Berlin Blockade, 1948-1949 was the first major crisis of the Cold War.

This was a time when both sides were trying to exploit the missile technology demonstrated by Germany at the end of WW II. The objective of both sides was to develop an intercontinental ballistic missile (ICBM) capability. The USSR was the first to do this, and trumped that when they launched Sputnik 1, an earth orbiting satellite proving they also had a guidance system necessary to make the ICBM a weapon system.

The missile race was on, the USSR was ahead, and the term "missile gap" was born. The Cuban Missile Crisis, October 15-28, 1962 was an important piece on the US/USSR chess board, but the major pieces were the inventory if ICBM missiles, and balance of their numbers, i.e. the Missile Gap. An explanation of this gap is known as the "Gilpatric's Principle." It is named after the US Deputy Secretary of Defense, Roswell L. Gilpactric. His principle articulates the ironic consequences for the USSR of Soviet secrecy and US openness, "The Soviets are forced to work very hard to keep up with what *they know* we are doing in order to keep up with what *we think* they are doing."

The significance of the Gilpatric Principle was its pertinence before sophisticated reconnaissance satellites, military and civilian, became normal eyes and ears in the skies. The impact of space-based information gathering satellites has transformed warfare, and the impact in civilian sectors is equally huge.

Things deep underground can still be hidden from cameras and radar, but if anyone talks about them more than once, secrets will be unlocked. This addresses a key problem in intelligence. Political leaders want to know what the "intentions" of a potential enemy are. Military Rule One: Weapons are issued to be used, but when, where and why usually remain to be answered.

This book is a tutorial on how all political leaders in the future will be able to get all of their questions answered, and voters will also be able to get all of their questions answered about political leaders.

In a relative sense, the messages of this book are simple: remote viewing and telepathy are real human "technologies," and they are very valuable. The real exciting and complex answers are ahead. Extraterrestrial races exist and are older than the human race. Some coexist on Earth with humans and were here first. From our small sample those who are normally in the physical dimension had one head, two arms and two legs but were distinctly different from Humans. All of them have mind skills far beyond the average Human. This predicts that a fully mature post contact world will be going through a complete social and economic transformation. Respect and cooperation will either be the new norm or Human civilization will self-destruct.

The Hollywood/ET Nexus

For years Hollywood has played a profitable role in keeping the alien threat idea alive. The U.S. Department of Defense is usually willing to provide locations, equipment and personnel as long as the military is presented in a favorable light. For example, the 1996 film *Independence Day* that featured the White House being destroyed by a fifteen mile wide alien spacecraft, such assistance was offered. However, that was subsequently withdrawn when the film's producers refused to remove the script's Area 51, and Roswell alien UFO and alien crew member references. The film predictably featured hideously looking aliens and a scene in which a Roswell ET crew member regains consciousness after fifty-years and revealed that its species mission was to travel from planet to planet, destroying all life and harvesting the planets natural resources. Of course, by film's end the U.S. military with significant civilian help defeated the aliens. The film's combined domestic and international box office gross was $816 million. While that is impressive, the Star Wars franchise is the third highest grossing film series of all times behind Harry Potter and James Bond. We are talking billions now. That is serious money being made on feeding the human appetite for fantasy. We can understand why the secret keepers and mind twisters are so delighted to have such a profitable partner; no extra pay for their services is required.

The simple messages of these films are direct and memorable. "There is a global threat to Earth from predatory aliens; U.S. military can handle it." It is fortunate that the threat hypothesis is false, because the capability claim of being able to handling it is preposterous.

The producers of *Independence Day* generously and shrewdly provided the White House a private screening of the film for Bill Clinton and his family before its nationwide release in the U.S.

The fictional movie claim of an alien threat is important. It has conditioned a generation of the world to the idea of "alien threat." Sometime in the future of most of the readers of this book a decision will be made by those currently maintaining a boycott on the reality of Earth/ET contact. The decision will be whether or not the formal announcement of ET/Earth contact will be made with a "threat spin." This is why the pre-disclosure dialogue about what disclosure will mean is so important. The dialogue will directly influence that decision.

We sincerely believe that the dialogue will result in affirming the capability of the needed transformation that earns for Earth an invitation to take its rightful place in the Cosmic Community.

Who Else is in the Game?

The world's great religions are major players, but only one has suited up for the game. Catholicism is the only major religion that has publicly stepped forward on the issue. A very brief account of the Vatican's current involvement starts with Monsignor Corrado Balducci. Balducci was a member of the Vatican Curia and starting in 1995 spoke openly about the possibility of extraterrestrial intelligences interacting with Earth. He identified that his interest and exploration into psychiatry and parapsychology led him into the UFO and ET field. He strongly defended the value of human testimonies using theological arguments for their acceptance and importance. He also drew from ancient church history to support his views. He quoted from the book *Thus Spoke Padre Pio* (author Don Nello Castello, 1974). "Someone in Padre Pio's confraternity asked him, 'Father, I thought Earth was nothing compared to the stars and all the other planets,' to which Padre Pio replied, 'Yes, and if we leave Earth we are nothing. The Lord certainly didn't restrict his glory to this little planet. On other planets, there will be beings without sin." Two other examples that Balducci used were from Cardinal Nicolo Cusano (1401-1464) who wrote, "There is not a single star in the sky which we can rule out the existence of life, even if different from ours," and the Jesuit astronomer, Father Angelo Secchi (1818-1866) who wrote, "it's absurd to consider the worlds that surround us as uninhabited deserts." (These quotes are from an interview with Monsignor Balducci by Adriano Forgione, Editor-in-Chief of the Italian UFO Magazine 'Dossier Alien' in April 1999).

Balducci's citation of Saint Pio's observation that, "On other planets there will be beings without sin," will be heard again from a Catholic spokesman who brings a modern scientific perspective joined with theology to the subject.

In April 2000, Zecharia Sitchin, a Hebrew scholar and researcher of ancient civilizations, a biblical archaeologist, and a descendant of Abraham met with Monsignor Balducci during an international conference held in Bellaria, Italy. Sitchin reported on his website that during their meeting they arrived at three common conclusions: extraterrestrials can and do exist on other planets; they can be more advanced than us; and materially, Man could have been fashioned from a pre-existing sentient being.

Monsignor Balducci died in September 2008, Zecharia Sitchin died in October 2010.

The Vatican's Close Look at the Heavens

The Catholic News Service lead news story in 14 May 2008 was headlined: "Vatican astronomers say if aliens exist, they may not need redemption." The quote was in reference to what Jesuit Father Jose Funes, director of the Vatican Observatory had said during remarks in an interview published May 13 by the Vatican newspaper L'Osservatore Romano. But that was old news as reported above. The new news from Father Funes was that Christians should consider alien life as an extraterrestrial brother. This was a very important theological statement and one with which millions of U.S. Christian evangelicals do not agree. Many Christians, largely Evangelicals, believe that the extraterrestrials are fallen angels, followers of Satan.

It is no coincident that this modern voice from the Vatican is coming from Jesuit priests. Since the foundation of the Jesuit Order in 16th Century, compared with other orders, Jesuits have more men, more flexibility in the type of work undertaken, and a tradition of scholarship. The Vatican Observatory is one of the oldest astronomical research institutions in the world.

Pope Francis, elected in 2013, became the first Jesuit Pope.

The Quran and ET Life

The world's great religions undoubtedly watch each other. Crudely put, they are concerned about their market share of souls. At this point in current history, only the Vatican has publicly made statements concerning where extraterrestrials fit according the Catholic theology. Calling them our Brothers is a bold theological and political statement. None of the other major religions have publicly commented about this. One reason for this silence may be the confidence that other religious leaders have about their followers understanding of their religion's belief on this subject, and the Quran has straightforward comments about this. The source for the following is Mirza Tahir Ahmad at, http://www.alislam.org/library/books/revelation/part_4_section_7.html and used with permission.

65:13 اَللّٰهُ الَّذِیْ خَلَقَ سَبْعَ سَمٰوٰتٍ وَّمِنَ الْاَرْضِ مِثْلَهُنَّ

Allah is He Who created seven heavens, and of the Earth the like thereof...

It needs to be explained here that the figure 'seven' can be treated as a specific term of the Quran in this verse and many other similar ones. As such it would mean that the universe comprises many units of heavens, each divided into groups of seven (a perfect number), each having at least one Earth to it which will be supported by the entire system of that heaven (galaxy). Referring to that system in general, a more specific verse on the existence of extraterrestrial life runs as follows:

وَمِنْ اٰيٰتِهٖ خَلْقُ السَّمٰوٰتِ وَالْاَرْضِ وَمَا بَثَّ فِيْهِمَا مِنْ دَآبَّةٍ

42:30

And among His Signs is the creation of the heavens and the Earth, and of whatever living creatures (da'bbah) He has spread forth in both...

Da'bbah covers all animals which creep or move along the surface of the Earth. It does not apply to animals which fly or swim. It is certainly not applicable to any form of spiritual life. In Arabic a ghost will never be referred to as *da'bbah*, nor an angel for that matter. The second part of the same verse speaks not only of the possibility of extraterrestrial life, but it categorically declares that it does exist—a claim which even the most modern scientific researchers have not been able to make so far with any measure of certainty. Yet, this is not all that this verse reveals. Wonder upon wonder is added when we read at the end of this verse, that He (Allah) will bring together the life in the heavenly bodies and the life on Earth when He so pleases:

وَهُوَ عَلٰى جَمْعِهِمْ اِذَا يَشَآءُ قَدِيْرٌ* 42:30

...And He has the power to gather them together (jam-'i-him) when He will so please.

Jam-'i-him is the Arabic expression in this verse which specifically speaks of bringing together of life on Earth and the life elsewhere. When this meeting of the two will take place is not specified, nor is it mentioned whether it will happen here on Earth or elsewhere. One thing however, is definitely stated: this event will most certainly come to pass whenever God so desires. It should be kept in mind that the word *jama'* can imply either a physical contact or a contact through communication. Only the future will tell how and when this contact will take place, but the very fact that more than fourteen hundred years ago such a possibility was even predicted is miraculous in itself.

This revelation of the Quran was made at a time when cosmology as a science was not yet born. A different age of conjectural visualization prevailed which had to go a long way before it could contemplate the existence of extraterrestrial life. Even today such claims are only found in science fiction.

Amazing is it not that what the Quran asserted as a fact, around fourteen hundred years ago, is just beginning to appear as a feasible reality to the scientists of today! The Quran goes a step further when it predicts that man shall one day make contact with extraterrestrial life.

The time for the full realization of this prophecy has not yet arrived, but its signs are appearing on the horizon. This demonstrates that the prophecies of the Quran run ahead of human scientific progress. Every new era witnesses the fulfillment of some more revelations which previous eras had no means to testify. Hence it should be clearly understood here that Quranic prophecies are intrinsically different in nature from those implied in science fiction. . .

The case of the Divine scriptures, however, is a different matter altogether and the knowledge expressed in them cannot be confined to any particular era. Moreover, chance has no role to play in their fulfillment. The scientific discoveries of subsequent ages have never proved any Quranic prophecy to be wrong.

So we must look forward with well-founded hope for the realization of even such prophecies as rest with the future to decide. The prophecy about the meeting of life here and the life elsewhere belongs to the same category which remains as yet unfulfilled. May we live long enough to witness the glorious day when life on Earth will establish some sort of communion with life in space."

The above discussion strongly suggests that formal disclosure of Earth/ET contact will not present a theological challenge to Islam. From this position of clear and strong doctrine confidence on the subject, White Papers from Islamic Universities on the anticipate impact of disclosure on all aspects of Islamic culture would presumably be positive.

A Failed Effort to Garner Islamic Academic Attention

In October 2003, I visited Doha, Qatar to meet with Dr. Saif Ali Al Hajari, Vice Chairman of the Qatar Foundation for Education, Science and Community Development. In 2003, Education City was a work in progress. With enlightened royal patronage from the Emir of Qatar, the Foundation was spending millions of dollars to replicate a premier Western university system. They selected and bought branch campuses from some of the world's leading universities. Six American universities and one each from the United Kingdom, France and Canada now are fully enrolled and operating. There are a number of additional educational and research units in Education City, including a Qatari university, the Qatar Faculty of Islamic Studies, the RAND-Qatar Policy Institute and Doha Debates, a public forum modeled on the Oxford Union debates.

There is no other Islamic facility with matching capability to introduce from scientific and Islamic religious perspectives what we current know about Earth/ET contact and what formal disclosure will mean to the Islamic world.

During my 2003 visit I introduced the P.E.A.C.E. Inc. Sustainable Peace and Development (SPD) program, and asked them to coordinate its introduction to Qatar University and other global Islamic Universities. Dr. Al Hajari was generous with his time and asked many excellent questions. He said he would present my proposal to the Chairman of the Foundation and I would receive a reply. Four months later I received a reply from a mid-level staff person that simply said that my proposal was outside of the Foundation's mission and objectives.

By 2008, Plan C had joined the SPD program, and in May of that year I wrote a letter to Dr. Ali Al Hajari introducing for the first time the ET connection to peace. This was followed by a letter a month later with additional details until in August when I received a rejection email message that noted "your program/project objectives do not align with the vision and objectives of the Qatar Foundation."

The dance with Qatar is not over. Our next approach will be designed to establish that our program not only is aligned with the vision and objectives of the Qatar Foundation, but it is importantly supportive of them.

In The Name of God – History's Sad Lessons

The complex history of the religious wars that waxed and waned in Europe for over a hundred years is generally dated from 1524 to 1648. It presents a legacy of important messages. The Reformation is easily identified as the major causative factor, but more than the stresses of religious change were involved. War provides opportunities to address and redress a host of political, economic, racial, and other issues. A compounding factor was the extensive use of mercenary armies that were paid by the privilege of looting and foraging. The consequences of this were devastation of large areas resulting in famine and disease and extensive loss of life. Some of the powers involved were bankrupted by the costs of extended war, and desperate peasants rose up in revolt.

A continuing consequence of the Reformation, over 300 years ago, is that "reformed" religions continue to transform into more and more Christian denominations. It is impossible to know how many there are today or will be tomorrow. All it takes is a charismatic (or conning) leader to convince a group that he or she has "the word," and a new church is born.

We believe that all the world's current large religions will be able to adjust to the impact of formal disclosure. They are smart and powerful. We also expect many small protestant religions will not survive the consequences of disclosure. However, they will be replaced by a larger number of new, fully enlightened religions with space related names.

There will be a period of serious spiritual confusion and wonderment. In countries with large protestant Christian populations, this unrest should be anticipated and prepared for.

Earlier in this section we presented quotes from the Quran that provided a theological base for followers of Islam to accept the reality of extraterrestrial life. The Bible provides a similar statement that oddly the Vatican has not used to support their current strategy to prepare Catholics for disclosure.

Paul Davies is an acclaimed physicist, cosmologist, and astrobiologist at Arizona State University. He also has been involved with the SETI program since it became a privately funded organization. He chairs the Search for Extraterrestrial Intelligence Post-Detection Taskgroup. He was awarded the 1995 Templeton Prize--the world's largest annual prize--for his work on science and religion. An author of more than twenty books, including *The Mind of God*, and *Are we Alone: Implications of the Discovery of Extraterrestrial Life* (London, 1995). In the preface of this book he writes:

"There is little doubt that even the discovery of a single extraterrestrial microbe, if it could be shown to have evolved independently of life on Earth, would drastically alter our world view and change our society as profoundly as the Copernican and Darwinian revolutions. It could truly be described as the greatest scientific discovery of all time."

In the book *Extraterrestrial Life and the Cosmic Christ as Prototype* by Martin Thomson, another theologian, John Jefferson Davis is extensively quoted about his assessment of Colossians 1:15-20. This material is used with permission from Martin Thomson.

Colossians 1:15-20
English Standard Version (ESV)
The Preeminence of Christ

[15] He is the image of the invisible God, the firstborn of all creation.[16] For
by him all things were created, in heaven and on Earth, visible and invisible,
whether thrones or dominions or rulers or authorities—all things were created
through him and for him.[17]And he is before all things, and in him all things
hold together. [18] And he is the head of the body, the church. He is the beginning,
the firstborn from the dead, that in everything he might be preeminent. [19] For

in him all the fullness of God was pleased to dwell, [20] and through him to reconcile to himself all things, whether on Earth or in heaven, making peace by the blood of his cross.

Davis comments that this passage in the Bible has received inadequate attention in connection with the authority of Christ over the Cosmos. Davis proposes that it alone is evidence that the:

"Redemptive effects of the atoning sacrifice of Christ are not limited to humanity, but extend in some way to the entire created order. The apostle stresses in the most emphatic way the absolute supremacy of Christ in every realm of space, time, and human experience."

Judaism and extraterrestrial life

Some caution is appropriate in presuming that the three great Abrahamic religions will move easily through the extended phase of acknowledging disclosure of Earth/ET contact. Such caution is particularly appropriate if knowledge gained during the post-disclosure era challenges a religion's fundamental assumptions of God and the relationship of God to believers. The reader will understand this point clearly when they read the interviews and dialogue with the different ET races in the chapters ahead. The fact that the ETs present a spectrum of belief and non-belief, even in our very small sample, may rationally lead to considering that God is unknowable. Perhaps when an ET does not answer the question about God, the issue of God's name being ineffable may arise. Additional telepathic contact and ultimately face-to-face meetings will build the needed knowledge base. P.E.A.C.E. Inc. is ready to work with theological leaders ready to prepare for the predictable and unexpected consequences of disclosure.

There is a paucity of information on Judaism's positions on extraterrestrial life. For any future researcher on this subject I recommend starting with the website Judaism 101. Founded in 1995 by Tracey Rich, he states that he writes the site from an Orthodox Jewish perspective because "I think that's the best place to start if you want to understand Jewish traditions." In his section: "What Do Jews Believe?" he summarizes – "Judaism has no dogma, no formal set of beliefs that one must hold to be a Jew."

Not necessarily a complication, but certainly a reality is the diaspora of Jews in the world, and the distinct spectrum of observance within these global communities. A reasonable estimate (because not all countries report this data) is that there are between 13 and 14 million Jews in the world. Most of these Jews live either in the United States or in Israel, both with Jewish populations of 5 to 6 million. According to Tracey Rich, "More than half of all Jews in

Israel today call themselves "secular," and don't believe in G-d or any of the religious beliefs of Judaism. Half of all Jews in the United States don't belong to any synagogue."

An example of current rabbinical comment on ET life suggests some challenges ahead for Judaism. In a search on ET life on the website www.torah.org, Rabbi Aryeh Kaplan cites the opinion of Sefer Habris who states that, "... extraterrestrial life does exist, but that it does not possess free will. The latter is the exclusive position of man, for whom the universe was created." In four pages of theological and philosophical argument he cites other contributions to the subject from Talmud teaching.

An argument can be made that in the end it will be the secular Israeli government based upon knowledge from actionable intelligence that will respond to the challenges and opportunities that flow from acknowledged disclosure. However, the heritage of the Jewish people, the Torah and its message are intertwined and that connection cannot be ignored. Neither should a dialogue about what we have learned be ignored.

Hinduism as a culture and religion is supported by well-known and respected epic literature that feature a host of celestial gods and equipment. Buddhism, on this subject as noted by the Dalai Lama, is also at ease. In an address at the University of Oregon on May 14, 2013, he took several minutes out of his speech, *The Path to Peace and Happiness in the Global Society,* to repeat what he has said many times. "Extraterrestrials are sentient beings and we should respect them as such."

It thus appears that for the billions of Earth's citizens who are under an umbrella of the world's great religions, the issue of sharing the universe with other intelligence life has, as a minimum, been considered. And, as noted, for some, it is an integrated part of their culture, and for one there has been an announcement of a potential large increase in the number of siblings in the family. On balance, this mixed bag of "understanding" is good news because it provides a foundation for a dialogue about what will actually happen when a formal and accepted announcement is made that "they" are here –now!

Does the reader get the point, if you do start the dialogue with your family. Take positions with the editor of your newspaper, your school board, and your spiritual leader. If you haven't already discovered, the Internet is a hazardous place to search for reality. It has become a favorite tool for disinformation. The safest place to look is inside. That takes discipline and perhaps learning some new skills. The payoff is confidence in discernment, and discernment is critical.

There are other important players in the game.

The Business Community Begins to Pay Attention

We have noted earlier that an elite group in the international financial community has been playing a controlling role in keeping information about ET/Earth contact out of the media. They also probably think that they control the timing of and how disclosure will be presented. We believe that the ETs will be the principals in making these decisions based upon action or lack of action by the nation state system to reform itself concerning institutionalized violence and other potential Earth-ending practices

Only recently has the public learned that attention is being shown to the ET/Earth contact subject by the broader business community. This is a very important step as it will be vital component to the needed global dialogue on the challenges and opportunities that will flow from a formal full disclosure.

Founded in 2006 by the Saudi Arabian General Investment Authority (SAGIA), the 5th Annual Global Competitive Forum (GCF) took place in January 23-26, 2011, in Riyadh, Saudi Arabia. Over three days, nineteen Panel sessions were heard by global business leaders, international political leaders, and selected intellectuals and journalists brought together for the stated purpose "to create a dialogue with respect to the positive impact organizational and national competitiveness can have on local, regional and global economic and social development."

On the first day, one of six panels was Contact: Learning from Outer Space. The participating invited panel members were: Stanton Friedman, a duel citizen of Canada and the USA, and has BSc and MSc degrees in physics from Chicago University. He was the original civilian investigator of the Roswell Incident and has lectured extensively at colleges and professional groups on UFOs in more than twenty countries. Dr. Jacques Valle, a French citizen received his BS in mathematics from the Sorbonne, his MS in astrophysics from Lille, and his Ph.D. in computer Science from Northwestern University. He has studied UFOs for many years and in his three books on the subject has advanced sophisticated hypotheses to explain their origin. Nick Pope, a United Kingdom citizen, worked at the Ministry of Defense for twenty-one years. Four of these years he was involved in investigating UFO sighting to determine their defense significance. Dr. Michio Kaku was born in the US to Japanese immigrant parents (with Tibetan DNA ancestry). Recognized by physicist Edward Teller as a young genius, Teller took Kaku as a protégé and awarded him with an engineering scholarship at Harvard University where he graduated summa cum laude with a BS in physics. He then received a Ph.D. in physics from the University of California, Berkeley. Currently a professor in theoretical physics at the City College of New York he is a prolific author in his field, and is noted for his skill in explaining complex science to the layperson.

He has stated that he is 100% certain of the existence of extraterrestrial life. Dr. Zaghloul El Nagger is a noted Muslim scholar and author. The main theme of El Naggar's books has been science in Quran. He is the Chairman of Committee of Scientific Notions in the Quran, Supreme Council of Islamic Affairs, Cairo, Egypt.

It is reasonable to assume that this subject was included because Saudi Arabia's economy is completely dependent upon its oil and gas riches. From the beginning of attention to UFO phenomena and suspected ET involvement, was a discussion that potential Earth-changing energy systems were involved. This obviously would be a vital issue for every country significantly dependent upon carbon based resources, and equally important to all other countries that have to import oil, gas and coal to meet their energy needs.

Keep Your Eye on Davos

The World Economic Forum (WEF) is a Swiss non-profit foundation based in Cologny, Geneva with the following mission statement:

"The World Economic Forum is an independent international organization committed to improving the state of the world by engaging business, political, academic and other leaders of society to shape global, regional and industry agendas."

There is nothing modest about the WEF. It was founded in 1971 by Klaus Schwab, a German-born business professor at the University of Geneva. At first it was named the European Management Forum, but in 1987, it was renamed The World Economic Forum, seeking to broaden its vision "to include providing a platform for resolving international conflicts." That would appear to make it a mini-UN with that objective. However, as it has turned out, the WEF has something critical that the UN lacks, a budget capable to match its objectives. The WEF is funded by its 1,000 member companies. These are mostly global enterprises with more than five billion dollars in turnovers. They rank among the top companies within their industry and/or country,

The annual five-day meeting takes place at the end of January in the delightful ski resort village of Davos, Switzerland. It is by membership and invitation only. While the WEF now has a number of other venues, principally regional meetings, the Davos affair is its flagship event where the CEOs from its 1,000 member countries hold court, mixing with selected politicians, members of academia, NGOs, religious leaders and the media. Around 2,200 participants gather and attend some of the 220 sessions in the official program. It is reported that private meetings have led to as many ideas and solutions as the scheduled ones.

The economic power represented at the annual WEF meeting is underwritten by successful managers of global corporations. It is highly unlikely that the international financiers who have fought their way to the top of their industry have ever missed a meeting at Davos. They appear as bankers and as CEO of businesses completely controlled by the bankers. Davos is a place where the seeds of needed global transformation could take place, provided that the harvesters of the current crop recognize that the new crop will be just as profitable as the one they currently tend. This is eco-politics, the game that really counts.

It was therefore very important that one of the products that came out of the 2013 WEF meeting was a discussion of Global Risks. Under a suggestive heading of X-Factors, the details are worth reading. The premise for looking at X-factors was this:

"In this section, developed in collaboration with *Nature*, a leading science journal, the Risk Response Network asks readers to look beyond our high-risk concerns of the moment to consider a set of five X factors and reflect on what countries or companies should be doing to anticipate them.

In a world of many uncertainties we are constantly on the search to identify 'X factors' – emerging concerns of possible future importance and with unknown consequences. Looking forward and identifying emerging issues will help us to anticipate future challenges and adopt a more proactive approach, rather than being caught by surprise and forced into a fully reactive mode.

X factors are serious issues, grounded in the latest scientific findings, but somewhat remote from what are generally seen as more immediate concerns such as failed states, extreme weather events, famine, macroeconomic instability or armed conflict. They capture broad and vaguely understood issues that could be hatching grounds for potential future risks (or opportunities)."

The five identified X factors were: Runaway Climate Change; Significant Cognitive Enhancement; Rogue Deployment of Geo-engineering; Costs of Living; and Discovery of Alien Life. Only the report on Discovery of Alien Life is presented in total below. (Source is the Global Economic Forum website www.weforum.org and is used with permission from the WEF.)

By: Risk Response Network Team

Jan 14th 2013

Discovery of Alien Life

"Given the pace of space exploration, it is increasingly conceivable that we may discover the existence of alien life or other planets that could support human life. What would be the effects on science funding flows and humanity's self-image?

It was only in 1995 that we first found evidence that other stars also have planets orbiting them. Now thousands of "exoplanets" revolving around distant stars have been detected. NASA's Kepler mission to identify Earth-sized planets located in the "Goldilocks Zone" (not too hot, not too cold) of sun-like stars has been operating for only three years and has already turned up thousands of candidates, including one the size of Earth. The fact that Kepler has found so many planet candidates in such a tiny fraction of the sky suggests that there are countless Earth-like planets orbiting sun-like stars in our galaxy. In 10 years' time we may have evidence not only that Earth is not unique but also that life exists elsewhere in the universe.

Suppose the astronomers who study exoplanets one day find chemical signs of life – for example, a spectrum showing the presence of oxygen, a highly reactive element that would quickly disappear from Earth's atmosphere if it weren't being replenished by plants. Money might well start flowing for new telescopes to study these living worlds in detail, both from the ground and from space. New funding and new brain power might be attracted to the challenges of human space flight and the technologies necessary for humanity, or its artificial-intelligence emissaries, to survive an inter-stellar crossing.

The discovery would certainly be one of the biggest news stories of the year and interest would be intense. But it would not change the world immediately. Alien life has been supposedly discovered before, after all. Around the turn of the 20th century, the US astronomer Percival Lowell convinced many people (including himself) that Mars was crisscrossed by a vast system of canals built by a dying civilization. But the belief that humankind was not alone did not do much to usher in an era of goodwill and Earthly harmony, nor did it stop the outbreak of World War I in 1914.

The discovery's largest near-term impact would likely be on science itself. Suppose observations point to a potential future home for humankind around another star, or the existence of life in our solar system – in the Martian poles, in the subsurface oceans of Jupiter's frozen moon Europa, or even in the hydrocarbon lakes of Saturn's moon Titan. Scientists will immediately start pushing for robotic and even human missions to study the life forms in situ – and funding agencies, caught up in the excitement, might be willing to listen.

Commercially built and operated spacecraft had a successful rendezvous with the International Space Station, and a host of celebrity billionaires declared intentions to make asteroid mining a reality. Discovery of an Earth 2.0 or life beyond our planet might inspire new generations of space entrepreneurs to meet the challenge of taking human exploration of the galaxy from the realm of fiction to fact.

If life forms (even fossilized life forms) are found in our solar system, for example, the origin of life is "easy" – that any place in the universe life can emerge, it will emerge. It will suggest that life is as natural and as ubiquitous a part of the universe as the stars and galaxies. The discovery of even simple life would fuel speculation about the existence of other intelligent beings and challenge many assumptions that underpin human philosophy and religion.

Through basic education and awareness campaigns, the general public can achieve a higher science and space literacy and cognitive resilience that would prepare them and prevent undesired social consequences of such a profound discovery and paradigm shift concerning humankind's position in the universe."

The above X factor assessment is surprisingly bold for a first mention of the subject. The last paragraph is particularly noteworthy – a recommended dialogue. A year earlier, Neil Freer and I offered to present on this subject in one of the 220 scheduled sessions. No response was received.

Reader Alert

The real heart of this book is ahead of you when you encounter what the ET races have shared with us. The importance of the other chapters is that they provide background and context information that is important to help you through some challenging times ahead. We have added a post script at the end of the book that will remind you of the material you have just read from the business community.

Every sector that currently defines Earth civilization will either transform or destruct. Those that move first and fast have the best chance of survival. Every political-ism will become dysfunctional. There will be a great opportunity for a heroic transformation of the global economic system. Go ahead and peek at the PS if you want to.

Chapter 4

The Conundrum of Consensus Trance.

C. B. Scott Jones

First Voice: "Have you ever visited __________ (fill in the blank), and noticed how different the people are?"

Second Voice: "Different? They are weird!! I couldn't wait to get home."

Consensus trance is the root of cultural shock and is a well-recognized phenomenon. The U.S. State Department, other government agencies that send personnel overseas in representational assignments, and savvy corporations with international business, pay attention to it. Perhaps the largest cohort of individuals exposed to culture shock is the thousands of college and university students that crisscross the globe in educational exchange programs. While it is important for a government to have its representatives in a foreign country represent the best of its culture, and particularly to avoid what became known as the "Ugly American" stereotype, it is far more important for student exchange programs to demonstrate that the stresses of cultural shock are a normal and more than a survivable situation. It will be an important model for what is ahead.

But there is a dark side to this subject, and important as to how we get to the post-disclosure world and maximize the potential of that future.

A pioneer researcher on the subject of consensus trance is Dr. Charles T. Tart. A psychologist and parapsychologist, he is known for his work on the nature of consciousness, and is one of the founders of the field of transpersonal psychology. He introduced the concept of consensus trance in his1986 book, *Waking Up, Overcoming the Obstacles of Human Potential.*

Tart identifies consensus trance as the everyday "normal" state of consciousness. That state defines all the cultural attributes of a Japanese, a Russian, a Pakistani, etc. This is the stuff of pride and honor and survival for each culture. If you want a stereotype definition of the population of the three countries noted in the previous sentence, ask a Korean, a Polish, an

India citizen. The process to achieve this normal state is enculturation, and the teachers are family, religion, history, geography, education, and others. A summary of Tart's description of enculturation shows why the results are so profoundly successful: This tutorial is used with permission from Tart.

"Each of us is born unto a culture, a group of people with a shared belief system, a consensus about how things are and how they ought to be...

Becoming "normal," becoming a full-fledged member of your culture, involves a selective shaping, a development of approved...potentials, an inhibition of disapproved...ones.

This interlocking set of beliefs includes a belief that we don't have a "belief system." Foreigners have strange "beliefs," but we know what's right!

Cultures almost never encourage their members to question them. Physical survival has been too precarious for too many people from most of our history, so there is a deep, if implicit, feeling that our culture has kept us alive in a rough world; don't ask questions, don't rock the boat. Cultures try to be closed systems."

We believe that the diversity of responses to the same questions asked of the ET cultures that we have interviewed is evidence that consensus trance is a universal condition. Why would we expect something else? Spatial issues, geographic separation of Earth's cultures are obvious factors in consensus trance. We now must consider distances in terms of light years, and additionally the issue of dimensionality.

Don't get discouraged, but seriously consider the need and importance to make room in the body of your consensus trance for what will be a "once in a world" event. Those who do will be on the path of discovery that is essential for the survival of Earth. From experience and wise ET counsel we know this is a long path, measured in terms of generation travel. Your boldness will be a profound gift to your consensus group.

If the reader is a member of a professional group within his/her culture, the challenges and opportunities are obvious. One example, if you are a scientist in the classical sense, you will embrace the leadership window opening for you to write the transition chapter in the new text book that says "goodbye" to the old hypotheses of your field, and launch into an academic adventure of ecstatic proportions.

There are examples when a window of potential change opens, and the results are anything but change.

The multi-million-copy bestseller that didn't dent the nation's consensus trance, *The Ugly American,* was written by William J. Lederer, a retired senior U.S. naval officer, and Eugene Burdick, a Professor of Political Science at the University of California, Berkeley. Published in 1958, their original plan was to write it as a non-fiction book during our build up to the Vietnam War. The intention was to challenge the policy decisions being made about South East Asia in our concerns about Communist moves in that area. Their publisher suggested that a novel based upon facts would be more effective. That advice was well taken, and the book spent 76 weeks on the best-seller list and sold approximately five million copies. After fifty-six years it is still in print, and in 2009, *The New York Times Sunday Book Review* published a1400 word essay by Michael Meyer, *Still 'Ugly" After All These Years.* Meyer pointed out that the Ugly Americans were not U.S. citizens wearing tube tops to the Vatican, or who speak English in a loud voice to assist understanding by a non-English speaking native in Uganda. The Ugly Americans are the occupying civilian and military elite and government contractors in Iraq and Afghanistan with buckets of bucks and a determination to nation building on a U.S. model. The problem, of course, is for that to work there would have to be a miracle conversion to the American consensus trance. Unfortunately, there is a direct relationship between power and hubris

The Ugly American became a runaway national bestseller boosted by numerous favorable reviews that combined the following points: It is a slashing exposé of American arrogance, incompetence, and corruption in Southeast Asia. Based on fact, the book's eye-opening stories and sketches drew a devastating picture of how the United States was about losing the struggle with Communism in Asia. Combining gripping storytelling with an urgent call to action, the book prompted President Eisenhower to launch a study of our military aid program that led the way to much-needed reform.

The Eisenhower action did not cause a ripple in the consensus trance. A young senator from Massachusetts, John F. Kennedy, was inspired by the book and mailed a copy of *The Ugly American* to each of his Senate colleagues. The message of the book was reflected in the Peace Corps. that Kennedy proposed in 1960.

When Kennedy became president in 1961, as Commander-in-Chief he directed that no U.S. military officer would be ordered to an overseas representational assignment unless he was linguistically qualified in the language of the country. At that time I was in the pipeline to become Assistant Naval Attaché to India and Nepal. My orders were modified and I spent eleven months learning Hindi. When I arrived in New Delhi I was met at the airport by my colleagues currently on duty in the Naval Attaché's Office, and two India Naval Officers from the India Naval Intelligence Directorate, our official host organization.

These two greeted me in Hindi and we had a short conversation in Hindi. I was the first military attaché in India to speak Hindi, and India Naval Officers were ordered to speak only in Hindi to me. That resulted in a significant improvement of my Hindi skills. Finally, after one month, at a social event the Chief of India Naval Staff, Admiral A. K. Chatterji, greeted me in English, "So Jones, what do you think of India?" I decided that the proper protocol would be to respond in the language of the question, and replied, "Admiral, I will never understand India." After a month in India I was finally emerging from cultural shock, and simply spoke the truth. Chatterji replied, "Good answer. We now know that you speak Hindi, but your technical vocabulary is weak, and our South India officers are complaining. You know that they also had to learn Hindi, and their English is much better than your Hindi. I think we should conduct our business in English, do you agree?" I replied that I could handle that. He smiled and ended the conversation with: "We knew that the U.S. was rich, but we had no idea that it was so rich to be able to waste a year of a professional office's career to learn a skill he did not need."

William Lederer retired from the navy as a Captain in the early 1950s and became the Far East correspondent for the Reader's Digest. His credentials as a Far East expert began in the early 1940s when as a junior naval office he served on a river gunboat in China. Now, as a foreign correspondent with still strong navy contacts he began reporting on the war in Korea. That brought him aboard the aircraft carrier USS Princeton (CVA-37), and into the home of my jet fighter squadron VF-191, in Ready Room 1. For two days he interviewed pilots after their return from combat missions, and as a gifted story teller told of his experiences in China where he served during the Japanese-Sino war. One story he told involved someone reaching out of his consensus trance in a bold attempt of radical change. Lederer subsequently wrote about this incident in *Our Own Worst Enemy*, published in 1968, ten years after writing *The Ugly American.* The details are simple. In 1940 in China he met a Jesuit priest who had a Vietnamese assistant. The priest asked Lederer if he had a copy of the U.S. Declaration of Independence on his gunboat. Lederer did and gave the copy to the priest who in turn gave it to his Vietnamese assistant who was eager to provide the document to Tong Van So. Whether that particular copy was delivered to Tong Van So is uncertain, but we do know that Tong Van So, better known as Ho Chi Minh, quoted from that U.S. document in his 1945 Proclamation of Independence of the Democratic Republic of Vietnam.

Here the tentacles of different consensus trances become impossible to trace, and that is not unusual. There are common components of virtually all consensus trances, security, control and independence being some of these. Was the term "Democratic Republic" simply words borrowed from the U.S.

document but actually meant something much different from the vision of the American founding fathers? There is reason to believe that Ho Chi Minh's vision was close to what our founding fathers shared. But the history of the Vietnam War ignores that possible window of peaceful transition from French Colonialism to a free and independent Vietnam. The U.S. already had articulated its Domino theory of what to fear in Southeast Asia, one country after another falling under Communist control. As Lederer predicted, our bet on a corrupt South Vietnam government in what was a civil war was a losing wager.

As a matter of strategy, Uncle Sam was playing Dominos while Ho Chi Minh was playing Xiangqi (Chinese chess is very popular in Vietnam).

Weapons of mass destruction exist for a reason – but there are other solutions. Well before the industrial revolution in Europe that harnessed the power of steam and shocked the environment with the foul residue of burning coal, other cultures at other times have experienced the consequences of technological advances. It is a hoary cycle of humanity. It is a simple fact of life. Once something is invented, it cannot be un-invented.

As you will shortly read, some of the voices from the cosmos talk about their fear of humans as well as their fear for humans. Of course through the lens of our consensus trance there are only as few nutty and dangerous countries on Earth, and most certainly MY country is not one of THOSE. Pakistan only has nuclear weapons because India has them. We will let the knowledgeable readers in Israel and Iran, the U.S. and Russia, etc., come up with their own proof of this reality.

However, there is an overarching reality on this issue that the ETs talk about. There are two bottom lines, the first is that countries have weapons of mass destruction for one primary reason – to use them, and secondly, the use of nuclear weapons has effects that our physics has not recognized, but the ETs know only too well.

Bombs are Made to Drop

What "nearly" happened in Vietnam years before the years of full U.S. military engagement there is not well known. And what did happen during the defeat of the U.S. is now rarely talked about. As a sad reminder, the war resulted in the death of 58,159 U.S. military and 303,635 wounded and over four million civilians killed in Vietnam, Cambodia and Laos. The intensity of the air war is likely forgotten, if ever generally known. The U.S. dropped 6,727, 084 tons of bombs during the Vietnam War. That was over twice the amount dropped by the Allies during World War II.

Operation Ranch Hand involved spraying nearly 20,000,000 gallons of Agent Orange, an herbicide, with the goal to defoliate jungle cover to expose guerilla forces and supply routes and to destroy food crops to force rural-to-urban migration. Unintended consequences were hundreds of thousands of civilians killed and maimed. The number of children born with birth defects is staggering.

Not to be forgotten is that the consequences of post-traumatic stress disorder remain a burden on the lives of uncounted thousands in Vietnam, Cambodia, Laos and the U.S. Additionally, in the U.S., suicide rates for Vietnam veterans are the highest of any other group.

When I became involved in naval intelligence, several assignments involved unique nuclear weapon issues. The first of these was when I was Intelligence Officer on the staff of Commander Carrier Division 14 (COMCARDIV 14, 1955-1957). One of the requirements of that position was to be a qualified Nuclear Weapons Deployment Officer. Training for this focused on weapon effects in order to maximize kill and damage rates as selected by the operational commander. In those years calculations were done on a slide rule, using values from lookup charts that had been created from hundreds of open-air nuclear tests shots at the Nevada Testing Grounds and in the Pacific Test Site. The final examination of the seven-week course was based upon a military situation where the friendly forces were surrounded in a basin by enemy forces on higher ground. We were given an 8X10 inch aerial photograph of the target area, and the commander's requirements for kill and damage. We could use up to three nuclear weapons to be delivered by carrier based naval aircraft. Our job was to select the desired ground zeros (DGZ), yields, and heights of burst. Intelligence elements included that the enemy was dressed in summer uniforms, short-sleeve shirts and shorts. Personnel were the principal targets, and thermal effects were to be maximized. Friendly forces would be underground, but expected to suffer light to medium levels of fatalities and injuries. When the examination was over I told the instructor that I recognized the photograph as Dien Bien Phu, circa March 13-May 7, 1954, and asked if the problem was theoretical or historical. He responded that he was the Nuclear Weapons Deployment Officer aboard a U.S. aircraft carrier deployed in the Gulf of Tonkin off the coast of Viet Nam and was directed to designate the weapons, yields, DGZs and heights of bursts in order to break the two-month siege of the surrounded French forces. He said that the weapons were prepared, moved to the flight deck, loaded aboard delivery aircraft awaiting launch orders to come from the Pentagon. The orders that came were to stand down and return the weapons to their Special Weapons Storage. I passed the final exam by selecting three MK-7 nuclear weapons, each with an 8 KT yield, and height of burst that maximized thermal effects without the fireball touching the ground. The expected outcome would have been that 50% of exposed personnel would have been instantly killed and an additional 30% would have died from severe burns within three days.

The politics of this event are detailed in Jules Roy's book, *The Battle of Dien Bien Phu.* The key participants are President Eisenhower and Chief of the Joint Chiefs, Admiral Arthur W. Radford. Radford was the navy's equivalent to General Curtis LeMay, USAF, in many pathological ways. During the subsequent U.S. Vietnam War, LeMay stated, "we're going to bomb them back to the Stone Age."

It was Admiral Radford's idea to use nuclear weapons to assist the French. He made this offer to the French ambassador in Washington, D.C., and after the French agreed, Radford ordered the navy to plan for the action. At that point Radford informed President Eisenhower of this grand plan. Only the president can authorize the use of nuclear weapons. Eisenhower told Radford then they needed to consult with the leadership of Congress about the plan. There is no public record of that meeting, but obviously cooler heads made the correct decision and Radford was told the tell the French ambassador that the attack was off. Roy's account of this moment is the French ambassador responded in disappointment, "That being the decision Admiral, I wish you had not made the offer in the first case."

The U.S. Vietnam War started in 1950 with the arrival of military advisors. U.S. involvement escalated in the early 1960's. U.S. combat troops were deployed beginning in 1965. Ho Chi Minh then warned that if the Americans "want to make war for twenty years then we shall make war for twenty years. If they want to make peace, we shall make peace and invite them to afternoon tea." Eight years later, June 1973, Congress passed the Case-Church Amendment prohibiting use of the U.S. military in Vietnam after August 15, 1973, without advanced congressional approval. President Ford announced the end of the war on April 23, 1975.

Earlier in this chapter the saga of the bestselling book, *The Ugly American* was given. The reader will not be surprised to hear that this cycle of high attention followed by minimum successful action to address the issue is not uncommon. The situation is that moving the consensual trance off its determined tract is the stuff of miracles. Never the less, within every consensus trance there are enlightened thinkers who are bold enough to stand up and declare, 'The emperor has no clothes,' listen to me, this is the universal reality. An outstanding contemporary example of this is David Korten who has written and lectured brilliantly on the need for global cultural transformation. His classic international bestseller, *When Corporations Rule the World,* is both a predictive warning about the current tragic economic conditions for most the world's population, and a blueprint for the needed transformation. But taking back control of the economy and politics from the corporations will take more will and skill than is currently available to mere citizens. Something more, a powerful ally is needed. The closing section offers hope and challenges. Read it carefully.

A Special Voice from the Cosmos

For centuries, Earth has been a battleground of wars: Hot, Cold, and Secret. The ETs have followed this closely, especially when our weapon technology became uncontrollable and crept into space. They have legitimate concern about the human fratricide taking place and want a dialogue about it.

It is obvious that Earth is at a tipping point, probably a situation not really rare in the magnitude of the cosmos. The solutions must come from the hearts and sweat of those who have caused the problems and from those who have closed their eyes and hearts and tolerated the excesses that now clearly predict the end of civilization, perhaps too grand a description of Earth's society.

The best that this book can do is to introduce some of the issues to be faced before it is reasonable to even expect that wise counsel, if offered, will be understood. To that end we asked a representative of a group that is a communication link between Earth humans and the Spiritual Hierarchy. This entity is a Pleiadean that uses the communication name Monitor.

"MONITOR: The organization of ET activities is simple in design, yet when applied to specific meetings and projects, can become rather complex. The Spiritual Hierarchy long ago set guidelines that are similar to the Prime Directive expressed in the Star Trek series. The principal responsibility for the growth of humans needs to be the responsibility of those humans. And therefore the tendency for people to seek a savior to save them from themselves needs to be avoided through ET interaction.

Protocols for working in cooperation with humans keep a focus upon human clarification of intentions. Many humans seeking contact with ETs seek not only to establish their point of communication and sense of reality in their contacts, but also tend to gain a sense of self-importance. The ego reactions attached to the need for self-importance are often challenging for participating humans to deal with. And thus there is a certain ego distortion that often accompanies human ET contacts.

Thus from the viewpoint of the Spiritual Hierarchy, ETs are encouraged to add experiences to their contacts with humans that bring about a neutralization of ego reactions. That can take several forms. It can at times lead to a sense that what the human wants, the human often has to wait and develop patience in order to achieve the goal.

The challenge in human and ET communication typically involves the great difference between the human mind and the cultivated ET mind. The human mind must stretch considerably to gain reasonable communication from the human standpoint. The challenge facing humans lies in the inadequate concepts or beliefs that the human holds as a result of cultural training.

In addition, most humans do not perceive beyond the physical easily. Yet they may, over a prolonged period of ET contact, gradually develop beliefs and skills in perceiving beyond the physical. ETs that exist in higher planes of existence find it quite difficult to relate to human concepts that stem from their experience in a physical plane. Communications between ETs and humans can often become distorted, with humans assuming physical plane concepts when ETs do not refer to them at all.

Thus a period of time involving small groups of humans and ETs is required to develop greater understanding between the two levels of consciousness.

The fears of humanity tend to arise when a human, on conscious or subconscious levels, feels that it deals with the unknown and the unknown generates feelings of vulnerability and threat. Human fears *must* arise and be purged during even short-term communication with ETs.

The human concept of *power* is focused upon physical plane experience and often quite at odds with the true expressions of power that have become commonplace skills of ETs. Humans tend to project human dynamics upon ETs, which is quite inappropriate.

With these challenges to communication between humans and ETs, a prolonged experience involving several separate groups is required to compile a variety of long-term interactions and conversations. Out of that compilation will come a greater understanding, yet it will likely require human generations.

That is our comment."

SCOTT: I think that is perhaps one of the most important responses that you have shared with me over the years. And I specifically ask permission to use this in a book that we are writing, *Voices from the Cosmos*.

MONITOR: We give our permission.

Chapter 5

The Exobiology Project

Angela T. Smith

From early 2003 through the end of 2011, I contracted, as a remote viewer, to an amazing man: a visionary CEO of a NY financial company. From January through December, 2006 we ventured on an unusual and innovative joint project, "interviewing" a series of twelve different alien races: the Exobiology Project. This work began with two simple questions: the first was, if remote viewers can perceive and assess on-Earth individuals and groups, why not off-Earth? We wanted to see if we could successfully contact ET races in order to learn about them.

The second question acknowledged that much off-Earth communication involved a telepathy-like channel. So, could this medium be useful to talk one-on-one with off-Earth races? The Exobiology project was very fruitful and now forms the second half of this book. My thanks go out, once again to this creative thinker and his farsighted projects.

Anonymity has been preserved for the client. His role in the financial world during the increasingly-troubled recession was valiant but he finally sold his businesses and retired. His position as sponsor, patron, and friend is truly appreciated and the nine years working for him were ones of exploration and discovery, "pushing the envelope", and excitement. Our work together focused mainly on conventional business matters but his brave approach to unconventional topics opened the doors to the Exobiology Project, as well as many others.

So, how did we do this? Many people would classify me as being a "channel." That word is correct, only in that I am acting as a conduit for the voices of the races. There is a difference between how I do what I do and how the public views what a channel does. A classic "channeler" is in an altered state, often sets their own self aside, and allows a discarnate entity (spirit, alien) to take over their physical body. The discarnate entity then uses the "channeler's" voice and body to relay information while the "channeler" is in deep trance. The channeler's voice often changes to reflect the gender, race, and personality of the channeled entity. How I work is quite different. Critics of works such as the Exobiology Project claim that individuals who report ET contact are either mentally ill, perpetuating a fraud, or are uneducated. This has not been the case in the majority of contact work. For the record, I have never suffered from a mental illness, have never had a criminal record, and I am educated at the post-graduate level. At some point, I believe that the accumulation of evidence on ET communication will prove the skeptics wrong.

My method had more to do with remote viewing and telepathy than channeling. At no point am I in deep trance, under hypnosis, and I do not let an entity take over my voice or body. My method is based on the intuitive, telepathic ability that everyone has to some degree. Much like math or music ability, some individuals have a lesser or greater capability to be intuitive.

I am, in a sense, "listening" and reporting. I pre-type the questions onto my computer, and then send out a request to the entity to be interviewed. As I read through the questions, I "listen" for the answers and type them into the computer document as they are perceived. I ask confirming and clarifying questions of the entity but, at no point, does the entity have control of my voice or body. This is very similar to a standard, human interview except that the method of choice is telepathy. A scientific review of telepathy and remote viewing is included in the Appendices at the end of this book.

The Exobiology Interviews are reported verbatim: that is the responses given by the ET races to questions have not been modified or edited in any way. The responses belong to the different Exobiology races. We wanted to use an interview protocol that was academically rigorous, so that its success or failure would guide us and other researchers in such other undertakings.

Finally, sociological questions from C. Wright Mills and Dan Brook's TSS Directory were asked in an effort to document information about the different races. Rather than repeat the same sociological questions for each race, their assessed responses have been summarized at the end of each interview.

This assessment model allowed a learning curve to develop over the year of interviews. Using a model that was designed to investigate human society, to assess ET culture was not the optimal method. But one that gave us the best information we could get under the circumstances. It should be remembered, too, that information from the ET races was filtered through the consciousness of the human interviewer.

Over the year, the questioning progressed from standard, philosophical, and sociological inquiries, to specific questions for each group; we asked races to talk about each other, and then invited the races to dialog as groups. We invited each ET group to recommend other groups to interview and finally, we did "site visits" to three ET home bases. This was definitely a learning curve!

Scott has written about the Consensus Trance Lens: how we filter reality through our own preconceptions. There is a huge problem with anthropomorphizing the ET races, when they are very different from us. However, until we have a Universal Decoder Ring, or meet them face-to-face, this is the best we can do. Regardless, of the method, what the ET races have revealed to us in their interviews is fascinating and informative.

By the late summer of 2012, my client had retired and emigrated, and the Exobiology Interviews had been sitting in my files for over seven years. I felt it was time for them to be published. Inquiries to individuals in the remote viewing and UFO worlds met with indifference, skepticism, and, even, alarm! One brave individual: Donald Ware, volunteered to send out the Exobiology Interviews: one each week, to Truthseekers, his 600+ email list. The response was very positive and the recipients wanted to read more! Thank you, Don.

During the months that the Exobiology Interviews were being shared with the Truthseekers group, a long-time colleague, C. B. Scott Jones, contacted me with the idea that the interviews could form the basis of a book that we could write together. Scott introduced me to two of his Exopolitics colleagues, the two Neils: Neil Freer and Neil Gould, and questions from the three of them formed the basis for a new series of interviews, with another ET race, the Anunnaki.

Thanks are extended to the representatives of the different ET races that came forward to be interviewed, sometimes, several times over many months. According to them, few humans reach out to them in this way but they are very interested in talking to us. So thank you to the Large Grays, Nordics, Small Grays, Hooded Reptilians (even though you didn't want to talk to me), the Indigo Hybrids, the Oranges, the Light Ones, the Dark Ones, the Anaka, the Lyrians, the Wing-Makers, the Duvel, the Sirians, the Rall, the Orbs, the Aldebarans, the Angels, and finally, thanks to the Anunnaki, for our latest interviews.

Chapter 6

The Exobiology Interviews

Angela Thompson Smith

Exobiology –The scientific field that investigates the potential for life on other planets.

Imagine that you were out in a pristine Amazon jungle and came across a group of indigenous people who had the ability to understand your language but had very limited one-on-one interaction with your world. How would you interact with them and what would you ask them? Now imagine that the race of people were not of this Earth? Could you apply the same sociological questions to them, as you would for any other group?

It is anticipated that this series of interviews will elicit critique, disbelief, and even ridicule. The series is published as a means to a greater understanding of and with our "off-planet" neighbors. In historic, recorded interactions with these mostly "off-planet" races there seems to have been a mind-to-mind communication known as telepathy. Telepathy has endured constant critique by science but has survived as one of the most robust of the anomalous human abilities. Telepathy is even cited by skeptics as possible explanations for other paranormal phenomena! Over the twelve month period, twenty different races were interviewed. All of the races were interviewed using a "stream of consciousness" remote viewing method.

Multiple sessions assessed which races are currently interacting with humankind. Factual information was requested and no placating responses were accepted. Null responses during an interview or silence on a topic was noted as NR – no response. It is to be remembered that these interviews involved non-human intelligence and much of it was not necessarily understandable to our human logic or understanding. We could not expect their logic to be the same as ours.

This was a difficult and prolonged project that was carried out with diplomacy and respect. Each project was concluded with a request for an introduction to another, possibly related, race to interview in a subsequent session.

The initial phases of the Exobiology projects focused on questioning five non-human races. This brought us into contact with many diverse races including Large Grays, Nordics (otherwise known as Whites), Small Grays, the Hooded Reptilians, an Indigo Hybrid, Orbs, Elementals, the Oranges, The Angels (also known as the Smooths), the Record Keeper race, The Gate Keeper race, Light Beings, the Tall Oranges, and the Anaka. More recently the projects have focused on the Lyrians, the Wingmakers or the Rall, the Sirians and more recent interaction with the Angels and more. As the Grays said "There are as many other races as stars in the sky."

Chapter 7

Prelude To The Interviews

Angela Thompson Smith

Everything has a beginning: this is how the interviews with the ET races began. I have always had a fascination with the concept of life existing outside the Earth: in particular Beings that may have visited our Earth or who had an interest in Earth. In 1990, I made a decision to use a newly learned skill, remote viewing, to investigate this idea. Over a series of purposeful remote viewings I made contact with an entity, that I will call the Monitor or Wise One, because of this entity's search for knowledge about the Human race.

February 25, 1990 Open Interface One

I decided to request a mental interface with the "Visitors" with several aims in mind:

1: To exchange information
2: To understand goals and
3: To achieve mutual cooperation.

At first I conveyed "Request Information" and "Request Interface" following a meditation period. However, I realized that those terms put us on an unequal standing and changed my thought to convey "Interface Open" to indicate openness for dialogue. I visualized myself before an open window through which an interface might take place and sensed interest and curiosity but nothing happened.

Then I found myself in a woodland scene, it was summer, and sunlight was streaming through the tall trees. I didn't understand at once, and then I realized that we were meeting on neutral territory. It was if we had to create a virtual meeting place that was neither theirs nor mine, although it did resemble an English woodland.

I walked through the woods and sat on a stone seat and waited. From out of the woods came "the Wise One" or Monitor, who I realized was one of their senior members, very wrinkled, and slightly stooped. We exchanged looks and each of us held out a hand. I decided to be honest and told the entity that his hand reminded me of a chicken claw and was repulsive to me. He (assuming a male gender) responded that, to him, my hand was just as repulsive. This got us off to a good start!

He asked whom I represented and I replied that, basically, I only represented myself, but indirectly represented many other people, both in close circles of friends and wider groups. But the decision to interface was mine alone. His reply was that he represented his entire kind, not that he was above or better than others, just a representative.

We agreed that there should be a sharing of information and a statement of goals but we would have to decide *what* information and *what* goals. This was easier for him as there was already a consensus on what could be represented by him. I was at a disadvantage as I spoke initially for myself but indirectly for others, a totally different process to theirs. We did decide that there should be mutual cooperation and that we should return to discuss other topics. At this point I was feeling exhausted and I decided to close the window - it was taking a great deal of energy to maintain the interface. However, it was agreed that the open window would be a signal to indicate openness to interface and we would meet again in a neutral mental setting. Some information would be given and translated by means of their technology and the entity and I would interface again when the next opportunity arose.

February 26, 1990. Open Interface Two

At 10 pm I entered a meditation state and visualized "Open Interface" as an open window. My mind wandered onto mundane thoughts about my daily work as I waited but my attention was brought back to the Monitor standing on his side of the window. He came to my side of the window into a virtual room. He stood and I sat. I asked if he wanted to sit. He replied that sitting and lying down were Human actions. He asked me why we had not adapted, over the centuries, to gravity and still had to counter its force by sitting. I said that I did not know. We agreed on the first of several ground rules:

1: We would each do what was normal for us: He would continue to stand and I would sit if I wanted. We would not expect the other to conform to our idea of normality.

2: We also decided that we would be honest, even to the point or risk of offending the other. This way we could learn without false pretense.

3: The Monitor said that my opening the dialogue was one-sided and that he should also have the opportunity to initiate open interface. At first I commented that this might not be convenient but realized how unilateral this was and agreed that we should both have the opportunity to initiate dialogue.

4: It was agreed that communication should be telepathic; sometimes in the form of reciprocal dialogue, sometimes in picture form.

I realized how unstructured I was being and I said "Where shall we begin?" to which the Monitor replied "We have already begun!"

At this point, when we had only been interfacing for about 5-10 minutes I said that I was tired and wished to end the interface. The Monitor responded that I was being unreasonable by calling him to interface for such a short time. I explained that I was tiring and that it was an effort for me to interface. I was basically multitasking; being in a meditative state, trying to keep some vigilant facility to dialogue and think, and trying to remember the dialogue in order to record it accurately. This was energy draining.

We agreed to close the interface and try again another time. Perhaps it will get easier with practice. However, I felt comfortable that we had been able to lay down some ground rules which are mutually agreeable. Although it seemed as if nothing major was accomplished I still felt that these two interfaces had been successful preliminary stages.

February 27, 1990. Open Interface Three

Later in February of 1990, I experienced a continuation of the Interfaces with the Monitor. I had decided not to Interface that day but perceived the Wise One or Monitor requesting an Interface around 10:35 p.m. So, I meditated and connected. We found ourselves in a lighted globe. The Wise One had a companion and requested that I bring another person to Interface. I explained that this was not going to be easy. Telepathy was not a strong characteristic of humans and I would have to arrange an Interface through physical means, such as the telephone. However, I tried to mentally contact "Mariah", whom I requested to Interface with us. I felt her to be present and visualized her wearing a purple warm-up suit. However, the contact was not maintained. The companion to the Wise One remained quiet.

The Wise One and I talked about our different concepts of time - - theirs communal, ours individual. The Wise One said that time was something that someone else measured and they received moment-by-moment instructions regarding what they should do. There was no planning ahead, time was related to *now* only.

I explained our concept of time as objective or linear, as well as time subjective or holistic. The Wise One could accept a holistic version of time. He asked me to describe clocks. I began by saying that clocks were devices for measuring time and took many forms. The earliest, simplest ones were just a stick in the ground measuring the shadow of the sun as it passed overhead. The Wise One queried "But you are measuring the passage of the sun only, not time." I tried to explain the idea that when the sun passed from point A to point B, that interval was accepted as a measurement of a unit of time.

There was a similar dialogue regarding clocks. I used the same argument that the interval between tick A and tock B was agreed upon as a unit of time. The response was that we were "only measuring sound." There was little acceptance of the concept of linear time - I almost said that the concept was alien to him!

This Interface presented two new issues:

1: The acceptance by them that more than one person could Interface but the realization that it was easier for them than for us; and

2: The dialogue regarding our concepts of time and its measurement showed the differences in our acceptance of those concepts.

I think we both realized that we only covered the surface of our queries. I started thinking personal thoughts towards the end of the dialogue and the Wise One abruptly terminated the session by stating "Interface closed." There was no reproach or anger, just a decision to end the dialogue until the next time. The next time turned out to be twenty-six years later!

Chapter 8

Talking With the ET Races

1: Talking With The Large Gray

This first series of interviews began the first week of January, 2006. Basically this project was carried out, with diplomacy and respect, as a study of different extraterrestrial races. These initial questions formed the basis of an inquiry to the first interviewed race: the Large Gray, and these same sets of questions were then asked of the other races as the Exobiology Project continued.

Part 1

Q: How do they (Large Grays) cooperate? Is there a Confederation that is acting together?

Large Gray: We act alone. We are one. We know of others. We are not part of the others. There is a Confederation. We are not part of the Confederation. The Confederation acts together.

Q: Can you first tell me which groups are part of the Confederation?

Large Gray: Too complicated.

Q: Please try.

Large Gray: Lights. Darks. Smooths (?) Greens (?) Propers (?) Roughs (?) Most of the void. We are not part of the Confederation.

Q: Why?

Large Gray: Not ready.

Q: What do races need to do in order to be ready?

Large Gray: Be prepared. Be obedient.

Q: You cannot be obedient to the Confederation?

Large Gray: We act alone. We are one.

Q: How can the Earth be included in the Confederation?

Large Gray: It will be invited.

Q: When?

Large Gray: NR (No response)

Q: Is there more to the Orbs and others and can they manifest responses? Are there different types of Orbs?

Large Gray: Orbs are energy and information. Orbs carry information. They are also pure information. They can be deciphered.

Q: How?

Large Gray: Mental intellect.

Q: Can they respond to requests?

Large Gray: Yes. Too complex. There are many different Orbs.

Q: Can you tell me some of the purposes of the Orbs?

Large Gray: Probes. Scouts. Play. Attracted by sound. Encode sound within structure.

Q: Is that shown by the rings and colors within the Orbs?

Large Gray: Yes. Everything has a frequency. Orbs absorb frequencies. Become information. Carry information.

Q: Do the Large Grays send Orbs?

Large Gray: Yes. Limited probes.

Q: Can the different extraterrestrial races also manifest responses and are they positively oriented? Are there inherent conflicts detrimental to our interests?

Large Gray: Yes. Races can manifest responses. They have been manifesting responses. Nobody listens or responds. Many positively oriented to each other. Some positively oriented to Earth. Few negatively oriented. Too basic and primitive. Some are detrimental to Earth interests. Earth too territorial and aggressive. Most races cooperative with each other. Question is too basic and too primitive.

Q: Do you mean that we are asking the wrong question or that our basic nature needs to change before we can ask that question?

Large Gray: Both.

Q: Can other alien races prevent abductions?

Large Gray: Yes but why?

Q: Abductions are mainly viewed as negative, as imposing on the free will of humans, and against our will.

Large Gray: Abductions are not negative. They are positive. They enhance the human.

Q: How?

Large Gray: Humans are limited.

Q: Who are the good guys, who are the bad guys and what can we learn from them?

Large Gray: Good guys, bad guys, unknown. There is mainly cooperation within and outside Confederation.

Q: Is there one group, at least, that is considered, outside the Confederation and negative?

Large Gray: Earth. Humans. Most others cooperate. Different but cooperate.

Q: Can some races render implants fallible?

Large Gray: Yes, but why?

Q: Humans consider implants to be imposing on free will and autonomy. They dislike the idea that implants locate and control.

Large Gray: Implants are fortunate.

Q: Does that mean that people with implants are fortunate?

Large Gray: Yes. Humans are limited.

Q: Can we interfere with the functioning of implants?

Large Gray: Yes, but why?

Q: The same as before.

Large Gray: Interference renders unfortunate.

Q: Are they the same races or different groups of the same race that are carrying out the abductions?

Large Gray: Two races carry out abductions. Grays and Nordics.

Q: Are the whites what we call the Nordics?

Large Gray: Yes. Others are interested and visit.

Q: Do the ones who visit carry out abductions?

Large Gray: No. They visit and interact.

Q: How do they travel and is this travel with or without vehicles?

Large Gray: Physics. Humans are limited. Frequency physics.

Q: Like crystals?

Large Gray: Crystals not involved. Frequencies carry information and energy.

Q: Could this information be conveyed to humans?

Large Gray: No. Humans are limited.

Q: Will there come a time when we are not limited?

Large Gray: Yes. In future.

Q: How long can hybrids stay on Earth and why has the hybridization program taken so long?

Large Gray: Hybrids have a limited stay. Earth is toxic. Oxygen is toxic. Hybrids adapted before Earth visit. Hybrids usually stay out.

Q: Out of Earth's atmosphere?

Large Gray: Yes. It is not complete.

Q: The hybrid program?

Large Gray: Yes. Going on. Not complete.

Q: When will it be complete?

Large Gray: Not known.

Q: What and who are the Indigo Children? Is there a specific race that is producing the Indigo Children?

Large Gray: Earth children. Less limited. Enhanced. No race producing them. They are noticed.

Q: Does this mean that there is no race that is producing the Indigo Children?
Large Gray: Yes.
Q: Have there always been Indigo Children?
Large Gray: Yes.
Q: Has any race enhanced the Indigo Children?
Large Gray: No.
Q: Are Indigo Children easier to communicate with?
Large Gray: Yes.
Q: Why are some species interested in hydrocarbons? Are they rare in the galaxy? What about other minerals and gases: hydrogen, boron? What purpose do these species put hydrocarbons to? Are we in conflict for these resources?
Large Gray: Goo.
Q: Is that what you call our minerals including hydrocarbons?
Large Gray: Yes. Not rare in galaxy. Convenient. Use varied. Baths. Study. No conflict. Abundant in universe. Convenient.
Q: Are you saying that minerals are mined from Earth because it is convenient?
Large Gray: Yes.

Part 2

In addition the following philosophical questions were addressed to each of the ET races.

Q: They obviously find our human civilization to possess valuable galactic characteristics, some of which they probably lost eons ago, or they wouldn't be interbreeding with us. They certainly possess the ability to destroy our human civilization, but have not, why?
Large Gray: Inbreeding not possible. Hybrids only possible. Emotions, hormones, functioning.
Q: Is that what you find interesting about us?
Large Gray: Yes. Hybrids not considered inbreeding. No need to destroy. Too interesting.
Q: Does that mean that no race will destroy Earth and humans?
Large Gray: Yes.
Q: What about the idea that some races lost valuable galactic characteristics that we might possess?
Large Gray: Humans are limited.
Q: Is this intergalactic ethics - being held to certain behavior by other ET civilizations? Or is it just that their self-interest benefits more by using us

for their own needs rather than simply destroying us (a similar model of how things operate on Earth)?

Large Gray: Not part of the Confederation, Repeating. Act alone. No need to destroy.

Q: Do certain races have a code of ethics?

Large Gray: No need, act alone or cooperate.

Q: Given the billions of likely planets in our galaxy alone, there couldn't be anything very unique and special about Earth. Although the need to mine some of the debris circling Saturn is puzzling - - the implications of which implies a gigantic civilization that is widespread in our galaxy with a vast need for ongoing raw material supply. I would very much appreciate your insights on what all this implies about the nature of intergalactic inhabitation, the inhabitants in a portion or all of our galaxy. Are they dominant or is there a cacophony of conflicting vested interests in our galaxy like here on Earth?

Large Gray: Earth is special and interesting. Intelligence is widespread. All of galaxy is inhabited. Humans are limited

Q: I take this phrase to mean that your answer would be beyond our intelligence?

Large Gray: Yes. Most act alone or cooperate. Not like Earth.

Q: What are the intentions of each race? What is each race's ongoing purpose and when will this be completed?

Large Gray: Ongoing. No final intention. Act alone or cooperate. No difference. Races different. Act alone or cooperate. No difference. No end completion. Ongoing.

Q: Will there be a scenario like a "shock wave" from a distant part of the galaxy that will wipe out Earth? Will it hit the Earth and its oceans?

Large Gray: Minimal. Ongoing. Will impact but not major. Always ongoing.

Q: What are the meanings of the "disaster scenes" that are shown to abductees?

Large Gray: Learning. How to cope. Emotions.

Q: Do you have emotions?

Large Gray: Yes. Limited.

Q: What does the future of the Earth look like, say in 2012? What types of scenarios, based on fact, will Earth experience?

Large Gray: Future not available.

Q: Does that mean you cannot see future events or that you are unwilling to share with us?)

Large Gray: Both.

Q: That is conflicting.

Large Gray: Yes. Humans are limited. You have the knowledge.

Q: Are there specific races that are influencing our leaders and the process of civilization? Does any one race or a combination control our civilizations? If so why is this permitted?

Large Gray: No race controls Earth. Visiting and interacting.

Q: We consider abductions and implants as controlling.

Large Gray: Abductions and implants fortunate.

Q: Do some leaders have implants and are abducted?

Large Gray: Yes. Fortunate. Permitted.

Q: Do individuals give permission or is this an implied permission?

Large Gray: All fortunate is permitted.

Q: Would other civilizations be able to counter possible Earth changes? Are the Orbs more positive to humans?

Large Gray: Earth changes minor and ongoing. No need to counter. Orbs energy and information, no emotions. No positive or negative. Just energy and information.

Q: Do we ascribe emotions to the Orbs, positive and negative?

Large Gray: Yes.

Q: Regarding other controlling civilizations, what can we do as humans to enter this chain of command?

Large Gray: Act alone or join. No chain of command. Most work alone.

Q: Is the chain of command idea solely an Earth one?

Large Gray: Yes.

Q: What about the Nordics, Large Grays, Small Grays and other races appearing to have a chain of command?

Large Gray: Work alone or join together.

Q: Does that mean that some of them work together, cooperate, and others work alone on specific interests?

Large Gray: Yes.

Q: Most religions of the world accept life after Earthly death. 96% of humans accept this as fact. What is the alien concept and is there an equivalent life after death for them?

Large Gray: Humans are limited.

Q: No, I would like to hear what you know about this!

Large Gray: NR

Q: What mutual benefits are in place between different civilizations?

Large Gray: Join or act alone. Join, work together. Strengthen purpose and outcome.

Q: Could I eventually put together a chart of who works together and who works alone?

Large Gray: Yes.

Q: Basically, as a start, which of the Small Grays, Large Grays and Nordics works together and which work alone?

Large Gray: Large and Small Grays together. Nordics (Whites) alone.

Q: But Whites are seen with both types of Grays on craft?

Large Gray: Yes, visiting, alone, working.

Q: They appear to be working in cooperation with the Grays?

Large Gray: No. Visiting, alone, working.

Q: What will help the human race survive? Is the human race expendable? Are we in danger of decimation some time in the future?

Large Gray: No. Humans limited but ongoing. Will survive. Not expendable. Valuable. Life. Ebbs and flows of life. Natural and expected.

Q: Would there be a sharing of resources with different species in the future. This could affect the Earth financially. Would our leadership agree to share resources? How best can we manage our natural resources without destroying ourselves?

Large Gray: Sharing in place. No need for leadership to agree. Sharing not in conflict with management of resources. Humans are limited and will cause conflict anytime.

Q: Are some races hindering or helping us? Do they have a respect for intelligent life?

Large Gray: All respect life. All respect Human life. No hindering or helping. Respect and sharing. Humans act alone, no need for cooperation to help or hinder sharing.

Q: That is difficult to understand.

Large Gray: Humans alone but sharing with others.

Part 3

1) Social Structure:

Large Gray: We are united. We are alone. We are not of the Confederation.

Q: I need more than that? How does your society differ from, say, that of one that is in the Confederation?

Large Gray: We are arranged in ninths. Top nine and down. There are always nine.

Q: You said before that there was no hierarchy.

Large Gray: We are sets of same born in ninths.

Q: Are you born in the same manner as humans?

Large Gray: No. We are taken as immature and grown. We have special needs.

Q: So, if you have no hierarchy, are you a democracy, with every one thinking for itself?

Large Gray: Yes, but linked together always in thought.

Q: So, by interviewing you, I am also interviewing all other Large Grays?
Large Gray: Yes, they all share.
Q: That is an awesome thought!
Q: How do you instigate change, is there a vote?
Large Gray: There is little change. We all decide.
Q: Who made the decision not to join the Confederation?
Large Gray: We were not ready. We were not invited.
Q: Are you physically scattered across the galaxy or mainly all in one place?
Large Gray: Mostly in one place, many scattered across the galaxy.
2) Social Change:
Large Gray: We have always been. Before human history. No place in changing human history
Q: Some say that alien races designed us? Is that so?
Large Gray: No. Natural beginning.
Q: How is history recorded in your race?
Large Gray: History remembered by all.
Q: Do you have writing, books, or documents?
Large Gray: No, all is remembered by all.
Q: Historically, what are some major events in which your race has interacted?
Large Gray: NR
3) Social Inequality:
Large Gray: Repeated. Confederate together, others alone.
Q: Are there traits that your race shares with the human race?
Large Gray: Yes, cooperation, trust, shared thought.
Q: In what ways are you different from us?
Large Gray: Independent yet unified as whole. All share thoughts. Able to travel.

Part 4

The following was taken from the TSS Director, an online effort to document general bodies of information, established by sociologist Dan Brook. The interview structures, originally designed for human cultures, also became part of the assessment of each alien culture. This introduction will not be repeated in subsequent interviews.

Q. What are people thinking and doing there?
Large Gray: All share thinking and doing. All know all. Thinking and doing the same. Nothing one does, others do not know.
Q: So there is no individuality?
Large Gray: All individuals.

Q: There is a difference in definition of individual. Humans think and act without everyone else knowing what they are thinking or doing, most of the time.

Large Gray: NR

Q: What kinds of people are there?

Large Gray: All one. No kinds of people except different races.

Q: How are you like the Small Grays?

Large Gray: Same. Thinking and doing shared. Some thinking and doing not shared. Cooperation. Working together.

Q: How are you and the Small Grays unalike?

Large Gray: Different travel. Some not sharing. Small Grays fortunate.

Q: Does that mean that they have implants?

Large Gray: Yes.

Q: Who is included and who is excluded?

Large Gray: None excluded, all included.

Q: What rules and norms govern behavior there?

Large Gray: No rules or norms, all included, all shared. No behavior.

Q: Here we include behaviors such as eating, sleeping, social customs. Do you have rules that govern those behaviors?

Large Gray: All share.

Q: How are roles assigned and tasks divided?

Large Gray: No. All share and none is divided.

Q: For example, you are answering my questions, so you are acting alone in an assigned task, you are divided in this task?

Large Gray: No. All answering, none acting alone, none divided.

Q: Who says so?

Large Gray: All say so. There is no division and none apart from the all.

Q: How are people socialized?

Large Gray: No, we are all one.

Q: For example, here children are taught the rules of society at an early age. Do you have the same rules?

Large Gray: No, the nutrients we share teach rules. Shared thoughts teach rules.

Q: Whose interests do these social arrangements serve?

Large Gray: The all serves the all. All interests are served.

Q: Who benefits and who loses?

Large Gray: All benefit, none lose.

Q: What powerful people, processes, institutions, and structures influence these arrangements?

Large Gray: All are the same. None different.

Q: In what ways are things changing there and in what ways are they staying the same?

Large Gray: All stays the same.
Q: When, how, and why do people resist?
Large Gray: None resist. All are one. None is different.
Q: Is this process or system relatively sustainable?
Large Gray: Yes.
Q: It all sounds boring according to Earth interactions.
Large Gray: All is as it is.

Assessment of the Large Gray

While this interview may have appeared stilted and, even, boring at times, it shows the mindset and mind-view of the Large Gray. The Large Gray didn't answer certain questions: this might have been because they did not know the answer, did not want to answer, or were prevented from answering for some reason. For example, the question about life after death was not answered. It is possible that there is no life after death for the Grays. Also the Gray could not come up with any estimates of when the Earth could join the Confederation. Also the commonly used phrase "Humans are limited" is often given when the Gray does not want to answer a question or feels that Humans will not understand the answer. This indicates a race that either considers itself superior or does not have the answers.

It is possible that there <u>is</u> some division of knowledge and not all knowledge is shared by the Grays. For example the Large Gray could not state which historical events the Grays had been involved in. It gave the excuse that answers were "too complicated" as "Humans are limited." It could not, or would not, give the physics of their travel!

A quick analysis of the Gray's interactions (I am not a linguist) indicated a scarcity of language and vocabulary, very little creativity, and a "high-handed", even flippant manner of speech. It is interesting that the Grays view abductions and implants as positive and "fortunate," despite my questions about autonomy and control. Also the continued use of "Humans are limited" was annoying and arrogant.

There was no face-to-face interaction with the Large Gray but there was definitely mutual awareness and focused interaction. As this was not a face-to-face interaction, personal space could not be assessed but the Large Gray did take verbal turns in the interview showing awareness of personal space. The Large Gray was able to give us some glimpses of its culture, however stereotypical.

In this brief encounter with the Large Gray, it seems that there is very little culture in their system. Earth culture and societies are varied, colorful, and vibrant compared with the life of the Large Gray. It is very tempting to judge alien cultures by our own Earth standards. We are so diverse and yet retain global norms, such as commerce, privacy rights, freedom of speech, humor, etc. None of these appear to be present in the Large Gray society. Perhaps that is why we are, as a species, so interesting to them.

Many researchers have discovered a correlation between symbols found in crop circles, UFO sightings, and symbols remembered by abductees to symbols such as rune glyphs and other ancient markings. A study of these symbols could tell us more about different alien cultures. This has been a fascinating first session. I have learned a great deal from it and hope that the Large Grays have also learned more about our Earth society.

This interview with the Large Gray opened up the interview process to other groups. The next two races to be interviewed were the Nordics and Small Gray.

2: The Exobiology Project: Talking With The Nordics

Part 1

Q: How do they cooperate? Is there a Confederation that is acting together?

NORDICS: We are part of the Confederation; in fact, we were part of the early group. We are distributed throughout the galaxy and very abundant in your Earth region.

Q: Did a group of us see a couple of Nordics over the Millennium New Year's Day at the Stratosphere?

NORDICS: Yes but we prefer to be called the Whites. You saw two of our group.

NORDICS: Yes.

Q: How was in that I only saw the female Nordic coming down the escalator and not the male?

NORDICS: We have abilities and physics that are, as yet, unavailable to Humans although you are near. We cooperate with all races, including the Small and Large Grays. They are not part of the Confederation and will probably never be.

Q: There has been documentation that you have been seen on craft with Grays? What has been your role?

NORDICS: Please refer to them as Grays, not grays, they are a distinct species. We refer to Humans, not humans. We work with them for our own purposes. They collect Humans; we take advantage of this collection for our own purposes.

Q: We call the collections, abductions. What is your purpose in working with Humans?

NORDICS: The Grays are interested in physical aspects of Humans; we are interested in the intellect and personality. We are not concerned with how Humans are collected. They are available for us. So we do our work with them.

Q: Does your work with Humans benefit us?

NORDICS: It neither benefits nor harms Humans. It is important to us.

Q: How is it important to the Nordics?

NORDICS: Humans will one day join the Confederation, we need to be aware of how they think, feel, react.

Q: Do the Grays sometimes offer some of your scenarios, for example, the Doomsday scenarios?

NORDICS: Yes. We act in cooperation with the Grays.

Q: Is there more to the Orbs and others and can they manifest responses? Are there different types of Orbs?

NORDICS: Orbs are energy and information. This is well known among the Grays and the Nordics. They do not have personalities or purpose, as is thought by Humans. They can transform into Human shapes or Gray shapes but they are not Humans or Grays. They act as scouts, probes, carriers of information across distances.

Q: Can the Orbs be called?

NORDICS: Yes, we call them to give them information that can be transported across distances. Think of them as workers, rather than individuals. Once their purpose has been carried out, they usually dissipate into the atmosphere.

Q: Some of them appear to have faces?

NORDICS: The faces are a form of recognition to the receiver of the information. They are the faces of the individuals who form the spheres and they are for identification only. The Orbs are not personalities themselves. Yes, there are many different types of Orbs.

Q: So, someone could call an Orb, imprint it with information, and this information could be sent to another individual? Can Humans do this too?

NORDICS: Yes, Humans can do this but they cannot yet perceive Orbs all the time with their eyes, only with technology. Nor can they decode the information that is carried by the Orbs.

Q: Can the different extraterrestrial races also manifest responses and are they positively oriented? Are there inherent conflicts detrimental to our interests?

NORDICS: Most of the races, not living on the Earth, are cooperative but separate. For example, the Nordics and the Grays work together, cooperate, but they have different roles. Positive and negative are Human terms and do not apply. We do what we have to do. Grays do what they have to do. We do not interfere with each other. The work of the Nordics and the Grays are not detrimental to Humans.

Q: Humans view abductions and what is done to abductees as detrimental.

NORDICS: That is a Human perspective. Abductions are not detrimental; in fact they are beneficial to Humans, in the long run.

Q: How?

NORDICS: They facilitate mental growth and development.

Q: Are you involved in forming the Hybrids?

NORDICS: Yes, we cooperate with the Grays. The Hybrids are not Human, they are not Gray, they are not Nordic, they are something else. They are their own species. They are called the New. We will continue to call then Hybrids. They contain aspects of Human, Gray and Nordic.

Q: What is their purpose?

NORDICS: They do work that Nordics, Humans, and Grays cannot do, or to go where Nordics, Humans, or Grays cannot go. They are emissaries, workers, travelers, pioneers.

Q: Can other alien races prevent abductions?

NORDICS: Yes, Humans can prevent abductions.

Q: How?

NORDICS: By requesting it. Humans are not always aware that they have been abducted and so cannot request that they be stopped. Some Humans are aware of the abductions but have a need to continue to be abducted because of the psychological links to the Grays and the Nordics. Much of this is below the surface of consciousness. Very few abductees want the abductions to stop. That is our experience.

Q: Human abductees may suffer from psychological and physical trauma because of the abductions.

NORDICS: No abductee has lost their life, no abductee has lost a limb, no abductee has lost their mind because of abductions. Trauma is minimal. It is Human society that creates the perception of trauma.

Q: Who are the good guys, who are the bad guys and what can we learn from them?

NORDICS: There are no good guys or bad guys. These are Human terms and irrelevant in our race. Each race has its agenda and mission. Some of these may be opposite what others do and say but there is cooperation. Territoriality and aggression are Human traits. Humans can learn from the Grays and the Nordics. They can learn cooperation and survival.

Q: Can some races render implants fallible?

NORDICS: Yes, Humans can render their own implants and those of others fallible, just by willing it. Humans have more abilities that they know about. That is why there are so many abductions. Implants routinely fail because of abductee will. Implants are specifically formed with this factor in mind. Multiple implants are in place because of this fact. It is not a weakness of the implants or the implanters, it was designed that way.

Q: We would call this a moral dilemma that abductees can make their own implants fail.

NORDICS: It is not a moral act; it is just the way it is.

Q: Can abductees ever be implant free?

NORDICS: For short periods of time. Implants will be replenished.

Q: Can we interfere with the functioning of implants?

NORDICS: The answer is as above.

Q: Are they the same races or different groups of the same race that are carrying out the abductions?

NORDICS: It is the Grays, usually the Small Grays, that carry out the abductions, as they have technology and skills that the Nordics do not have.

Q: Such as?

NORDICS: They have the technology to counter Earth's gravity, they have the ability to dissolve matter, to pass through matter, they have the ability to interact with the Human mind.

Q: Nordics do not have these abilities?

NORDICS: We let the Grays carry out these functions. We have other abilities.

Q: Such as?

NORDICS: We can become invisible, as you saw with the male Nordic at the Millennium, we can travel non-materially long distances, and we can perceive many minds at one time.

Q: How do they travel and is this travel with or without vehicles?

NORDICS: Usually we travel non-materially.

Q: We call that teleportation.

NORDICS: We also travel in the Gray's craft and other races' craft.

Q: Are there physics that we don't know yet, by which you can achieve these abilities?

NORDICS: Yes, but Humans are getting there. Humans are too afraid of this technology. They worry about losing individuality, the soul, the mind but these go along with the body. The body is only matter and can be reconstructed anywhere. The mind or soul is what travels and goes into the reconstructed body at the destination.

Q: I have often wondered about that.

NORDICS: Humans have to overcome many mental and physical barriers before being able to travel in this way.

Q: Some Humans can travel mentally outside their body and can sometimes perceive the world from another Human body. Is this a form of teleportation?

NORDICS: Yes. In Nordic technology, a whole new body, which is a complete copy of the original, is provided for the mind, it is not owned by another individual.

Q: How is the new body formed?

NORDICS: It is manufactured from available energy in the atmosphere according to a pattern that is sent ahead of the mind.

Q: Fascinating!

Q: How long can Hybrids stay on Earth and why has the hybridization program taken so long?

NORDICS: Some Hybrids remain on Earth for a short time. Please refer to them as Hybrids, not hybrids, as they are a separate race. Many are sent as emissaries, travelers, explorers, to other parts of the galaxy. The hybridization process will continue, as it has continued, until there is no more need of the Hybrids.

Q: What and who are the Indigo Children? Is there a specific race that is producing the Indigo Children?

NORDICS: The Indigo Children are named by Humans. They are not formed by us. They are not Hybrids. They have always existed on Earth. Children with special abilities have always been born. What they become depends on their socialization. Some become criminals and murderers, these Indigo Children are never talked about.

Q: Are the Nordics and Grays especially interested in the Indigo Children?

NORDICS: Yes. They have many traits that we need in the Hybrids. They are also easier to interact with.

Q: The Tall Gray said this too.

NORDICS: More Indigo Children, than regular children, are collected by the Grays.

Q: Why are some species interested in hydrocarbons? Are they rare in the galaxy? What about other minerals and gases: hydrogen, boron? What purpose do these species put hydrocarbons to? Are we in conflict for these resources?

NORDICS: Nordics do not mine minerals or other substances. They have no need for these substances. The Large and Small Grays and others collect these substances. The Grays need them for food, for soaking, for feeding, for manufacture, and for trade. There is no conflict in collecting these substances. They are freely available in the galaxy and can be collected anywhere. There is no conflict.

Part 2

Q: They obviously find our human civilization to possess valuable galactic characteristics, some of which they probably lost eons ago, or they wouldn't be interbreeding with us. They certainly possess the ability to destroy our human civilization, but have not, why?

NORDICS: Interbreeding involves three races: the Nordics, the Grays, and Humans. The Nordic portion of the Hybrids includes their intelligence, other mental abilities, and some physical characteristics such as the white hair and blue eyes. What is valuable about the human portion is the ability to generate emotions, the ability to think in abstract ways, to reason about the past and the future, and the Human quest for exploration and discovery. There has been no need, and probably will continue to be no need, to destroy Human civilization.

Q: Is this intergalactic ethics - being held to certain behavior by other ET civilizations? Or is it just that their self-interest benefits more by using us for their own needs rather than simply destroying us (a similar model of how things operate on Earth)?

NORDICS: There is no ethical reason for destroying the Earth civilization, either our own or from other civilizations. It just is. When there is no reason to destroy, destruction doesn't happen. We do not destroy when there is no reason. There is self-interest in that the Hybrids will continue to be produced if Earth continues.

Q: Given the billions of likely planets in our galaxy alone, there couldn't be anything very unique and special about Earth. Although the need to mine some of the debris circling Saturn is puzzling - - the implications of which implies a gigantic civilization that is widespread in our galaxy with a vast need for ongoing raw material supply. I would very much appreciate your insights on what all this implies about the nature of intergalactic inhabitation, the inhabitants in a portion or all of our galaxy. Are they dominant or is there a cacophony of conflicting vested interests in our galaxy like here on Earth?

NORDICS: The inhabitants of the galaxy fall into two groups: those who work together and those who don't. There is no conflicting for raw materials, they are everywhere. It is not like on Earth. Earth is a closed system with the mistaken belief that resources are limited. There are resources that can be mined from the sea, from the air, from the water on the land. Humans restrict themselves to one or two ways to obtain resources, even though there are many. There is the mistaken belief that those who can control the resources control the Earth. This is not the case as these same resources can be found everywhere. It is small thinking. The galaxy is not like the Earth but the Earth could be like the galaxy.

Q: What are the intentions of each race? What is each race's ongoing purpose and when will this be completed?

NORDICS: The main intention of the Nordics is to explore, either as they are or through the Hybrids. The Nordics have no limit on their exploration but the Hybrids add other dimensions to the exploration such as a sense of inquiry. Other intentions of the Nordics are to maintain themselves as a species, to support other species in the Confederation, to grow in knowledge, and to encourage other species to grow and join the Confederation.

Q: When will the Earth be ready to join the Confederation?

NORDICS: In its current state the Earth is not ready. There has to be a sense of cooperation instead of territoriality, working together rather than war, and hands open in acceptance instead of closed in anger.

Q: Will there be a scenario like a "shock wave" from a distant part of the galaxy that will wipe out Earth? Will it hit the Earth and its oceans?

NORDICS: This scenario has happened before. It is possible that it will happen again. The Nordics show scenarios such as this to abductees to prime the Earth for such events. There is the mistaken idea that the scenarios are actually predictors of real future events. That isn't so. They are shown as possibilities so that Earth can take precautions. For example, a shock wave from a distant part of the galaxy could be ameliorated by underground living spaces with water, food, and other necessities, available under the ground. A shock wave could hit the Earth's oceans and could be a major blow to the Earth but it has survived before and it will survive again. Humans think very much in 50 and 100 year cycles and do not take into consideration distant past and distant future events.

Q: What does the future of the Earth look like, say in 2012? What types of scenarios, based on fact, will Earth experience?

NORDICS: The Nordics do not speculate on near future events. The Nordics think more in terms of long term consequences. In the short term, Earth will be much as it is now, with increased misuse and hoarding of resources. The Nordics do not see the Earth being very much different than it is now.

Q: Are there specific races that are influencing our leaders and the process of civilization? Does any one race or a combination control our civilizations? If so why is this permitted?

NORDICS: Nordics have more of an effect on Earth civilization and leadership. Unlike the Grays, the Nordics are able to blend in with Earth's inhabitants, they are not nocturnal (like the Grays), and have a command of Earth languages. There is no agenda to influence Earth's leadership although there is an interest in how the Earth is governed. No one race or combination control Earth's civilization.

Q: Would other civilizations be able to counter the possible Earth changes? Are the Orbs more positive to humans?

NORDICS: While the Nordics are interested in and interacting with Humans, we do not have any wish or need to counter Earth changes. Humans are an intelligent species that often acts in unintelligent ways. That is how it is. Orbs are no more positive to humans than to any other species. Humans are able to summon Orbs and to interact with Orbs from other sources but have little understanding of their function or purpose. Orbs simply carry information and energy and are not autonomous.

Q: Regarding other controlling civilizations, what can we do as humans to enter this chain of command?

NORDICS: The Confederation is a collection of species throughout the galaxy that have come to certain understandings. There is no hierarchy or chain of command. The species within the Confederation have come to understand that the best results come from shared interest rather than conflict, from cooperation rather than competition, and from shared resources rather than territoriality. To enter the Confederation, Earth needs to be united in these understandings.

Q: Most religions of the world accept life after Earthly death. 96% of humans accept this as fact. What is the alien concept and is there an equivalent life after death for them?

NORDICS: There is no equivalent belief in Nordic thinking to the human concept of reincarnation. There is a belief that the Hybrids carry part of the Nordic soul on their travels. The fact that the Nordics can transfer their mind/soul to a body copy, that has been sent on ahead, is equivalent to a continuation of life. If the original body dies, while the mind/soul is in its body copy, it can carry on functioning as if they were in their original body. So, there is no death as seen on Earth when the physical body dies.

Q: What mutual benefits are in place between different civilizations?

NORDICS: The mutual benefits that take place are between the members of the Confederation in that there is a sharing of information between the species. There are also mutual benefits that take place between other species, too, such as that between the Nordics and the Grays in the sharing of Humans and Earth resources.

Q: What will help the human race survive? Is the human race expendable? Are we in danger of decimation sometime in the future?

NORDICS: The Human race will always survive but in different numbers and at different times. There will always be a Human race, whether they survive as inhabitants of Earth or as part of the Hybrids in some other part of the galaxy. There will always be the danger of decimation, as there have been throughout Human history and well into the future. The Human race is not expendable neither is any other race, but races ebb and flow as do other Earth inhabitants.

Q: Would there be a sharing of resources with different species in the future. This could affect the Earth financially. Would our leadership agree to share resources? How best can we manage our natural resources without destroying ourselves?

NORDICS: It does not matter whether the Earth leadership approves or does not approve of sharing resources. The resources are there for everybody. The resources are ubiquitous through the galaxy. Humans, too, could share in the resources that are available outside of the Earth. Humans can learn to manage natural resources without destroying themselves by the realization that resources are not limited.

Q: Are some races hindering or helping us? Do they have a respect for intelligent life?

NORDICS: There is a respect for Human intelligence and life but the only help that other races give is to encourage Humans to embody the qualities needed to join the Confederation.

Q: How is the collecting of Abductees helping the human race? Most see it is hindering Humanity.

NORDICS: Abductees are not harmed during their abductions; they are helped as they help the Nordics and the Grays. They can have the satisfaction that part of their race is exploring the stars. This is respect.

Q: Most Humans would not see this as respect.

NORDICS: It is respect for Humans.

Part 3

1) Social Structure:

NORDICS: The structure of Nordic society is that we are all responsible to the whole but have autonomy in our actions. There is a lot of communication between Nordics, most of it on a mind-to-mind basis but some of it, particularly in Human public, voice-to-voice. There is a group consensus on most things, this consensus changes minute to minute, and from situation to situation. Personal decisions are discussed, agreed upon, and then acted upon. The essential components of Nordic society are communication and consensus. This differs from Gray society where there is total mind-to-mind communication, no voice-to-voice communication, and group mind-think. What this means for Nordic society is that it can be more flexible for the individual compared with Gray society.

Q: Does this mean that you discussed my request for an interview with other Nordics before we communicated and came to a consensus that this was OK?

NORDICS: Yes. Yes.

Q: Does communication take place between the whole of Nordic society or just a particular group?

NORDICS: It depends on the situation. A minor decision requires a small group consensus. A larger decision requires a larger group consensus.

2) Social Change:

NORDICS: Nordic society has been around for the whole time that Humans have had a history and even prior. Human/Nordics, as might be imagined, came from an early experiment to produce Earth-based Hybrids. The modern Human/Nordics do not now possess any Nordic or Gray characteristics, just the physical characteristics of coloring. We make history by discussing, and then acting, seeing what happens, discussing, and then acting again. Nordics have not had a significant effect on Human history although we have been present for a long time.

3) Social Inequality:

NORDICS: In Nordic society there are not many inequalities as we all possess the same abilities. Individuality is not as strong as in Human society. However, we can pass as Human, in Human society, are adept at languages and social customs, we do not have as much humor or emotionality as Humans. If there is more than one of us in a group, we may seem to be conferring with each other more than Humans. We consider it a great honor to be present in Human society and as part of the Hybrids. Some Nordics bilocate into Earth society to study and learn about Human society.

Part 4

Q. What are people thinking and doing there?

NORDICS: Nordics think and do by group consensus and are most everywhere in the galaxy. Our home is TS3490 on a map coordinate system designed by your NASA.

Q: I am not sure of this designation or of the system. I Googled "NASA Map Coordinates" and came up with a Galactic Coordinate Map that has coordinates between 90 and 180 degrees. Not sure how to read this map. 90 would be somewhere halfway along the lateral line and 34 possible towards its inner center?

Q: Where do the Grays come from?

NORDICS: RB457Q:

Q: What kinds of people are there?

NORDICS: The Nordics consider themselves a people under every definition. They are physical but can bi-locate a spirit/mind into a prepared physical body at another location.

Q. Who is included and who is excluded?

NORDICS: All Nordics are included in Nordic society. No Nordic is excluded. If a Nordic is impaired or damaged they cannot communicate, cannot function, and do not survive.

Q. What rules and norms govern behavior there?

NORDICS: The rules and norms are communication before action. Level of communication before action are decided by the complexity of decision.

Q. How are roles assigned and tasks divided?

NORDICS: Again, roles are assigned through communication, mostly mind-to-mind and action by one or more Nordics.

Q. Who says so?

NORDICS: The group says so.

Q. How are people socialized?

NORDICS: The group socializes.

Q. Whose interests do these social arrangements serve?

NORDICS: The group.

Q. Who benefits and who loses?

NORDICS: Mostly the group benefits, sometimes a Nordic loses due to inability to communicate. Sometimes there is a glitch in the prepared body that is to receive a bilocated mind/soul. If the glitch involves the ability to communicate, that one is lost. It happens rarely.

Q. What powerful people, processes, institutions, and structures influence these arrangements?

NORDICS: All of these arrangements have been put in place long ago and work efficiently. As mentioned, there is sometimes a glitch but rarely.

Q. In what ways are things changing there and in what ways are they staying the same?

NORDICS: Most things stay the same, little changes.

Q. When, how, and why do people resist?

NORDICS: There is group consensus and very little resistance.

Q: Is this process or system relatively sustainable?

NORDICS: Yes, very sustainable.

Assessment of the Nordic

The Nordics seem to be much more vocal and communicative than the Large Gray. They seem to have many unusual talents and the ability to merge with Human society. The Nordics have complete mastery of time and space.

They are not "zoned" in one time and space. They appear to communicate before they act and are able to pre-fabricate bodies into which they can bilocate. Nordics operate on a system of norms that are pre-agreed by discussion among varying sizes of groups. There is consensus before action. It would be interesting to "hang out" with a group of Nordics who have bilocated. Having a new understanding of the Nordics would ensure this was a more uneventful meeting.

There do not seem to be individuals within Nordic society that violate the norms, nor do there seem to be varieties of Nordics, however, they do seem to form a society according to our understanding of the term.

The Nordics do not appear to have or need a written language as all Nordics mentally communicate information to each other, either through small groups or larger groups. They are able to communicate voice-to-voice when in Human society and it is possible that they can also read and write in Human languages. The Nordic who was interviewed was quite open, although I suspect there is more than what was conveyed. The Nordic was much more open than the Gray. A handwriting sample from a bilocated Nordic would be interesting!

We thank the Nordics for their cooperation and thoroughness in answering our questions. The next group to be interviewed is the Small Grays.

3: The Exobiology Project: Talking With The Small Grays

Part 1

Q: How do they cooperate? Is there a Confederation that is acting together?

SMALL GRAYS: We have always been. We have always been here. We are not part of the Confederation. We do not need to act together but we do, with the other Grays and the Whites (referred to in this transcript as Nordics) and many others. We were here before you and will be here after you. We tolerate you. The Earth is home to many species not just Humans. The Earth is for everybody, for Humans and others. Humans and others claim the Earth as their own but it belongs to everybody: Grays, Nordics, Humans and many others. Humans do not have any priority claim to the Earth. Humans need to tolerate other species as well as tolerate other Humans.

Q: Are you a mechanical species, as some Humans claim?

SMALL GRAYS: No, we are biological but different in our biology than Human and other species.

Q: Are you part plant, as some Humans say, that your tissues contain chlorophyll?

SMALL GRAYS: We are not plant but use chlorophyll in a symbiotic way. Chlorophyll provides us with energy and nutrients.

Q: Is that why you look bluish-Gray in white light?
SMALL GRAYS: Yes, the chlorophyll in our skins colors our appearance. We are also able to bioluminescence.
Q: I once "observed" a Gray in captivity. Did this one die and what could have been done to keep it alive?
SMALL GRAYS: It did die. It needed other Grays and it needed nutrients.
Q: Do we have these nutrients on Earth?
SMALL GRAYS: Some of them. Chlorophyll, boron, but others you do not have.
Q: So, that means that captured Grays will always die?
SMALL GRAYS: Not always. Some may have enough reserves to survive.
Q: Are you mainly nocturnal?
SMALL GRAYS: Yes, we work by night. Bright light, unless it has special filters, damages us. Both heat and light damage us.
Q: How does the chlorophyll provide nutrients if it does not have sunlight?
SMALL GRAYS: We have special illumination.
Q: Is there more to the Orbs, observed by others and can they manifest responses? Are there different types of Orbs?
SMALL GRAYS: There are different types of Orbs. Some have intelligence. Some are able to act independently.
Q: The Nordics said that the Orbs were mainly messengers and probes. Are they wrong?
SMALL GRAYS: No, they are not wrong. The Orbs that they work with do not have autonomy but go where they are sent.
Q: Is this comparable to someone having a domesticated dog and another person owning a semi-wild wolf?
SMALL GRAYS: No. It is like keeping one dog chained, yet allowing another to roam.
Q: That could be dangerous.
SMALL GRAYS: Only if the roaming dog is aggressive. Orbs are not aggressive. They do not carry weapons. They are able to materialize and dematerialize. They carry information and energy and are useful.
Q: Could we learn to harness the Orbs?
SMALL GRAYS: That is a Human concept. Orbs are intelligent. They will come or go when asked. They will carry information.
Q: Can the different extraterrestrial races also manifest responses and are they positively oriented? Are there inherent conflicts detrimental to our interests?
SMALL GRAYS: There are species that are detrimental to Humans.
Q: Which ones?

SMALL GRAYS: More later.
Q: (Upon reviewing this questions, it was not answered later.)
Q: Aren't abductions detrimental to Humans?
SMALL GRAYS: No. They are beneficial.
Q: They can be very traumatic to Humans.
SMALL GRAYS: It is for research, for Human growth.
Q: Is it true that the Hybrids are a combination of Human, Gray and Nordic?
SMALL GRAYS: Yes.
Q: Can alien technology harm Humans?
SMALL GRAYS: Yes, propulsion systems and fields can harm Humans if they are in the way. We need Humans to not get in the way.
Q: Can other alien races prevent abductions?
SMALL GRAYS: Yes, other races could prevent the abductions but do not.
Q: Why not?
SMALL GRAYS: Because it is beneficial for them too.
Q: Are you talking about the Nordics?
SMALL GRAYS: Yes, mainly but others benefit, too.
Q: Who?
SMALL GRAYS: Humans, Lights, Smooths.
Q: Who are the good guys, who are the bad guys and what can we learn from them?
SMALL GRAYS: Good and bad are Human terms. Humans are different than Nordics and Grays and others. You can learn to be tolerant and work together.
Q: Can some races render implants fallible?
SMALL GRAYS: Yes but why would they? Humans can render implants fallible but they would be replaced. Always, they would be replaced.
Q: Can we interfere with the functioning of implants?
SMALL GRAYS: Yes, Humans can interfere with the functioning but they would be replaced, always.
Q: Are they the same races or different groups of the same race that are carrying out the abductions?
SMALL GRAYS: We carry out most collections and the Large Grays and Nordics sometimes help, if there is resistance.
Q: Do you ask the Nordics to help if the abductee is scared of the Grays?
SMALL GRAYS: Yes.
Q: How do they travel and is this travel with or without vehicles?
SMALL GRAYS: We travel with vehicles, large and small.
Q: Are these manufactured someplace?
SMALL GRAYS: Partly manufactured and partly grown.

Q: Does that mean they have plant-like qualities?

SMALL GRAYS: No, they grow like crystals but they are not crystals. They grow to a form which we put together.

Q: Our knowledge of physics is growing, is there some point in our near future, when we will understand your travel physics?

SMALL GRAYS: There are some who already know, others who are learning but it will be a long time before being put into use.

Q: The Nordics are able to bi-locate into prepared bodies that are waiting for them. Can you do this?

SMALL GRAYS: No.

Q: How long can Hybrids stay on Earth and why has the hybridization program taken so long?

SMALL GRAYS: Hybrids stay on Earth for very short periods. All Hybrids have varying amounts of Gray, Nordic, and Human. Some Hybrids have more Human and can stay on Earth for longer time periods; some have more Nordic and Human than Gray. Most Hybrids, especially those with more Gray, stay away from Earth. Hybrids have always been and will continue to be for a longer time.

Q: What and who are the Indigo Children? Is there a specific race that is producing the Indigo Children?

SMALL GRAYS: No race is producing the Indigo Children. They have always been. They interest us and we collect them more often. They have been in every culture and at every time but have not always been recognized.

Q: Why are some species interested in hydrocarbons? Are they rare in the galaxy? What about other minerals and gases: hydrogen, boron? What purpose do these species put hydrocarbons to? Are we in conflict for these resources?

SMALL GRAYS: You are not the only species that needs these minerals and gases. They are for everybody. Grays and others took these resources before Humans were on Earth. No conflict.

Part 2

Q: They obviously find our Human civilization to possess valuable galactic characteristics, some of which they probably lost eons ago, or they wouldn't be interbreeding with us. They certainly possess the ability to destroy our Human civilization, but have not, why?

SMALL GRAYS: Humans are a novelty. They came along, long after we were already here. There is no need to destroy. We add the Human characteristics to the Hybrids. We are the ones who were here first on the Earth, before Humans. Humans are interesting. There is no need to destroy them.

Q: The Nordics say that they started a Nordic Hybrid that has become the Human/ Nordics. Is that correct?

SMALL GRAYS: We do not know.

Q: I have read that the Grays do not always know what Humans are doing or saying, that they only pay attention to certain things? Is this so?

SMALL GRAYS: Yes. There would be too much data. We perceive most but not all.

Q: Is this intergalactic ethics - being held to certain behavior by other ET civilizations? Or is it just that their self-interest benefits more by using us for their own needs rather than simply destroying us (a similar model of how things operate on Earth)?

SMALL GRAYS: Each group lives by its own rules. We use Earth for our own needs but we do not need to destroy.

Q: There have been stories of Humans being hurt during abductions, for example broken limbs.

SMALL GRAYS: This is true. Accidents happen. Humans get broken sometimes. We try not to do this.

Q: Is it true that there is a hierarchy: hooded, robed ones, down to reptilian, Nordics, Large Grays, then small Grays?

SMALL GRAYS: No, we all have our own tasks and levels. We work together but there is no hierarchy. Hierarchy is a Human concept. This is how Humans see our races. We are not the aliens, Humans are the aliens. Some Grays collect the Humans and prepare them for procedures. The Humans are then given to the Grays and others for their use while they are with us.

Q: Given the billions of likely planets in our galaxy alone, there couldn't be anything very unique and special about Earth. Although the need to mine some of the debris circling Saturn is puzzling - - the implications of which implies a gigantic civilization that is widespread in our galaxy with a vast need for ongoing raw material supply. I would very much appreciate your insights on what all this implies about the nature of intergalactic inhabitation, the inhabitants in a portion or all of our galaxy. Are they dominant or is there a cacophony of conflicting vested interests in our galaxy like here on Earth?

SMALL GRAYS: There are many species. We all have our interests. There is no conflict among the ones who work together.

Q: Is there pressure for the Grays to join the Confederation?

SMALL GRAYS: No. We join when we are ready. There are species that do not work with us but they have their own interests.

Q: Would that be the robed Reptilians, and others?

SMALL GRAYS: Yes.

Q: What are the intentions of each race? What is each race's ongoing purpose and when will this be completed?

SMALL GRAYS: Too many to tell. The Grays collect Humans, gain knowledge, construct Hybrids, travel, learn, and work together.

Q: There is still a question in my mind that small Grays are robot-like and perhaps mechanical?

SMALL GRAYS: No. We have become as one because we share everything. We appear insect-like and cannot survive alone. There is no completion date.

Q: Will there be a scenario like a "shock wave" from a distant part of the galaxy that will wipe out Earth? Will it hit the Earth and its oceans?

SMALL GRAYS: There have been and will be shock waves. Humans are new and will have to learn how to avoid these. Our races know how to avoid them by going into the Earth. It will hit the Earth and the oceans. Humans are always concerned about what may or may not happen instead of living now.

Q: That sounds very Zen-like!

SMALL GRAYS: It is how we survive.

Q: What does the future of the Earth look like, say in 2012? What types of scenarios, based on fact, will Earth experience?

SMALL GRAYS: No Response.

Q: Do the Small Grays create such scenarios in their "Mind scans?"

SMALL GRAYS: Yes, but not to predict the future, to see what emotions arise. These scenarios are always possible. They have happened and they will happen. Earth will experience all of them in the future.

Q: Are there specific races that are influencing our leaders and the process of civilization? Does any one race or a combination control our civilizations? If so why is this permitted?

SMALL GRAYS: There is no race that controls all other races. That is Earth-thinking. We all control ourselves. There is no permitting because it is not so. There are no races that purposely influence the Earth's leaders except if they are collected. Then they are the same as all others who have been collected. Some leaders have been collected, others not.

Q: What decides who you will collect and who you will not collect?

SMALL GRAYS: We have criteria: physical, mental, and emotional. We do not recognize social or racial groups as you do. All are equally collected.

Q: Would other civilizations be able to counter the possible Earth changes? Are the Orbs more positive to Humans?

SMALL GRAYS: Other civilizations have been around and will be around during Earth changes. Change is always happening on Earth. We do not counter any Earth changes. Most Orbs do not have personality that is positive or negative. Positive and negative are Earth judgments.

Q: Regarding other controlling civilizations, what can we do as Humans to enter this chain of command?

SMALL GRAYS: There is no chain of command. Chain of command is an Earth concept. Humans can become another species that works together. It can join the Confederation. It can be part of the species that work together.

Q: Most religions of the world accept life after Earthly death. 96% of Humans accept this as fact. What is the alien concept and is there an equivalent life after death for them?

SMALL GRAYS: Death is a physical concept. Even after our physical stops, the remainder of our race assimilates the memories of us and that remains to be used by others. So we may stop in the physical but remain living as information.

Q: What mutual benefits are in place between different civilizations?

SMALL GRAYS: We work together. Most races work together. There is a sharing of resources including Humans. We do not see these as benefits. There is just sharing.

Q: What will help the Human race survive? Is the Human race expendable? Are we in danger of decimation sometime in the future?

SMALL GRAYS: Humans are always wondering about being less. There are always times when Humans are less and sometimes they are more. More or less, it does not matter. The Human race is not expendable. The races need Humans to collect and produce Hybrids. The races will always need Humans but the Humans do not always need the other races.

Q: Would there be a sharing of resources with different species in the future. This could affect the Earth financially. Would our leadership agree to share resources? How best can we manage our natural resources without destroying ourselves?

SMALL GRAYS: Humans have a backward-looking view of resources. We have a forward-view of resources. Other races were collecting Earth resources before Humans. Humans have claimed Earth resources as theirs, they are not theirs to own. The resources belong to everybody but belonged to the other races first.

Q: When you say other races, do you mean the Native Americans or other alien races?)

SMALL GRAYS: Not Native Americans, before them. Humans can avoid destroying themselves by sharing resources.

Q: Are some races hindering or helping us? Do they have a respect for intelligent life?

SMALL GRAYS: There is no hindering or helping. There is sharing and collecting. We have a respect for intelligent life. We have a respect for Human life.

Part 3

1) Social Structure:

SMALL GRAYS: Our race, the Small Grays, is a group society. We share all thoughts, all actions, and all consequences.

Q: It seems that some groups of Grays do not share the same information. For example a group that collects Humans in Montana, may not know information about Humans that are originally collected in New Jersey?

SMALL GRAYS: Yes, it is true; there is localized information and greater shared information. When Humans are collected from a new area, we do not know about them until we are in close contact with them. We do not have leaders, as we all share decision making. Decision-making is carried out by a group consensus. When something unexpected happens, when a Human behaves erratically during collection, we have to stop and regroup and concur before continuing. There is no individual decision-making or autonomy as with Humans. This is seen as a benefit and a detriment.

2) Social Change:

SMALL GRAYS: The Grays were around before Humans and will be around after Humans. There is no social change in Gray society. Gray society has a meaning for Humans due to the collections and the fact that part of Humans is incorporated into the Hybrids that then are spread around the galaxy. This social period is the same as other social periods, it is no different. The Grays have always done things this way. Humans think that they are the only species in the galaxy. They are Earth-centric and must expand their viewpoint.

3) Social Inequality:

SMALL GRAYS: All Grays are equal: thoughts, actions and consequences are shared. There are no Grays that are less or more than other Grays. Sometimes a Gray becomes injured or damaged. They naturally stop but their information remains to be shared by all others. The conduct and characteristics that are like "Human nature" are that we have some emotions, we have compassion, we have a sense of order, we have memory, we learn, we appreciate diverse forms of life and we can plan in the short term.

Part 4

Q: What are people thinking and doing there?

SMALL GRAYS: Grays act and think together as one unit. No Gray thinks or acts by itself.

Q: What kinds of people are there?

SMALL GRAYS: The Grays are one people among many races.

Q: Who is included and who is excluded? What rules and norms govern behavior there? How are roles assigned and tasks divided?

SMALL GRAYS: None are excluded unless they are damaged. Roles are assigned and tasks divided according to group consensus.

Q: Who says so? How are people socialized? Whose interests do these social arrangements serve?

SMALL GRAYS: The group decisions and group consensus affect the whole of Gray society.

Q: Who benefits and who loses? What powerful people, processes, institutions, and structures influence these arrangements? When, how, and why do people resist?

SMALL GRAYS: There is consensus. If there is resistance, it is assumed that a Gray is damaged and he stops. Change only occurs through new learning and consensus.

Q: Is this process or system relatively sustainable?

SMALL GRAYS: Yes, sustainable.

Assessment of the Small Grays

Both species of Grays appear to be nocturnal with an aversion to daylight and strong artificial light sources. Unlike the Nordics they do not normally appear on Earth during daylight hours. There are reports that, if they do, they bundle up in some sort of clothing.

There was definite mutual awareness and an attention to what the other said and answers came reciprocally: turns were taken However, the Grays are strongly connected to the point of there being no individuality. Gray society is pure socialism, with no autonomy. Everything is consensus: all values are shared and agreed upon. Grays live by prearranged rules and norms that are mutually agreed upon by all.

Material goods are produced by the Grays, i.e. medical instrumentation, transportation and implants but very little value is placed on cultural items such as art, music or writing.

Grays seem to judge each other in terms of their own culture but are very aware that there are other races and cultures that are very different and act very differently from the Grays. The Grays accept these differences and do not seek to impose changes on Humans and include Human characteristics into

Hybrids. Also, Grays do not judge other races and accept that other races have different ways of being and doing. It was assumed that by interacting with one Gray that I was interacting with the group.

Grays do not appear to have a spoken language or social prohibitions as seen on Earth. They do not appear to have religion and see the universe as property belonging to all. The concepts of marriage and life after death, as accepted on Earth, do not seem to exist in Gray society.

While the Grays do not have a spoken language, they are quite capable of making themselves understood. Both abductees and others who have contacted Grays have been able to understand them. They appear to be more "vocal" than the Large Grays, and to have a wider range of concepts and understanding.

It has been noted by other researchers that the Grays employ a great many symbols that have meaning to them. Some of these symbols have been incorporated into Human understanding and culture i.e. the Rune glyphs. Some of these Rune glyphs have been noted in crop circles. This might be a useful study but direct communication with the Grays appears to gather more information, than from symbols alone.

We thank the Small Grays for their cooperation. The next race to be interviewed will be the Robed or Hooded Reptilians.

4: The Exobiology Project: Talking With The Hooded Reptilian

Part 1

Q: How do they cooperate? Is there a Confederation that is acting together?

HOODED REPTILIAN: We do not cooperate. We are not part of the Confederation. The Confederation acts together. It also works with us.

Q: Will you become part of the Confederation?

HOODED REPTILIAN: No.

Q: Why not?

HOODED REPTILIAN: NR: (No Response.)

Q: Are there rules for joining the Confederation?

HOODED REPTILIAN: Yes.

Q: Will you be honest with your answers?

HOODED REPTILIAN: Yes.

Q: Do you have a code of ethics or a morality that you uphold?

HOODED REPTILIAN: Yes.

Q: Can you tell me some of the principles?

HOODED REPTILIAN: Those who do not work together, are not in the group, and are excluded.

Q: The group known as the Hooded Reptilians has an Earth reputation as being aggressive and negative. Is this so?

HOODED REPTILIAN: Yes.

Q: Can you explain how you came by this reputation?

HOODED REPTILIAN: We do not have emotions like the Grays and the Whites (Nordics). When we work it is with no emotion. We do not offer compassion. We do not offer options. We do not offer kindness. We do not offer calm. We do not offer emotions that are offered by the other groups. We do not have emotions.

Q: Thank you.

Q: Are the Reptilians cooperative?

HOODED REPTILIAN: No. We have no emotions. Cooperation involves emotions. We have no emotions and do not cooperate.

Q: Is there more to the Orbs, observed by others and can they manifest responses? Are there different types of Orbs?

HOODED REPTILIAN: We do not discuss the Orbs.

Q: Can you tell me if others have Orbs and what or who they are?

HOODED REPTILIAN: Others have Orbs, we do not. We have never had Orbs. We will never have Orbs. We will never talk about the Orbs

Q: For an emotionless species you get quite irritated with my questions!

HOODED REPTILIAN: No.

Q: Can the different extraterrestrial races also manifest responses and are they positively oriented? Are there inherent conflicts detrimental to our interests?

HOODED REPTILIAN: There are many conflicts within and between the different races. There are disagreements between those species that have emotions and those who do not have emotions. We manifest responses but we do not manifest emotions.

Q: Is there a hierarchy of races, for example between the Nordics, Grays, and Reptilians?

HOODED REPTILIAN: No. There are many more of the Small Grays, fewer of the Nordics, and even less of the Reptilians. It seems as if there is a hierarchy because the larger Reptilians and Nordics move around the small Grays, Reptilians are taller and more oriented. Each of the races has its own routes and purposes.

Q: Can you explain to me the Reptilians routes and purposes?

HOODED REPTILIAN: We assist the Grays in the movement of Humans.

Q: When you say move, do you mean physically, as in craft?

HOODED REPTILIAN: Yes.

Q: Do you own the craft?

HOODED REPTILIAN: We do not own the craft. No race owns the craft. They are made by the Grays. We are the ones who make the craft move.

Q: We often see the Small Grays but not the Reptilians on Earth, why is this?

HOODED REPTILIAN: We rarely come to Earth. We move the craft and move the Humans.

Q: There have been Reptilian insignia seen on craft, does this imply ownership or some other reason.

HOODED REPTILIAN: Not ownership, we move the craft. The insignia are signs to certain parts of the craft.

Q: Would that be like the Grays are in this part of the craft and the Reptilians are in this other part?

HOODED REPTILIAN: Yes.

Q: Can other alien races prevent abductions?

HOODED REPTILIAN: No.

Q: The other races said that Humans could prevent abductions by asking for them to stop.

HOODED REPTILIAN: No that is not so.

Q: Are you sure?

HOODED REPTILIAN: Yes.

Q: Who are the good guys, who are the bad guys and what can we learn from them?

HOODED REPTILIAN: These are Earth emotions. There are only those races that have emotions and races that do not have emotions. You can learn from all of them.

Q: Can some races render implants fallible?

HOODED REPTILIAN: No.

Q: Again, other races said that Humans could render their own implants fallible.

HOODED REPTILIAN: No. If they fail, they are replaced. Nothing is infallible. The only way that something can be rendered infallible is if it is made that way. Implants are fallible as they are made and can fail.

Q: So Reptilians cannot render implants fallible?

HOODED REPTILIAN: No.

Q: Can we interfere with the functioning of implants?

HOODED REPTILIAN: Yes. Humans can interfere with the functioning of implants. They also become fallible on their own. They are replaced.

Q: How can Humans render implants fallible?

HOODED REPTILIAN: They can take them out.

Q: Do the Reptilians take part in the collection of Humans, the examinations, the implants and the scenarios?

HOODED REPTILIAN: No. We move the craft. We can also be seen alongside the Grays as we determine where to go next.

Q: Are they the same races or different groups of the same race that are carrying out the abductions?

HOODED REPTILIAN: The Grays and the Nordics carry out the abductions. There are no other races that collect Humans.

Q: The Grays and Nordics speak of the Hybrids as a race.

HOODED REPTILIAN: They are not a race.

Q: I have noticed that you do not insist on the races' names being capitalized. (I have capitalized them in this transcript.)

HOODED REPTILIAN: This is a Confederation matter. We do not place importance on races as does the Confederation.

Q: Would you prefer it, as Earth is not part of the Confederation, not to capitalize?

HOODED REPTILIAN: NR.

Q: How do they travel and is this travel with or without vehicles?

HOODED REPTILIAN: We move with physical vehicles. We take the Grays and the Nordics where they need to go.

Q: Can you travel like the Nordics, sending your non-physical body into a prepared body ahead of you?

HOODED REPTILIAN: No.

Q: How long can Hybrids stay on Earth and why has the Hybridization program taken so long?

HOODED REPTILIAN: Hybrids belong to the Grays and the Nordics. We have no interest in or information about the Hybrids. They are not a race. They are a by-product.

Q: What and who are the Indigo Children? Is there a specific race that is producing the Indigo Children?

HOODED REPTILIAN: We are not interested in these children. They are human. They have always been human. All Humans are the same.

Q: What are you interested in then?

HOODED REPTILIAN: Travel, craft, our own race.

Q: Do you have culture, such as music, arts, song?

HOODED REPTILIAN: No.

Q: You sound mechanical, according to Earth characteristics, are you mechanical or physical?

HOODED REPTILIAN: We are physical. We are not mechanical.

Q: Why are some species interested in hydrocarbons? Are they rare in the galaxy? What about other minerals and gases: hydrogen, boron? What purpose do these species put hydrocarbons to? Are we in conflict for these resources?

HOODED REPTILIAN: The Grays bring Earth matters to us for fuel, for nurture, for cleansing, for breathing, for sustenance, for "greening".

Q: What is "greening"?

HOODED REPTILIAN: We have chlorophyll in our skins for nutrition.

Q: Like the Grays?

HOODED REPTILIAN: Yes. There is no conflict for resources. Resources are everywhere.

Q: That is what the other races have said.

HOODED REPTILIAN: That is true.

Part 2

Q: They obviously find our human civilization to possess valuable galactic characteristics, some of which they probably lost eons ago, or they wouldn't be interbreeding with us. They certainly possess the ability to destroy our human civilization, but have not, why?

HOODED REPTILIAN: The Reptilians do not possess any Human characteristics. The Reptilians do not possess any Gray or Nordic characteristics. The Reptilians are their own species. We do not breed with other races. There is no need to destroy Human civilization. We do not have any plans to destroy Earth. The Confederation would not allow it.

Q: So you follow some of the Confederation rules, although you are not part of the Confederation?

HOODED REPTILIAN: There are simple Confederation rules that apply to all races.

Q: Is this intergalactic ethics - being held to certain behavior by other ET civilizations? Or is it just that their self-interest benefits more by using us for their own needs rather than simply destroying us (a similar model of how things operate on Earth)?

HOODED REPTILIAN: Each race has its own self-interest. Those races who belong to the Confederation act within Confederation rules. All those who are not in the Confederation still have Confederation rules.

Q: Can you tell me some more of the Confederation rules that non-Confederation races have to follow?

HOODED REPTILIAN: Certain areas that we can and cannot travel in.

Q: So Earth is an area where travel is allowed?

HOODED REPTILIAN: Yes.

Q: If Earth joins the Confederation will Reptilians and Grays still be allowed to travel near Earth?

HOODED REPTILIAN: NR.

Q: Can you tell me more about the Confederation. Is there a Council, as we have been told? Are there representative members of each race represented, such as our United Nations?

HOODED REPTILIAN: NR.

Q: Is your answer because you cannot answer or do not know?

HOODED REPTILIAN: We do not know.

Q: Given the billions of likely planets in our galaxy alone, there couldn't be anything very unique and special about Earth. Although the need to mine some of the debris circling Saturn is puzzling - - the implications of which implies a gigantic civilization that is widespread in our galaxy with a vast need for ongoing raw material supply. I would very much appreciate your insights on what all this implies about the nature of intergalactic inhabitation, the inhabitants in a portion or all of our galaxy. Are they dominant or is there a cacophony of conflicting vested interests in our galaxy like here on Earth?

HOODED REPTILIAN: There are many more races than the Grays, Nordics and Reptilians but we do not know anything about them.

Q: What are the intentions of each race? What is each race's ongoing purpose and when will this be completed?

HOODED REPTILIAN: Reptilians do not have an intention. We move other races and are interested in our race. This will always be and will not be completed at any time in the future.

Q: Will there be a scenario like a "shock wave" from a distant part of the galaxy that will wipe out Earth? Will it hit the Earth and its oceans?

HOODED REPTILIAN: We do not know.

Q: Thank you. Is that true?

HOODED REPTILIAN: Yes.

Q: What does the future of the Earth look like, say in 2012? What types of scenarios, based on fact, will Earth experience?

HOODED REPTILIAN: We do not know. We do not look at future times. We live now. We carry and go from place to place. We cannot give you any information about these scenarios.

Q: Are there specific races that are influencing our leaders and the process of civilization? Does any one race or a combination control our civilizations? If so why is this permitted?

HOODED REPTILIAN: There is no race that controls Earth civilization. Humans are collected by the Grays and the Nordics and we carry everybody.

Q: Some Humans have said that they have interacted with Reptilians on craft. Is that so?

HOODED REPTILIAN: Yes, from time to time, we interact if they are in our way or prevent us from moving the craft. Sometimes we are confused with the Large Grays. Some Large Grays wear hoods and are mistaken for Reptilians.

Q: Part of me believes you and part of me still believes that you have interacted with Humans in a negative way.

HOODED REPTILIAN: It is not true. We have our duties.

Q: If a Human gets in your way and you cannot carry out your duties, what do you do?

HOODED REPTILIAN: We move the human. We make a loud noise at them. We move them out of the way so that we can move the ship.

Q: How do you move the Humans?

HOODED REPTILIAN: We push them.

Q: Humans would consider being pushed and made a loud noise at, as aggressive.

HOODED REPTILIAN: We are not aggressive. We move them.

Q: Would other civilizations be able to counter the possible Earth changes? Are the Orbs more positive to Humans?

HOODED REPTILIAN: We do not know about Earth changes. We do not discuss Orbs.

Q: So, Reptilian owned Orbs might be different than those managed by Grays or Nordics?

HOODED REPTILIAN: We do not own or discuss Orbs.

Q: Are Orbs a separate species?

HOODED REPTILIAN: No. They are a nuisance.

Q: Regarding other controlling civilizations, what can we do as Humans to enter this chain of command?

HOODED REPTILIAN: There is no chain of command. There is the Confederation. Some races are part of the Confederation. Some are not. Humans might become part of the Confederation. Now they are not.

Q: Most religions of the world accept life after Earthly death. 96% of Humans accept this as fact. What is the alien concept and is there an equivalent life after death for them?

HOODED REPTILIAN: There is no equal concept of life after death. We are now and then we are not. There is nothing after.

Q: What mutual benefits are in place between different civilizations?

HOODED REPTILIAN: Each race does what it does. Reptilians carry, Grays collect Humans, Grays and Nordics create Hybrids.

Q: What do Humans do?
HOODED REPTILIAN: Nothing.
Q: What will help the Human race survive? Is the Human race expendable? Are we in danger of decimation at some time in the future?
HOODED REPTILIAN: We have no information about any of this. It does not matter if Humans survive.
Q: Humans think it matters if we survive. How can we assure this?
HOODED REPTILIAN: NR.
Q: Would there be a sharing of resources with different species in the future. This could affect the Earth financially. Would our leadership agree to share resources? How best can we manage our natural resources without destroying ourselves?
HOODED REPTILIAN: We have no information about any of this.
Q: Other races said that there were plenty of resources for everybody to share. Is this true?
HOODED REPTILIAN: Yes.
Q: Are some races hindering or helping us? Do they have a respect for intelligent life?
HOODED REPTILIAN: There is respect between races. There is respect for Humans. There is respect for Grays. There is respect for Nordics. There is respect for all other races. It is one of the Confederation rules.

Assessment of the Hooded Reptilian

The Reptilians appear to be a single-minded race that has certain roles, such as carrying other races in craft. They claim to be non-aggressive but will push and make loud noises at Humans, if they are in the way. Reptilians claim to live in the now and do not know about future events. They claim to have no emotions but admit to Orbs being a "nuisance" and react to some questions with irritation. They do not appear to have an after-life. They do not belong to the Confederation but work alongside the Grays and the Nordics. They claim that Large Grays can be mistaken for Reptilians.

The Reptilians do not appear to be interested in making history. They have probably been around as long as the Grays. Their history appears to be linked with the Grays and the Nordics. Despite their short answers, they appear to be intelligent; in fact, they must have some intelligence to pilot craft and have knowledge of space destinations.

They claim not to have any Human characteristics or any from other races. In this way they are unique. Their physiology does not form part of the Hybrids. They consider the Hybrids to be by-products. They have a role that they fulfill single-mindedly, that of moving the craft. They do not appear to have a sense of humor, or cultural activities of any kind.

Reptilians move craft and are seen with the Grays and Nordics. They have the knowledge of how to move the craft although there have been reports of Grays doing so, on occasion.

They act single-mindedly and react with aggression (pushing, making a loud noise) if not allowed to carry out their work. Reptilians consider themselves a unique race and unlike any other. I would agree.

Reptilians are not part of the Confederation but live under some of its rules i.e. respect for all races. The interests are those of the Reptilians only. There did not appear to be any indication of juvenile Reptilian. It was not possible to interact with a group of Reptilians. They only appear in small numbers, perhaps one or two to a craft but their system appears to have been and will remain sustainable.

There were turns taken in conversation but there was a feeling that there was irritation with doing this. Reptilians have no compunction to moving Humans and I am sure there was great restraint employed by the Reptilian to "take turns". They probably think Humans are very annoying! Reptilians obviously "respect" Humans but will also use aggression to complete their work of moving the craft. They appear to have a need for personal space in which to carry out their work. They will "move" Humans to complete their work, using aggression if necessary.

Reptilians do not appear to create any material goods but are service-oriented, they move craft. They are a race but do not appear to have a culture, do not have abstract concepts such as life-after-death, and appear to be rule-bound: they are not interested in anything outside those rules.

Reptilians appeared to be a specific race with no subcultures or members that differ from each other. While Reptilians realize they are part of a race, they do not seem to connect with each other and they do not appear to be socially telepathic among their own group, as are the Grays and Nordics.

They do not appear to reveal any abstract concepts such as marriage, religion, family but they obviously have a language that can be understood by the Grays and the Nordics. It is possible that they have a limited telepathic ability to interact with Grays, Nordics, and Humans. They have some vocal mechanics as they are able to make "a loud noise" at Humans who get in their way. The only symbols related to by the Reptilians are the signs that indicate which part of the craft are accessible to each race. It is unknown whether the Reptilians understand writing although they do understand symbols and obviously understand enough about the galaxies to direct craft to destinations. They can probably read maps that are developed by their race and others.

Respect and thanks is offered to the Hooded Reptilian for their cooperation. The next race to be interviewed will be an Indigo Hybrid.

5: The Exobiology Project: Talking With The Indigo Hybrids

Part 1

Q: How do they cooperate? Is there a Confederation that is acting together?

INDIGO HYBRID: We cooperate with the Grays and the Whites, that you call the Nordics. It is OK with us if you call then the Nordics. As we have many races represented in our physiology, we understand them all, even Human. There is a Confederation and the Hybrids are part of the Confederation.

Q: I am surprised. The Grays and Reptilians are not part of the Confederation.

INDIGO HYBRID: Yes. As the Nordic part of us is part of the Confederation, we are too.

Q: So far, as I understand it, the Nordics and the Hybrids are part of the Confederation, but the Small Grays, Large Grays, Reptilians, and Humans are not part of the Confederation?

INDIGO HYBRID: That is correct.

Q: I have asked this question to other races, but when will Humans be part of the Confederation. If the Nordic part of you entitles you to be part of the Confederation, could not the fact, that you have some Human, entitle Humans to be part of the Confederation?

INDIGO HYBRID: It does not work that way. Humans will join the Confederation when they are ready. Most of Humanity does not even admit that we exist.

Q: Which is true!

INDIGO HYBRID: The Confederation acts together with all races regardless of whether they are part of the Confederation.

Q: Does being part of the Confederation bestow special privileges on its members?

INDIGO HYBRID: Yes but I cannot discuss that.

Q: How would we know it would be worth joining the Confederation unless we know what it is worth?

INDIGO HYBRID: That is a very Human attitude. Joining the Confederation is not about gaining something but knowing things.

Q: Is there more to the Orbs, observed by others and can they manifest responses? Are there different types of Orbs?

INDIGO HYBRID: The orbs are problematic. They were a race at one time but became subservient to other races and became messengers and servants. Not exactly slaves but they are altruistic and subsume their own interests for the interests of others.

Q: The other races say that the Orbs carry energy and information. Is that so?
INDIGO HYBRID: Yes.
Q: Are some Orbs independent?
INDIGO HYBRID: They are all independent but subservient to other races.
Q: Could Humans call them and ask them to carry information or for help?
INDIGO HYBRID: Yes, but that would be adding to their subservient role.
Q: Is this role something that they have chosen?
INDIGO HYBRID: Yes.
Q: Is there a way that Humans could interact with Orbs in a way that would enable them to be more independent, yet cooperating with Humans?
INDIGO HYBRID: Yes. By stating to other races that Humans are cooperating with the orbs.
Q: Are the Orbs part of the Confederation?
INDIGO HYBRID: Yes.
Q: That surprises me.
INDIGO HYBRID: Yes, they are members.
Q: You refer to the orbs, rather than the Orbs I learned from the Nordics that those races that belong to the Confederation had their names capitalized, i.e. Nordics, Whites.
INDIGO HYBRID: It is the choice of the race. We respect the orbs' decision and do not call them orbs.
Q: Would calling them Orbs, give them more respect?
INDIGO HYBRID: They do not want it.
Q: Can the different extraterrestrial races also manifest responses and are they positively oriented? Are there inherent conflicts detrimental to our interests?
INDIGO HYBRID: Almost all of the races have knowledge of Humans and give them respect. As long as there is cooperation between the races, it is not detrimental to any interests. Humans do not like to cooperate. That is why the Hybrids, who are a combination of Human, Gray and Nordic are more balanced and more cooperative. Each race has its own interests.
Q: Can other alien races prevent abductions?
INDIGO HYBRID: If the abductions were prevented, we would cease to exist. We would not do anything to deny our own existence. The Grays have worked out a good program. We are happy with what they are doing.
Q: Are you in constant communication with the other Hybrids, Grays, and Nordics?
INDIGO HYBRID: Yes, we are also in some communication with Humans. Why do you refer to the Grays with a capital letter as they are not part of the Confederation?

Q: It is our custom to refer to other persons' names with Capitals. We also refer to major place names with Capitals?

INDIGO HYBRID: I will accept that.

Q: Who are the good guys, who are the bad guys and what can we learn from them?

INDIGO HYBRID: We do not have references for good and bad, although we understand the Earth concept of good and bad but it seems to change according to who or where you ask. One part of the world sees something or someone as good or bad and another part of the world sees the opposite. We can learn from everybody. Everybody has something to teach us.

Q: Can some races render implants fallible?

INDIGO HYBRID: Yes, all implants can become fallible.

Q: Is it true that if an implant fails, for whatever reason, that it is always replaced?

INDIGO HYBRID: Not always. Some implants are only needed for a specific time. They are not replaced.

Q: Do they stay in the body, dormant?

INDIGO HYBRID: Yes, sometimes they are removed.

Q: Can we interfere with the functioning of implants?

INDIGO HYBRID: Yes.

Q: Some races say that we can interfere with the implants, others say that we cannot?

INDIGO HYBRID: Some races understand the implants better. They can be interfered with by removal and other means.

Q: Can you tell me some of these means?

INDIGO HYBRID: No.

Q: Are they the same races or different groups of the same race that are carrying out the abductions?

INDIGO HYBRID: The races that are carrying out the abductions, which the Grays call collections, are the Small and Large Grays, the Nordics help the Grays when the Humans are on the craft and Hybrids also help when needed.

Q: There are stories, related by abductees, that Hybrids interact quite readily and frequently with Humans.

INDIGO HYBRID: Yes, when it is necessary.

Q: Is it true that the Hooded Reptilians just move the craft and do not collect Humans?

INDIGO HYBRID: Yes, that is correct, although we refer to them for other purposes, such as information about our destinations. They carry a great deal of information about the destinations.

Q: How do they travel and is this travel with or without vehicles?

INDIGO HYBRID: We can travel in many different ways related to what percentage of races we have in us. If a Hybrid has more Nordic, it may be able to travel as a Nordic does, by sending a body plan on ahead. If the majority of the Hybrid is Gray, they must travel by craft. If the highest percentage is Human, then we stay with the Grays, in the craft, or are sent to some destination that is Earth-like.

Q: It must be quite exciting, the prospect of exploration and travel?

INDIGO HYBRID: It is what we do. We go where we are sent. We are not explorers or travelers; we go to live at that location.

Q: Can you breed?

INDIGO HYBRID: Not in Earth terms. We can create other Hybrids when we arrive. We work with the Grays.

Q: How long can Hybrids stay on Earth? Why has the Hybridization program taken so long?

INDIGO HYBRID: Hybrids can stay on Earth as long as they have a high percentage of Human in their physiology. Even so, they can only stay for a short time. The best percentage is 50% or more Human and about 25% Nordic and 25% or less Gray.

Q: Are you all blond haired and blue eyed?

INDIGO HYBRID: No, it depends on our Human part and on our Nordic part. Some of us can have quite dark hair and dark eyes. Not all Hybrids have Caucasian features.

Q: What and who are the Indigo Children? Is there a specific race that is producing the Indigo Children?

INDIGO HYBRID: The Indigo Children belong to Earth. If an Indigo child is collected by the Grays, the Hybrid may have varying percentages of that Human's characteristics.

Q: The Grays have said that Indigo Children are easier to communicate with and, perhaps more are collected?

INDIGO HYBRID: Yes.

Q: So, would that mean that more Hybrids contain Indigo Children characteristics?

INDIGO HYBRID: No. The Indigo Children are easier to communicate with but not all are collected.

Q: Does that mean that some Indigo Children can have communication with different races but may not be collected?

INDIGO HYBRID: Yes, that is right. We can communicate with them but they may not be collected.

Q: Who makes the decision who to collect?

INDIGO HYBRID: The Grays.

Q: How do they decide who they collect?

INDIGO HYBRID: They know who to collect, we do not.

Q: Do you know what produces an Indigo Child? They are special to the Earth, but why do they appear?

INDIGO HYBRID: They just do.

Q: Why are some species interested in hydrocarbons? Are they rare in the galaxy? What about other minerals and gases: hydrogen, boron? What purpose do these species put hydrocarbons to? Are we in conflict for these resources?

INDIGO HYBRID: The Grays and the Nordics, and sometimes the Reptilians need Earth resources for many different purposes.

Q: Do they need these resources, minerals etc to help create the Hybrids?

INDIGO HYBRID: Yes. Also to replenish and nourish themselves.

Q: Most of the races say that there is no conflict for these resources?

INDIGO HYBRID: There is no conflict. These resources are available everywhere.

Q: Then why take them from Earth?

INDIGO HYBRID: Because we have always done so.

Q: You say, "We", does this mean that you need these resources too?

INDIGO HYBRID: Yes, to develop and subsist.

Part 2

Q: They obviously find our Human civilization to possess valuable galactic characteristics, some of which they probably lost eons ago, or they wouldn't be interbreeding with us. They certainly possess the ability to destroy our Human civilization, but have not, why?

INDIGO HYBRID: Yes, the Grays and the Nordics realize that Humans possess a great deal that is useful and that is why this third race is included in the Hybrids.

Q: What is it about Humans that is important enough to be included in the Hybrids?

INDIGO HYBRID: Many things such as: intelligence, humor, many ways of looking at situations, able to carry out several tasks at once, ability to make quick decisions, critical thinking, and emotions, which are considered very important.

Q: It seems that some of the races see emotions as dangerous or unpredictable?

INDIGO HYBRID: In Hybrids, emotions are only a minor part of the overall mixture, so it is neither dangerous nor unpredictable.

Q: Did the Grays and the Nordics possess these abilities and then lose them?

INDIGO HYBRID: No, they never had them. Why would we want to destroy a civilization that helps produce our race? (Referring to part of Question 1).

Q: Is this intergalactic ethics - being held to certain behavior by other ET civilizations? Or is it just that their self-interest benefits more by using us for their own needs rather than simply destroying us (a similar model of how things operate on Earth)?

INDIGO HYBRID: Each of the races follows rules that are imposed by the Confederation and those races that join the Confederation have other rules. This may be thought of as a moral code or ethics but it is just what works best. Many races work for their own self-interest but this is respected if it is within the rules.

Q: Given the billions of likely planets in our galaxy alone, there couldn't be anything very unique and special about Earth. Although the need to mine some of the debris circling Saturn is puzzling - - the implications of which implies a gigantic civilization that is widespread in our galaxy with a vast need for ongoing raw material supply. I would very much appreciate your insights on what all this implies about the nature of intergalactic inhabitation, the inhabitants in a portion or all of our galaxy. Are they dominant or is there a cacophony of conflicting vested interests in our galaxy like here on Earth?

INDIGO HYBRID: There are multitudes of different races, some which we don't even know about. The Hooded Reptilians know many of them but don't interact with them. Reptilians are great sources of information.

Q: But don't get in their way?

INDIGO HYBRID: Right. There are vast stores of resources throughout the galaxy, this and others, so there is no need for conflicting interests. There is no one species or race that is dominant.

Q: What are the intentions of each race? What is each race's ongoing purpose and when will this be completed?

INDIGO HYBRID: We cannot speak for other races' purposes; you will have to ask them. Our purpose is to learn and to interact, to travel, and to settle.

Q: Does that mean to "settle" in another location?

INDIGO HYBRID: Yes. There is no end date for the completion of our purpose.

Q: Will there be a scenario like a "shock wave" from a distant part of the galaxy that will wipe out Earth? Will it hit the Earth and its oceans?

INDIGO HYBRID: Yes, there will be shock waves that emanate from the sun and other distant celestial objects. Most will bypass the Earth. Some may hit but in a minor way. Your atmosphere will deflect most of the force, which will be spent by the time it reaches Earth. We encounter these all the time when traveling and go right through them with no harm.

Q: What does the future of the Earth look like, say in 2012? What types of scenarios, based on fact, will Earth experience?

INDIGO HYBRID: This is a difficult question to answer as we do not have answers. Hybrids are developed and, after a short period of socialization with the Grays and the Nordics, we travel to other parts and do not know about Earth after that.

Q: Are you ready to travel or are you still being socialized?

INDIGO HYBRID: Still being socialized.

Q: What percentages of Human, Nordic, and Gray do you have in your system?

INDIGO HYBRID: Mostly Human, perhaps 57% and the remaining balance of equal parts of Nordic and Gray. I am able to travel to Earth and can also communicate with the Grays and the Nordics but not enough to travel like the Nordics. You would have to ask the Reptilians about future scenarios.

Q: I did but they said they had no knowledge.

INDIGO HYBRID: They do.

Q: Are there specific races that are influencing our leaders and the process of civilization? Does any one race or a combination control our civilizations? If so why is this permitted?

INDIGO HYBRID: There is no race that is influencing Earth leaders or Earth civilization. Humans are collected and some leaders are among that collection process. The leaders are collected for their potential to produce Hybrids and not for any knowledge or information that they possess. There is no need to permit or not permit.

Q: Would other civilizations be able to counter the possible Earth changes? Are the Orbs more positive to Humans?

INDIGO HYBRID: Humans live on the Earth and use its resources. Many other species and races live on the Earth and use its resources. If there was the possibility that changes to the Earth would be detrimental, all races would try to prevent these changes. We have talked about the orbs before. They are poor things that have been used. Leave them alone.

Q: Regarding other controlling civilizations, what can we do as Humans to enter this chain of command?

INDIGO HYBRID: Even if Humans were to join the Confederation, they would not be in any chain of command. There is no chain of command. There are no controlling civilizations.

Q: Most religions of the world accept life after Earthly death. 96% of Humans accept this as fact. What is the alien concept and is there an equivalent life after death for them?

INDIGO HYBRID: Life after death is a Human concept and not one that is accepted by most races outside of Earth. Humans live in a different time restraint than other races. They are confined to a one-time dimension. Other races live in multipl-time dimensions and so have no need for a life after the physical stops.

Q: What mutual benefits are in place between different civilizations?

INDIGO HYBRID: Respect is the main benefit. This assures cooperation between the races. There are other mutual benefits that do not involve the Human race but affect other races.

Q: What will help the Human race survive? Is the Human race expendable? Are we in danger of decimation sometime in the future?

INDIGO HYBRID: There is no risk of decimation in the near future. If the Human race ceased to be, there would still be Hybrids out in the universe living and producing other Hybrids.

Q: Would there be a sharing of resources with different species in the future. This could affect the Earth financially. Would our leadership agree to share resources? How best can we manage our natural resources without destroying ourselves?

INDIGO HYBRID: As mentioned earlier there are plenty of resources in the galaxy and no need to worry about running out or destroying yourselves. What Humans and other races take from the Earth is a blip.

Q: Do you mean that what we and other races use is negligible?

INDIGO HYBRID: Yes.

Q: Are some races hindering or helping us? Do they have a respect for intelligent life?

INDIGO HYBRID: There is always respect for intelligent life. Most races have their own path or plan and it is incidental that these hinder or help the Human race.

Assessment of the Indigo Hybrid

Hybrid socialization appears to be totally tied to that of the Grays, the Nordics and Humans. It is unusual for one race or species to be so reliant on other species for so much. Depending on the proportions of each race that is incorporated into the Hybrids, they have differing abilities and characteristics. They appear to be bred for several reasons: the main reason to travel to other locations to produce more Hybrids. Interestingly, the Hybrids are members of the Confederation. Interestingly, they also noted that the Orbs are also members of the Confederation, which was a surprise.

On the surface, Hybrids have not had a place in Human history except for the taking of Human reproductive materials for incorporation into the Hybrids. Sometimes leaders are collected (abducted) but just as regular folk, not because of their position or information that they may have. Hybrid development seems to have been around for as long as Humans have been on the Earth. Hybrids contain differing percentages of each of the three races and this determines what insight they have into the other races.

Hybrids contain varying quantities of Human reproductive material and thus show differing Human characteristics. It is possible that some Hybrids on Earth could pass as Human. Hybrids do not see themselves, Grays, Nordics or Humans as inferior but do see the Orbs as inferior.

Hybrids seem to have respect for Humans and other races. They interact with all other races and have a unique insight into other races as they are formed from three of them. They are formed to eventually travel and spread to other location. And, according to this Indigo Hybrid, they are a chimera of three different races: Gray, Human, and Nordic.

Hybrids interact with and obtain direction from the Grays and the Nordics, perhaps sometimes Human and their tasks appear to be predetermined, in that they accept their role of travelers. The Grays seem to do most of the socialization and the socialization ultimately benefits the Hybrids. There does not seem to be any powerful processes that shape the Hybrids, the processes appear to be institutionalized and ongoing. The Hybrids do not seem to resist any of their socialization.

The flow of communication with the Hybrid was seamless, even though I took breaks from the conversation. It was picked up easily after the breaks and the interaction with the Hybrid was easy, perhaps because of the high Indigo Human component of the Hybrid. Of all of the races interviewed, it was only the Hybrids that asked questions back. The Hybrid do not seem as concerned about personal space or the invasion of personal space as the Reptilian.

Hybrids appear to live by certain norms and behaviors and thus form a society. They mentioned that they were part of the Confederation. The nature of the Confederation has not yet been established. It could be some great, all powerful, controlling body or some simple, intergalactic AAA organization.

Hybrid society does not appear to have abstract concepts such as life after death.

Hybrids do not appear to be as connected to each other like Grays or Nordics but are cultural composites - a population made up of a number of groups from diverse cultural, ethnic, and linguistic backgrounds. Hybrids are able to interact telepathically with all other species but not as completely as Grays and Nordics. It is highly possible that those Hybrids with Human characteristics could converse normally and pass in Human culture. It is unknown whether Hybrids can read or write but it is highly likely that they can. It is also highly possible that Hybrids possess a symbolic system.

With many respectful thanks to the Indigo Hybrid. The next project will include additional questions regarding Consensus between the five races that have been interviewed to date: the Large Grays, the Nordics, the Small Grays, the Hooded Reptilian and the Indigo Hybrid.

6: The Exobiology Project: Consensus Forum

"There are as many other races as stars in the sky."

—Large Gray

Introduction – Consensus Forum

Previous interviews focused on five different ET races: Large and Small Gray, Nordic, Hooded Reptilian, and Indigo Hybrid with additional races remaining to be interviewed. This new forum brings together these five races to answer additional questions. As before, this new project is carried out with diplomacy and respect.

Q: The alien races appear to operate on a consensus basis. That is, the races act as one mind, conferring before responding or acting. Is this a stumbling block in communication between alien races and Human? Does this affect alien races/Human relations? Humans act more independently, usually act alone, does this difference matter?

Large Gray: We act as one. All know what one thinks. This does not affect our relations with Humans. One interacting with a Human is like all interacting. All know. It is the Human that is at a disadvantage. It is a disadvantage because the one Gray cannot share with all other Humans.

Nordic: We share information with other Nordics, with Hybrids and with the Grays as one mind. We cannot share with all Humans, only several. It can be a detriment to alien/Human communication and relations.

Small Gray: We are of one mind. Everyone shares each thought, each decision. Think of it as a graph with millions of points: as agreement or disagreement is reached, the graph goes up and down. There is no stumbling block for Grays, only for Humans and hybrids that have more Human in their composition.

Hooded Reptilian: Communication is limited. We have our purpose. It cannot be shared with Humans. So there is no need for communication with Humans.

Indigo Hybrid: We have an advantage. We can interact with all races including Humans. Not all Humans can communicate with us. If we are on Earth for some time we can reach more people. Not everyone will listen.

Q: How many different Confederations are there beyond our galaxy? How many different races are there beyond our galaxy? Are they highly intelligent? Do they operate on pure intelligence, rather than having a physical body? The size of the universe is beyond our Human knowing? What can the five races tell us about the rest of the universe, other galaxies, other races, and other Confederations? How do they communicate? Would we be able to communicate with them? The races, so far interviewed, appear to respect Human intelligence. Do the other races also respect Human intelligence? How would other races differentiate between Humans and other animals on Earth?

Large Gray: All races respect intelligence and other races. Humans are at the bottom of the chain. Some like the Whites (Nordics) operate on pure intelligence. Others are more physical. There are as many other races as stars in the sky.

Nordic: Other races would not differentiate between Humans and other Earth animals. We see the difference but other races would not. The difference is that the Earth has had a limited span of being from other parts of the void.

Small Gray: We know the difference between Humans and animals. Others, distant races, may not. We know that Humans and Earth animals have different uses.

Hooded Reptilian: We know all races, all who communicate. We communicate with them. Most respect us and other intelligent races. Humans and Earth animals are the same to us.

Indigo Hybrid: We are just learning about all the other species, who is friendly and who is not. The Reptilians have the information about other races and they share some with us. Often we have to wait until we have traveled to a new location. Then we can learn about the other races there.

Q: All abductees appear to be subject to "video" presentations that present cataclysmic scenes. How are the different races able to project these scenes? Humans have the ability to predict future events either through psi means or through statistics. The races, interviewed so far, do not seem to be able to predict beyond a short time period. Are there races that are able to predict beyond the near-term, and can predict events up to 50-100 years into the future? The Nordics (Whites) appear to have some predictive abilities. Can the Nordics predict up to 50-100 years into the future? If so, to what extent is the Earth at risk over the next 50 years? Is the Earth, itself at risk, or just Humans?

Large Gray: We can predict based on previous events. There is no quality to predictions. Humans give more value to predictions than Grays. You will not be around in 50 to 100 years, so what is the concern? We do not think about the future or plan, we do what is necessary now, not for the future.

Nordic: The Nordics can only predict for short time periods but we do plan. We have to plan ahead to send our body copies and to know where to bi-locate. We have to plan where we will be next and where to send the Hybrids. We cannot predict long periods of time ahead.

Small Gray: Predictions are made short-term by all on a consensus basis. This is usually accurate for us. We predict where and when a Human will be, to be collected. We can plan what tests and treatments to make to collect materials from Humans and to implant. We do not predict further than that.

Hooded Reptilian: We are long-range planners to predict travel. We can move a craft to a distant location with prediction. Time dimensions are different. They are not linear.

Indigo Hybrid: It is impossible for Hybrids to predict long range unless they have a very large percentage of Human in them (70% plus) and they have been trained by Humans. In that respect they are very like Humans themselves. Not every Human can predict ahead that far. Once Earth has been left time and space differences confuse the question and it cannot be answered.

Q: The events written about at the Skinwalker Ranch showed that many races, while frightening and threatening Humans, appeared to attack animals. It is obvious that Humans are being watched by different races? How many are watching us? There was evidence of shape-shifting at the Ranch. Which races are able to shape-shift? Was the Big Foot creature seen at the ranch an individual species or a race that was shape-shifting? What use are the harvested blood/organs to those harvesting them? Are there other species that are harvesting these animal parts?

Large Gray: We are not able to shape-shift unless it is to move through solid objects to get to a location to collect Humans. We can only materialize and dematerialize. We do not shift into other creatures or beings. We retain our shape. We harvest animal parts.

Nordic: We can shape-shift. We have shape-shifted into animals and other races when we need to. We may frighten but we do not harm Humans. Many people were frightened at the Ranch but none were physically harmed. We can bi-locate to a Nordic shape body or we can send ahead a proxy body, such as an animal and we can bi-locate to that body. We can bi-locate to wolf, hairy creature, Earth creature, tree creature, and others. We can even bi-locate into a proxy Orb body, if we need to. These proxy bodies are physical and we need to be careful. We can abandon a proxy body and re-bi-locate to a Nordic body somewhere else. We assist the Grays when we shape shift.

Small Gray: We cannot shape-shift into other forms, only to move through dense materials. We merge through these materials when we collect Humans. We retain our Gray shape before and after we merge.

Hooded Reptilian: There is no need for us to shape shift. We rarely leave the craft. We know about the shape-shifters but we do not shape-shift. We only leave the craft to transfer to another craft.

Indigo Hybrid: We do not shape-shift. We retain the shape in which we were produced and that shape is determined by the percentages of the races that make up our characteristics.

Q: Most alien races, interviewed so far, have abilities to travel outside of the Earth, either in craft or, as in the Nordics, bi-locating themselves to body copies at their destination. Will Humans ever have these abilities? What other abilities are dormant in Humans that we could further develop? What abilities, that we currently have, are we not using?

Large Gray: Humans are limited. They have limited abilities. Humans do not have the abilities that other races have. If Humans had these abilities they probably would not use them or they would fight over them.

Nordic: Humans are limited in what they use of their minds. They have the ability to bi-locate with their mind but have not yet learned how to send a proxy or duplicate physical body. Some Humans are able to bi--locate to a light body that feels like the physical body. Humans also have the ability to make themselves invisible. Some can do this at will, others it happens to accidentally. Humans have the ability to use telepathy but not how to use it at will.

Small Gray: Humans are very limited and are based in the physical. They do not share thoughts and cannot live in the communal mind. There is the potential for a less limited existence.

Hooded Reptilian: We would not want Humans to have more powers. They are only useful to the Grays and Nordics. There are dormant abilities but they will probably stay that way. Humans just get in the way of other races.

Indigo Hybrid: Humans have great potential. As Hybrids we have characteristics that are from Grays and Nordics. This gives us greater abilities than just being Human. But Humans have the potential to do all these things. It will take time.

Q: What other races should we be interviewing? Are there other races that are producing Hybrids? Are there other Hybrids that are different races than Human/Nordic/Gray? What characteristics and abilities would these other Hybrids exhibit?

Large Gray: Other races would include the Smooths, the Greens and the Oranges. There are other smaller animal-like races but they would not understand Humans, they are on another level of communication. We cannot communicate with them.

Nordic: There are many races to communicate with. It would be good to send out an invitation and see who responds. Be careful that you are not bringing in Nordics in a proxy body.

Small Gray: There are many races but we do not have that information.

Hooded Reptilian: NR

Indigo Hybrid: The Orbs are a species but a poorly defined one. They are also part of the Confederation. They would be one race that you could interview and you could also ask about the Confederation. They might tell you.

Q: If Humans can request that they not be abducted (collected) is just one request enough for all the times they might be abducted? Could one abductee request that all abductions of other abductees be stopped?

Large Gray: To ask that an abduction be stopped is frail (?) It is the way it has been. No Human who is collected needs to ask for it to be stopped. It can be asked but it will not happen. It is frail thinking.

Nordic: Abductions can be stopped but they will resume. A Human can ask for themselves for the one time and multiple times and they will stop but they will resume. One Human can ask that all Human abductions be stopped and they may be for a very short time but they will resume. They cannot be stopped for ever.

Small Gray: We would not allow the collections to be stopped. If one group stopped then we would go to another group and come back for the first group. There is no need for them to be stopped.

Hooded Reptilian: It is not important to the Reptilians. We will still move craft. It is important to the Grays and the Nordics. If the collections do not take place, the hybrids cannot be formed. Less Humans means less problems.

Indigo Hybrid: Humans can ask for the abductions to stop, both for a limited and an extended time and they can ask for the abductions of others to stop. Humans need to understand that once in the collection process, Humans change in their physiology and need the collections to stay healthy. There are processes during the collections that ensure that Humans stay healthy. There is a benefit to Humans, as well as Hybrids, during the collections.

Q: What capabilities do we need to be accepted into the Confederation? What do Humans need to do to be ready to join the Confederation?

Large Gray: We are not part of the Confederation. We do not know what is needed. Humans have less knowledge about what is needed. Only when you know will it happen.

Nordic: There is an invitation offered. This invitation enters many minds at the same time. It is resisted many times before it is accepted. It may take generations before the invitation is accepted. There is a natural progression that takes place, which cannot be explained, before the invitation is extended.

Small Gray: We are not part of the Confederation but we are waiting. We have produced the Hybrids who are part of the Confederation, with the help of the Nordics, who are part of the Confederation. One day we will be part of the Confederation. We listen and wait.

Hooded Reptilian: We have no need of being part of the Confederation. We move all those whether they are part of the Confederation or not. It is not important to us.

Indigo Hybrid: We cannot tell you about the Confederation. We are part of the Confederation because we have achieved certain mental levels and physical abilities. There will be an awakening in the Humans and, when the time is right, the invitation will be given and accepted.

Q: Are there Orbs that are autonomously intelligent? Are the majority programmed or are some intelligent and able to act on their own? What kinds of information do the Orbs carry? If a Human calls them and asks for help, will it be given? Will they respond to an individual Human? Are they individuals? Are they protectors? There are Indigenous peoples on Earth who believe that the Orbs are protectors of Humans. Is this so? Can the energy and information, that Orbs carry, be useful to Humans? Can the Orbs enter Human chakras or energy points on the body?

Large Gray: Orbs are messengers and are composed of energy and information. They have some rights. They do belong to the Confederation. They have abilities that we do not have, such as the ability to move long distances in very short time periods with much information. We do not want them to act on their own. They carry our information.

Nordic: Orbs are important to us. They carry our body copies and proxy bodies for us. Sometimes we have other means of sending the body copies. We send information to each other and to other races. They serve us well.

Small Gray: Orbs are useful but we do not bother with them much.

Hooded Reptilian: NR

Indigo Hybrid: Orbs can be independent and autonomous. Yes, they can carry out all the activities listed above. They can carry information. They can protect Humans. They can enter chakras. They can help Humans if asked. But they are more needed by the other races. You do not understand the Orbs and could subjugate them. They do not need this.

Q: On some craft, abductees have noted a serpent-shaped insignia. Is this indicative of control by any one race? Are the ships manufactured by the Reptilians? In many Earth cultures there is a Reptilian motif in their mythology. For example, in Egypt, there is a myth that a disabled craft was incorporated into a pyramid that was built around it by Humans. Is there a relationship between different insignia seen on different craft?

Large Gray: Insignia are seen on craft to indicate many things. These insignia show us where to be and how to get there. The craft are produced by the Large and Small Grays and moved by the Reptilians. They are not owned by any race but shared.

Nordic: We share the craft. We do not make the craft. We do not need the craft as we are able to bi-locate. We only share the craft when we need to participate in Hybrid development and to help with Human collection for the Grays.

Small Gray: We help make the craft and they are shared by all and moved by the Reptilians. The Reptilians do not own the craft.

Hooded Reptilian: The insignia show that we can move the craft. We can take other species to other places. It shows places that only we can go. No others are allowed there.

Indigo Hybrid: There are insignia and pictorial signs all over the craft. They vary from maps, to directions, to decorations. The decorations are for the Hybrids. Those that have more Human in them appreciate them. They are based on ancient Earth designs. The designs differ from craft to craft. Sometimes the Hybrids create the designs themselves. We are very proud of this. We like to be creative.

Q: Many Earth cultures believe in a Power that created the galaxies. Do any of the races have similar believes in a Creator, either now or in the past? Is there an intelligent source in the Universe?

Large Gray: All races have intelligence. There is no one individual with intelligence that is larger than the Large and Small Grays together. There is no one being that created the whole universe. We do not have such a belief.

Nordic: There are races that are more intelligent than the Grays and the Nordics but they live far away from this galaxy and do not have control over the whole universe. Each part of the universe has its own galaxies, its own races and its own needs.

Small Gray: There is no match for this belief with the Grays.

Hooded Reptilian: NR.

Indigo Hybrid: What Humans call God is what we can do ourselves. We learn about God-like beings from Humans who have been collected but we cannot understand such a concept. Many of the abilities, that this being can do, we can do. We do not understand this concept.

Q: Are there Rules of Communication, that we should know about, when interacting with different races. For example, the Nordics prefer for us to use Initial Caps when referring to other races but not places, this does not seem so important to the Grays. The Large Gray refers to Humans as "limited" are there things that we should know that are not being told to us? Are there things that the different races do not want to tell us? Are there rules within the galaxies, such as honesty? It has been reported by some abductees that some races lie, is this so? What about cooperation? Do the races not tell some things because it would be harmful to Humans? Are there other reasons?

Large Gray: We do not lie but we do not always give all the information that there is to tell. Some information is not safe for Humans. When we collect Humans they are asleep and cannot understand what we tell them. We tell them many things, but they don't understand because they are asleep. We tell then enough for them to cooperate. Some things that Humans would like to know, we do not know ourselves.

Nordic: Humans are naturally curious. When they are collected by the Grays they are curious about the craft and the other races. But we have to only give them a little information. They would not be able to understand all of the information, so we only give them a little information. We do not lie but we do not give the whole of the information.

Small Gray: We may give information that is not correct so that the Humans will cooperate. We sometimes appear to them as others that they know so that they will not be frightened. We give them pictures in their minds of places they know so that they will not be frightened. We do this so they will cooperate and not be frightened.

Hooded Reptilian: We do not need to lie. We have accurate information. There is no need for us to lie.

Indigo Hybrid: Humans are often lied to but the lies are for their safety and comfort. Grays will appear as an animal such as a bird or deer in the forest. The Human remembers the eyes of an animal and not the Gray. Grays will pretend to be loved ones during sexual encounters. This ensures cooperation and comfort. It is not intended for lies to harm Humans. They do not cooperate if they are scared and uncomfortable.

Q: Humans have a strong sense of time, which is related to the revolutions that the Earth makes around the Sun, the Moon around the Earth, and Earth's rotation through the galaxies. How do the different races think about time? If there is a sense of time, is there any information about the future of the Earth in 3, 6, 9, 12, 13, 16, 19 revolutions of Earth? Can we help different races understand how we use time? Do all races have no sense of the future? Do races act in self-interest only, or is there some altruism? If most races act on a group consensus basis, why is there an NR response? Is it that the races do not have the information or do not want to answer?

Large Gray: Sometimes we do not have the information that is needed. We do not know everything. Often, if we meet a new group of Humans to collect, we have to assess them anew. Sometimes we miss things that we should see, we are not perfect. Time is irrelevant to us. We sense when it is dark and we can perform our collections. We sense when there are conditions when collections would be difficult such as thunderstorms and solar storms. We do not have a linear sense of time as Humans do.

Nordic: Time and space to us are factors to be used to bi-locate and move ourselves around. Time is not linear for us. Time is multi-dimensional and we can use that to move around. Linear time is a Human concept. Humans have not yet accepted a different concept of time and space.

Small Gray: Sometimes we do not want to answer. Humans do not always understand what they want to know. We cannot give small bits of knowledge. Human thinking works in small chunks, Gray minds work in large maps. We do not know how to chunk!

Hooded Reptilian: We do not give information to Humans.

Indigo Hybrid: Outside of the Earth time ceases to be linear but is omni-directional. That is how we can travel. There are layers of time and space that is difficult to understand. We do not understand all the mechanics. The Reptilians know how to move the craft through these layers. They do not give us information either.

Q: What other species should we be contacting and interviewing? What other questions should we be asking of these races?

Large Gray: We do not know. There are many races that would cooperate. Send out a signal. See who answers. Ask the Confederation.

Nordic: We will ask when we travel. We will ask who is willing to cooperate. Most will. Most have respect for Humans and Nordics.

Small Gray: There is no need to interview others. We have given you the views of most of the other species. We do not know everything. What we do not know is probably small. Other races would probably not give you this other information.

Hooded Reptilian: NR

Indigo Hybrid: The Reptilian does know of other races but will not say. The reptilians keep such information to themselves and do not share it with other races. We share what we can and agree that you should send out an invitation to other races, the Orbs and to the Confederation.

Q: Human evolution is said to be going through some major changes, for example with more Indigo Children being born and recognized. Is there a Higher Order of living that we should be searching for? Is there a connection with a source that we should be looking for?

Large Gray: There have always been special children born on the Earth. We have collected them and noticed them. They are the vanguard for the development of the Earth. They display the ideal for Humans, who are generally mediocre. These children are generally ignored by Humans.

Nordic: In every race there are "children" that are special. They have finer characteristics. They should be nurtured. We communicate with them and most of them hear us. But they are ridiculed. They are thought to be sick in the mind. The Human race does not recognize their abilities and talents. They could teach Humans to be greater.

Small Gray: We collect all Humans and not special ones. If there is a special one, they are easier to communicate with and are more cooperative. We do not need to lie to them. They accept us as we are. We prefer to work with cooperative Humans.

Hooded Reptilian: It is not important to us whether Humans are special or not. All Humans are the same to us. They are on the craft and then they are gone.

Indigo Hybrid: It is quite an honor to become a Hybrid that has Indigo Child characteristics. It makes it easier for us to communicate with other races and to understand Human thought and action.

Q: Another remote viewer has perceived that the Gray race was once an autonomous race and that another, more aggressive, race subdued them to what they are today. Is there any more information on this?

Large Gray: Each race has a history of being autonomous. Many races became linked with other stronger races. They subdued some of their autonomy for the sake of cooperation. Humans consider them-selves autonomous but are not. The Grays collect them when they want.

Nordic: There are races that were autonomous, but had to become weak in order to stay strong. The Nordics had a much greater freedom but had to follow the rules and norms to exist. We are not as autonomous as other would see us.

Small Gray: We consider ourselves autonomous and not under great rules. We also live in cooperation with other races.

Hooded Reptilian: We consider ourselves autonomous. We have information and we can move the craft. That is all we need to have.

Indigo Hybrid: The history of these races is complex. There is too much for Humans to fully know and understand. Humans are not autonomous either. No race can stand by itself. One day all the history will be understood.

Q: This has been an awesome experience bringing you all together. Thank you!

7: The Exobiology Project: Talking With The Orbs

"Talking to an Orb is like talking to a Thesaurus."

We know quite a bit about the Orbs from the other races that have been interviewed. An invitation was extended to the Orbs to participate in this project and an Earth-bound Orb, calling itself Orb1, responded. Orb1 was invited to comment on these findings. Specific questions were also asked of Orb1, including questions that were unanswered by the other races. This session then directly interviewed an Earth-bound Orb with particular questions. Specifically, how can we facilitate communications with them, are there some activities that they enjoy, what abilities can they help us develop, and what different types of Orbs are there and what are there functions? Are the Orbs always the same or different Orbs, are they carrying messages. and are they independent or where do they come from?

What we know about the Orbs from the Other Races.

Large Gray

Large Gray: "Orbs are energy and information. Orbs carry information. They are also pure information. They can be deciphered through mental intellect. They can respond to requests. There are many Orbs and they are: probes, scouts and they play. They are attracted by sound. Encode sound within structure as manifested by the rings and colors within the Orbs. Everything has a frequency. Orbs absorb frequencies. Become information. Carry information. The Large Grays are able to send Orbs that are limited probes. Orbs are energy and information, no emotions. No positive or negative. Just energy and information. Humans ascribe emotions, both good and bad to the Orbs."

Orb1 Responds to the Large Grays

Orb1: The Large Gray is correct in many aspects of this dialogue. We carry both energy and information that is encoded into our structure. We consider ourselves *spiritual* and we do not act on our own volition. We act as messengers and *servants*

Q: This is the closest word I could find to what they mean. They appear to be altruistic. The words in *italics* are my perception of their meaning. Talking to an Orb is like talking to a Thesaurus.

Q: Some words that the Orbs relay are "noisy" and have many meanings, so I have written the closest word in *italics.*

Orb1: Most races can interpret the information that we carry. There are very few Humans that can interpret the information.

Q: Have you come at my request?

Orb1: Yes.

Q: Thank you.

Orb1: The Large Gray is correct in stating our functions: we are probes as we can encode information at the destination and take it back to our starting point. We can play, if we are requested to, but we do not play autonomously. Yes, we are attracted by sound, specifically low frequencies. We have emotions but these are only expressed according to the sender and the receiver of the information. For example, if an Orb is called and asked to play, the Orb will do so, until it is called away or sent to another destination.

Q: When Humans pray or want to send positive thoughts, blessings and other thought messages to another, do you carry them?

Orb1: Yes. But there are other *micro-elementals* that also do this work. Orbs can also carry negative thoughts, as can the smaller entities.

Q: Are the faces seen on photographs of Orbs, the faces of those who sent them?

Orb1: Many times but the faces can also be of the person who is to receive the information. Sometimes, we get delayed on a journey by another person calling us. So, the face on the Orb is not the face of the one sending but the one ultimately receiving the information. We wish this did not happen. Please only call the ones closest to you! Not the ones that are on a journey! This can be done with the *mind.*

Nordic

Nordic: "Orbs are energy and information. This is well known among the Grays and the Whites. They do not have personalities or purpose, as is thought by Humans. They can transform into Human shapes or Gray shapes but they are not Humans or Grays. They act as scouts, probes, carriers of information across distances. The Orbs can be called. The Nordics call them to give them information that can be transported across distances. Think of them as workers, rather than individuals". "Once their purpose has been carried out, they usually dissipate into the atmosphere. The faces see in some Orbs are a form of recognition to the receiver of the information. They are the faces of the individuals who form the spheres and they are for identification only. The Orbs are not personalities themselves." "Yes, there are many different types of Orbs. Humans can also imprint an Orb with information but cannot yet perceive Orbs all the time with their eyes, only with technology. Nor can they decode the information that is carried by the Orbs. Orbs are no more positive to Humans than to any other species. Humans are able to summon Orbs and to interact with Orbs from other sources but have little understanding of their function or purpose. Orbs simply carry information and energy and are not autonomous."

Orb1 Responds to the Nordic

Orb1: This is *nonsense*! We cannot change into other shapes, as the Nordics can. They have an *inflated sense of themselves*. They can change shape and assume that all other races can do this. They are the ones changing into other shapes. Not us. They are correct that we carry information. Yes, we carry information for the Nordics, who like to call themselves *Whites*. They are *pompous*! Yes, we have personalities but these are *subsumed* so that we can *serve*. Some Humans can see us as small lights and we are often seen on *media*. We are autonomous but choose to be *messengers*. Nordics are members of the Confederation, as we are, but the Nordics have an *inflated sense of self*.

Small Grays

Small Grays: "There are different types of Orbs. Some have intelligence. Some are able to act independently. The Orbs that the Whites (Nordics) work with do not have autonomy but go where they are sent. Orbs are not aggressive. They do not carry weapons. They are able to materialize and dematerialize. They do carry information and energy and are useful. Could we learn to harness the Orbs? That is a Human concept. Orbs are intelligent. They will come or go when asked. They will carry information. Most Orbs do not have personality that is positive or negative. Positive and negative are Earth judgments."

Orb1 Responds to the Small Grays

Orb1: Yes, we have intelligence. It is *nonsense* that we are sent by the Nordics because we do not have intelligence or autonomy. We have both. They are right that the Orbs cannot be harnessed or *detained*. We do have personalities but these are *subsumed*. We recognize each other Orb's personalities and intelligence. They are right that we do not carry weapons and are not aggressive but we can choose not to come and choose not to deliver information, or even to deliver the wrong information when we decide. There have been accidents when a Human has walked into us and we have knocked them over.

Hooded Reptilian

Hooded Reptilian: "We do not discuss the Orbs. Others have Orbs, we do not. We have never had Orbs. We will never have Orbs. We will never talk about the Orbs. We do not discuss Orbs. We do not own or discuss Orbs." When asked, are Orbs a separate species, they replied, "No. They are a nuisance."

Orb1 Responds to the Hooded Reptilian

Q: Here I perceived something like the Earth-based saying: "Don't talk to us about the Reptilians!" It was perceived in a tolerant yet sarcastic manner. There seems no "love lost" between the Orbs and the Reptilians.

Q: Do you carry information for the Reptilians?

Orb1: Yes but under *duress*.

They do not like to talk about each other or to each other.

Q: What caused this difference in opinion and dislike?

Orb1: NR – No Response.

Indigo Hybrid

Indigo Hybrid: "The orbs are problematic. They were a race at one time but became subservient to other races and became messengers and servants. Not exactly slaves but they are altruistic and subsume their own interests for the interests of others."

Q: The other races say that the Orbs carry energy and information. Is that so?

Indigo Hybrid: "Yes."

Q: Are some Orbs independent?

Indigo Hybrid: "They are all independent but subservient to other races."

Q: Could Humans call them and ask them to carry information or for help?

Indigo Hybrid: "Yes, but that would be adding to their subservient role."

Q: Is this role something that they have chosen?

Indigo Hybrid: "Yes."

Q: Is there a way that Humans could interact with Orbs in a way that would enable them to be more independent, yet cooperating with Humans?

Indigo Hybrid: "Yes, by stating to other races that Humans are cooperating with the orbs."

Q: Are the Orbs part of the Confederation?

Indigo Hybrid: "Yes."

Q: That surprises me.

Indigo Hybrid: "Yes, they are members."

Q: You refer to the orbs, rather than the Orbs. I learned from the Nordics that those races that belong to the Confederation had their names capitalized, i.e. Nordics, Whites.

Indigo Hybrid: "It is the choice of the race. We respect the orbs decision and do not call them Orbs."

Q: Would calling them Orbs, give them more respect?
Indigo Hybrid: "They do not want it. We have talked about the orbs before. They are poor things that have been used. Leave them alone."
Orb1 Responds to the Indigo Hybrid
Q: There also appeared to be some problem with obtaining information from the Orb regarding the Hybrid. The only information was that this particular Hybrid had some dealings with the Hooded Reptilian and was *suspect*.
Orb1: The Hybrids do not understand us. They have little to do with us. They hear about us from the Grays, Nordics and Reptilians and do not understand us. They have pity for us but do not understand us. We are part of the Confederation, we have autonomy, we have intelligence, and we have personality. Do not pity us.
Q: I don't pity you. I respect you and your race.
Talking to Orb1 – Direct Questions
Q: How can we facilitate communications with them?
Orb1: We can interact in many ways, through thought, by changing the *density* of items so that they appear or disappear. Mostly, we interact, with Humans, through thought. Other races have *machines* that can download the information that we carry.
Q: Are there some activities that they enjoy?
Orb1: We enjoy traveling to distant places. We do not need craft, like the other races. We are totally *amorphous* and can travel whenever and wherever we want. We like this freedom. We go where others need to us to go, we go where we are called, and we enjoy this.
Q: Do you enjoy dancing with Humans?
Orb1: Yes, but it often calls us away from other destinations. You must call local Orbs to dance: they will become your Orbs.
Q: Will they relocate?
Orb1: Yes.
Q: Will they carry information?
Orb1: Yes, but others will not know how to *perceive* the information.
Q: What abilities can they help us develop?
Orb1: We cannot help with this. Humans have varying degrees of information and understanding but their *prejudices* hinder them developing and understanding more about their gifts.
Q: What different types of Orbs are there and what are their functions?
Orb1: Orbs are one race but have many differences. Our destinations define our differences. We carry messages, information, and energy. We take these from one location to another.
Q: If you are an Earth-based Orb, do you only carry information around the Earth?

Orb1: That is a *mistake*. We are all the same race. We can all go *off-Earth* and none of us is *confined* to the Earth.

Q: One of the things that I perceive about the Orbs is that many words that you use have multiple meaning, like a Thesaurus. I have given the nearest equivalent in this report. Is this correct?

Orb1: Our language contains many *interpretations*. We work with many races and therefore have many *interpretations* of each *word/meaning*.

Q: While still respecting your race, it is like interacting with a Thesaurus.

Orb1: True.

Q: How do they cooperate?

Orb1: We *cooperate* with all races but more with some than others. *Cooperate* implies an equality. We are equal with some and not equal with others. We carry information for everyone but do not *cooperate* with everyone.

Q: Is there a Confederation that is acting together? Are the Orbs part of the Confederation?

Orb1: All Orbs are part of the Confederation. We have been part of the Confederation for all time. We have always been.

Q: A thought has crossed my mind to ask? If you have always been, and interact with all races, were you once part of these races?

Orb1: Yes. It is similar to *reincarnation*. As other races fade away we become part of the Orb race.

Q: I have asked the other races about "Life after Death" and they have been unable to answer this question.

Orb1: There is no death. Life continues but in different forms.

Q: So were you once a Gray or a Nordic?

Orb1: It is not that simple. The energies mixed and we are formed.

Q: Is there more to the Orbs observed by others, and can they manifest responses?

Orb1: There is nothing more to the Orbs that others have observed except that they have been interrupted in their journey. There are Orbs available to be called and which will interact with them, use *peripheral vision*.

Q: Some say that they can put out their hands and feel the energy of the Orbs. Is this so?

Orb1: Yes, but the Orbs they are interacting with are then disturbed and have to return to the *source* to regain their information. You can do what you want with the Orbs that you call from the *layers*.

Questions asked of the Forum of Races

Q: The alien races appear to operate on a consensus basis. That is, the races act as one mind, conferring before responding or acting. Is this a stumbling block in communication between alien races and Human? Does this affect alien races/Human relations? Humans act more independently, usually act alone, does this difference matter?

Orb1: Orbs do not act as one *mind* and are like Humans in this. But when conveying information for another race, the Orbs are able to act like that race and share information with many other races. Communicating as one *mind* or as individual minds is not important to communication.

Q: How many different Confederations are there beyond our galaxy? How many different races are there beyond our galaxy? Are they highly intelligent? Do they operate on pure intelligence, rather than having a physical body? The size of the universe is beyond our Human knowing? What can you tell us about the rest of the universe, other galaxies, other races, and other Confederations? How do they communicate? Would we be able to communicate with them? The races, so far interviewed, appear to respect Human intelligence. Do the other races also respect Human intelligence? How would other races differentiate between Humans and other animals on Earth?

Orb1: All races respect Human intelligence, even the Hooded Reptilian, or they would not communicate with you. The Human race is able to communicate with all of them. The Human race can communicate both with the mind and with *the voice*. All races are able to *differentiate* between Humans and other animals on Earth. There is too much information to share in this one *communication.*

Q: Will you communicate these answers in another session, which would have been devoted to an off-planet Orb?

Orb1: Yes.

Q: All abductees appear to be subject to "video" presentations that present cataclysmic scenes. How are the different races able to project these scenes? Humans have the ability to predict future events either through psi means or through statistics. The races, interviewed so far, do not seem to be able to predict beyond a short time period. Are there races that are able to predict beyond the near-term, and can predict events up to 50-100 years into the future? The Nordics appear to have some predictive abilities. Can the Nordics predict up to 50-100 years into the future? If so, to what extent is the Earth at risk over the next 50 years? Is the Earth, itself at risk, or just Humans? Do the Orbs have predictive abilities?

Orb1: Only in the information that we can carry. Humans are the most predictive as they can reason, plan, remember, and think independently. They have the ability to *set aside extraneous* information and look at future events. Orbs can tell you information that they are carrying, they can be sent to access information about future events and their consequences but cannot predict events of their own *volition.*

Q: The events written about at the Skinwalker Ranch, UT showed that many races, while frightening and threatening Humans, appeared to attack animals. It is obvious that Humans are being watched by different races? How many are watching us? There was evidence of shape-shifting at the ranch. Which races are able to shape-shift? Was the Big Foot creature seen at the ranch an individual species or a race that was shape-shifting? What use are the harvested blood/organs to those harvesting them? Are there other species that are harvesting these animal parts?

Orb1: The Orbs carry information; we do not harvest parts or *shape-shift*. The Nordics are the only ones visiting Earth on a regular basis that can *shape-shift*. The animal *remains* are used by the Grays. There is a *reciprocal* arrangement between the Grays and the Nordics.

Q: Most alien races, interviewed so far, have abilities to travel outside of the Earth, either in craft or, as in the Nordics, bi-locating themselves to body copies at their destination. Will Humans ever have these abilities? What other abilities are dormant in Humans that we could further develop? What abilities, that we currently have, are we not using?

Orb1: Humans can bi-locate with their minds only. It would be very difficult for Humans to bi-locate with their bodies. They are too *dense*. Humans can further develop their ability to bi-locate with their minds.

Q: Are there Orbs that are autonomously intelligent? Are the majority programmed or are some intelligent and able to act on their own? What kinds of information do the Orbs carry? If a Human calls them and asks for help, will it be given? Will they respond to an individual Human? Are they individuals? Are they protectors? There are Indigenous peoples on Earth who believe that the Orbs are protectors of Humans. Is this so? Can the energy and information, that Orbs carry, be useful to Humans? Can the Orbs enter Human chakras or energy points on the body?

Orb1: We are all intelligence and autonomous as *explained* before. We can carry information for any race. Orbs can be protectors of information. They cannot be aggressive protectors of Humans from other Humans. We can protect from other races by the information that we carry. All information is useful but information for another race will not be given to a Human. Orbs can enter the Human body but prefer not to do so, it is too *dense*.

Q: Are the Orbs that visit some the same or different Orbs, are they carrying messages that can interpreted, are they independent or where do they come from?

Orb1: The Orbs that are called are on their *journey* to other places. They are from many places. You must call other Orbs that are specific to you; you can just *mentally* call them.

Q: On some craft, abductees have noted a serpent-shaped insignia. Is this indicative of control by any one race? Are the ships manufactured by the Reptilians? In many Earth cultures there is a reptilian motif in their mythology. For example, in Egypt, there is a myth that a disabled craft was incorporated into a pyramid that was built around it by Humans. Is there a relationship between different insignia seen on different craft?

Orb1: We do not have information, *currently*, about these insignia. We will *ask*.

Q: Many Earth cultures believe in a Power that created the galaxies. Do any of the races have similar beliefs in a Creator, either now or in the past? Is there an intelligent source in the Universe?

Orb1: We do not have such a *belief*. We do not know of such a *creator* of the universe.

Q: Are there Rules of Communication, that we should know about, when interacting with different races. For example, the Nordics prefer for us to use Initial Caps when referring to other races but not places, this does not seem so important to the Grays. The Large Gray refers to Humans as "limited": are there things that we should know that are not being told to us? Are there things that the different races do not want to tell us? Are there rules within the galaxies, such as honesty? It has been reported by some abductees that some races lie, is this so? What about cooperation? Do the races not tell some things because it would be harmful to Humans? Are there other reasons?

Orb1: Each race has its own rules of communication. Some races consider Humans as "limited", because they are different and do not share a group mind. There are *strengths* in both ways of being.

Q: Humans have a strong sense of time, which is related to the revolutions that the Earth makes around the Sun, the Moon around the Earth, and Earth's rotation through the galaxies. How do the different races think about time? If there is a sense of time, is there any information about the future of the Earth in 3, 6, 9, 12, 13, 16, 19 revolutions of Earth? Can we help different races understand how we use time? Do all races have no sense of the future? Do races act in self-interest only, or is there some altruism? If most races act on a group consensus basis, why is there an NR response? Is it that the races do not have the information or do not want to answer?

Orb1: Orbs do not have predictive powers as explained. Like us, many races do not have the information that you look for. But we can go and find some information if asked.

Q: What other species should we be contacting and interviewing? What other questions should we be asking of these races?

Orb1: Humans are *better at this.*

Orb1: You have asked questions of the main races that are *currently interacting* with Earth and Humans. Questions will arise as the races emerge for questioning.

Q: Human evolution is said to be going through some major changes, for example with more Indigo Children being born and recognized. Is there a Higher Order of living that we should be searching for? Is there a connection with a source that we should be looking for?

Orb1: There is no *source* that we know about except the other races and ourselves.

Q: Another remote viewer has perceived that the Gray race was once an autonomous race and that another, more aggressive, race subdued them to what they are today. Is there any more information on this?

Orb1: This is not so. The Gray races can be aggressive; they did not arise from another aggressive race nor were subdued by them. Grays are not usually aggressive to Humans but they can be if provoked. They have weapons. They are strong. That is why Humans are *altered* before interacting with the Grays. This is not to prevent Humans from becoming aggressive but so that the Grays do not have a *reason* to be provoked and to become aggressive.

Unanswered Questions from the other Races.

When interviewed individually, two of the races were unable to answer some of the questions posed to the races. The Large Gray and the Hooded Reptilian were unable to answer the following questions and these are now asked of the Orbs.

Large Gray.

Q: The Large Gray was asked if the Earth would be invited to join the Confederation and the Large Gray answered that the Earth would be invited but could not answer when. It was also asked about concepts such as "life after death" and it gave its standard "Humans are limited" response. It would not elaborate. The Large Gray could not answer complex questions, such as the difference in beings acting and thinking as individuals. It could not state if there were any major, Earth, historical events in which their race had interacted.

Orb1: We do not have that answer either as it is too far into the future for us to perceive. We do not have that information. Large Grays and Reptilians will not answer complex questions. It is beyond the group mind. Simple questions and answers are *preferred.*

Hooded Reptilian

Q: In addition, the Hooded Reptilian was asked if his race would become part of the Confederation and answered, "No", and did not know answer why this was so. They did not seem to care whether races names, that were part of the Confederation, were capitalized, as the Nordics insisted. They also did not answer the question regarding if Grays and Reptilians would be allowed to travel near the Earth if Earth joins the Confederation. They also did not seem to know much about the Confederation. Finally, the Hooded Reptilians did not think it mattered if Humans survived and would not answer how we could assure that we would survive.

Orb1: As mentioned the Grays and the Reptilians have a limited understanding. They cannot react autonomously. They cannot predict the future. They act very much *in the now*. The Reptilians do not care if any species survives. Humans are respected because they are able to communicate with their minds and their bodies.

Q: With thanks and respect to Orb1: We will return with more questions at a later date.

8: The Exobiology Project: Talking With The Oranges

The following group, the Oranges, is not traditionally extraterrestrial as they are mostly found within the Earth's surface. However, as they interact with all other extraterrestrial races and provide minerals to other races they have been included in the interview process.

Q: Who are the Oranges and where do they fit into the scheme of other races?

The Oranges: Please read through all the questions first so that we can peruse them and decide what we want to answer. When all the questions have been read through, please start at the beginning and we will answer where we can.

Q: Thank you, I will do that.

The Oranges: Please wait...we, the Oranges are chemists, you would call us chemists. We are also vulcanologists, we are metallurgists: we are people who study and mine minerals and metals. We fit into the scheme of other races by providing raw materials. We are very practical and we provide a service.

Q: But who are the Oranges, where did you come from?

The Oranges: We have always been here. We are a separate race from the Grays and the Nordics although we know all of these races.

Q: If you mine these minerals and metals how is it that we haven't seen these metals being transported to craft?

The Oranges: The craft come underground through their physics.

Q: Do you ever come above ground?

The Oranges: Rarely and only to transport members of our race to other locations. We do not come out, just to come out.

Q: Where are there others of your race?

The Oranges: We are everywhere there are minerals to collect.

Q: Do you use mechanical means to collect the minerals?

The Oranges: Sometimes mechanical, other times electrical, sometimes molecular. We have many ways to collect the minerals. Please read through our answers. Have we covered all your questions?

Q: (At this time the Researcher stopped to read through the questions and answers for the Oranges.) - Yes.

Q: You seem very practical and efficient and able to understand the Human mind. Have you had interactions with Humans?

The Oranges: Yes, in mines and deep underground. Many ancient Humans went into caves to meet us but we rarely meet Humans now that want to interact with us.

Q: What is the main purpose and intent of the Oranges? Do you have a group-mind like the Grays?

The Oranges: Our main purpose is to mine and that is our only purpose. If you need an approximation of who we are, we are cousins to the Grays, that is the closest we can come to who we are. We look a lot like the Grays but we are taller and thinner.

Q: Do you actually have an orange skin?

The Oranges: It is more of an Earth tone, as we are constantly interacting with different minerals and we absorb many minerals. Yes, we have a group mind like the Grays and can interact and communicate with them very easily.

Q: How do the Oranges work with the Nordics, the Grays, the Orbs and any other race?

The Oranges: We provide minerals for their use for food and nourishment and for maintenance and for fuel. We interact with them all but we are not them. We work in a cooperative manner to provide what they need.

Q: Do they provide something that you need?

The Oranges: Yes, but it cannot be expressed.

Q: Please try.

The Oranges: It is a form of energy exchange, an information exchange. It is similar to Humans receiving telecommunications, we learn about what is happening across the galaxy but there is much more than that.

Q: Is there a Central Being, a Universal Source, which we refer to as God?

The Oranges: This is a concept that we do not understand. If you are asking which is the strongest race, then the Reptilians are the strongest. If you are asking which race is the most powerful, then it is the Confederation, not one race. If you are asking which is the most altruistic, it is the Orbs. There is not one race that is all of these things.

Q: Are the Elementals a manifestation of what we call God?

The Oranges: As we understand the Human notion of God: that God is omnipresent: everywhere and knows everything. The closest races that come to that are the Orbs and the Elementals. Yet, they still do not come close to what you call God. It seems to us that what you call God has different interpretations across Earth. It could be that all races, including Humans, are manifestations of God? Is this answer sufficient?

Q: Yes, thank you.

Q: The other races have talked about other races such as the Darks, the Greens, the Propers, and the Roughs. Are there other races that are interacting with Humans that we need to contact?

The Oranges: Each solar system has its own life and some can interact with Humans as we are communicating. Some cannot and you would not want to communicate with them, they would see you as food, or a threat. There are other races, or what you call races that interact with Humans but they are not easy to communicate with. Be very careful, some of them have dark selves.

Q: I have interacted with dark selves before and have been able to manage the interaction and disconnect afterwards.

Q: Be very careful. We do not interact with them. We choose not to interact with them, although some live close to us in the Earth.

Q: What is your opinion of Humans?

The Oranges: Do you really want to know?

Q: Yes.

The Oranges: Humans are greedy. They have the whole surface of the Earth, they have all of the seas, they have all of the air but they still want more. They have some of the underground but want more even though they can only handle some depths. They do not want to share or give acceptance to races that have been here for ever and only mine what the Humans cannot mine and take what the Humans do not need.

Q: Thank you for your opinion.

Q: What percentage of Humans is interacting telepathically with non-Human races?

The Oranges: It is very small.

Q: I felt that it was between 5-10% of the Human race.

The Oranges: It is greater than that but only a few can interact with us and the other races. To interact with us needs a motivation and a need. We do not communicate with everybody who has the ability. Many are sleeping in this regard and we do not communicate with them.

Q: So there is a potential to communicate, like so many two-way radios that are not switched on?

The Oranges: Yes.

Q: At the Skinwalker Ranch, UT, were the Oranges active and interacting with the other races?

The Oranges: Yes, we have always been there and many other places. We interacted mostly with the Grays at that ranch.

Q: Is there anything else that you can tell us about the ranch and the interactions that scared the rancher and investigators?

The Oranges: The rancher created most of his own fear. He was fearful for his animals.

Q: What about the caution not to dig at the ranch. Did the previous owners know about the Oranges?

The Oranges: They did not have knowledge of us directly but knew that important work was going on below the ground. They heard the noises and smelled the smells and felt the hot air.

Q: Why are other races at that specific location?

The Oranges: Multiple reasons: to collect Humans, to convey messages between races, to provide access to the site, to mine (we), to collect animals and many other reasons.

Q: Why and how do these races interfere with Humanity?

The Oranges: To interfere means, to Humans, to interact, to make their lives difficult to carry out in the ordinary way. Just by our races being there interferes. There are levels of interference. On a minimal level, we just are there and being there interferes. We collect Humans

Q: So Oranges also collect Humans?

The Oranges: Yes, sometimes but only if they come underground.

Q: That sounds very quick and trite.

The Oranges: It is so.

Q: What else?

The Oranges: We sometimes interfere in a way by creating a lack of minerals so that Earth movement happens.

Q: Does this mean Earthquakes?

The Oranges: Some of them.

Q: Why are the Oranges helping the Nordics and Orbs?

The Oranges: They bring us information. We need the information to do our jobs. What is it you are doing?

Q: (Here I was sneezing). Sneezing. Something irritates the nose and we sneeze.

The Oranges: We do not sneeze.

Q: Are there other locations where the Oranges are either working alone or with other races?

The Oranges: Everywhere.

Q: Are under the sea?

The Oranges: Under the land, under the sea. We like mountains and Earth that has many layers. It is easier to work.

Part 1

Q: How do they cooperate? Is there a Confederation that is acting together? Who do they act as messengers for? Why cannot Humans access information that they are carrying? How best can Humans communicate with the Orbs? Does the information that the Orbs carry, bubble-up into consciousness? Are the Orbs autonomous? What is their intent? How do they work? What can the Orbs tell us about the Confederation?

The Oranges: There are many questions. Please read them over and we will respond. These questions are mainly about the Orbs. We interact with them but do not understand everything about them. You must ask the Orbs.

The Oranges. We have.

Q: Are the Oranges part of the Confederation?

The Oranges. No. We are close but it takes a long time.

Q: What do you need to belong to the Confederation?

The Oranges. We need to stay where we are until the Confederation asks us to belong.

Q: Is there more to the Orbs, observed by others and can they manifest responses? Are there different types of Orbs?

The Oranges: These are questions for the Orbs. We cannot answer them.

Q: Can the different extraterrestrial races also manifest responses and are they positively oriented? Are there inherent conflicts detrimental to our interests?

The Oranges: Most races work together. Most races are positive to each other except the Darks and the Reptilians and the mix of them.

Q: Does that mean that the Darks and the Reptilians breed?

The Oranges. No, it is not a breeding but a mixing.

Q: I don't understand that, is it like the Hybrid program?

The Oranges. Something like that.

Q: Can other alien races prevent abductions?

The Oranges: No. The Oranges help the collections. Most other races will help with the collections when needed.

Q: Even the Darks and the Reptilians?

The Oranges. Yes, if there is a need.

Q: Who are the good guys, who are the bad guys and what can we learn from them?

The Oranges: Those are Earth concepts. In your interpretation the Darks and the Reptilians are bad guys, everybody else is good or neutral. We do not have these distinctions.

Q: Can some races render implants fallible?

The Oranges: Not that we know about. We do not install the implants. You must ask the Grays.

Q: Can we interfere with the functioning of implants?

The Oranges: Not that we know. Again, you have to ask the Grays. Please wait. (Here the Researcher had to wait a short time before proceeding.)

Q: Are they the same races or different groups of the same race that are carrying out the abductions?

The Oranges: Come. (Interview resumed) The races that are carrying out the collections are the Grays and the Oranges assisted by the Nordics and the Reptilians. You know this already.

Q: How do they travel and is this travel with or without vehicles?

The Oranges: We do not have our own craft. When we hear of a need to mine somewhere else we go with the Grays on their craft. We cannot travel without craft.

Q: How long can Hybrids and Oranges stay on Earth? Why has the Hybridization program taken so long?

The Oranges: Oranges cannot stay above the land for very long. We can exist for a short time to quickly move to a nearby location in the night.

Q: Does ultraviolet radiation hurt you?

The Oranges. Yes. We can exist for a very long time under the land. We do not know about the Hybrids. Ask the Grays.

Q: What and who are the Indigo Children? Is there a specific race that is producing the Indigo Children?

The Oranges: We do not know about the Indigo Children.

Q: Have you heard other races talking about them?

The Oranges. Yes but we do not know any.

Q: Why are some species interested in hydrocarbons? Are they rare in the galaxy? What about other minerals and gases: hydrogen, boron? What purpose do these species put hydrocarbons to? Are we in conflict for these resources?

The Oranges: Please read the questions. (Researcher stops to read questions for Oranges.) There is no conflict. There are plenty of resources. Humans have the whole Earth, the seas, the skies and they talk about conflict? The hydrocarbons are fuel and nutrition for the Grays and for us too.

Part 2

Q: They obviously find our Human civilization to possess valuable galactic characteristics, some of which they probably lost eons ago, or they wouldn't be interbreeding with us. They certainly possess the ability to destroy our Human civilization, but have not, why?

The Oranges: Please read to us. (Researcher stops to read questions.) There is no need to destroy Humans. There are plenty of resources. Humans have many qualities that the Grays need for the hybrids. We help them but we do not know what for. We do not often interact with Humans.

Q: Is this intergalactic ethics - being held to certain behavior by other ET civilizations? Or is it just that their self-interest benefits more by using us for their own needs rather than simply destroying us (a similar model of how things operate on Earth)?

The Oranges: We do not interact with Humans because few Humans come underneath the Earth. Some who come down to our levels hear us and go away. They do not stay to interact with us so we do not know about them. This is not ethics but the facts.

Q: Given the billions of likely planets in our galaxy alone, there couldn't be anything very unique and special about Earth. Although the need to mine some of the debris circling Saturn is puzzling - - the implications of which implies a gigantic civilization that is widespread in our galaxy with a vast need for ongoing raw material supply. I would very much appreciate your insights on what all this implies about the nature of intergalactic inhabitation, the inhabitants in a portion or all of our galaxy. Are they dominant or is there a cacophony of conflicting vested interests in our galaxy like here on Earth?

The Oranges: There are many galaxies that even we do not know about.

Q: Is that why the Grays are producing the hybrids to travel to these unknown locations?

The Oranges: We do not know. We do not ask the Grays. You should ask the Grays.

Q: What are the intentions of each race? What is each race's ongoing purpose and when will this be completed?

The Oranges: We only know our own intentions, our own ongoing purpose and this will go on forever. Our intention and purpose is to mine.

Q: You also said that you help the Grays collect Humans that come under the ground.

The Oranges. Yes, that too.

Q: Will there be a scenario like a "shock wave" from a distant part of the galaxy that will wipe out Earth? Will it hit the Earth and its oceans?

The Oranges: We do not know about this. If this happens we will learn about it and go to another location until it passes.

Q: What does the future of the Earth look like, say in 2012? What types of scenarios, based on fact, will Earth experience?

The Oranges: We do not know. We only know what is now and what information is brought to us. If there is anything that will harm us we can go elsewhere.

Q: Are there specific races that are influencing our leaders and the process of civilization? Does any one race or a combination control our civilizations? If so why is this permitted?

The Oranges: None that we have heard about. Most races stay away from Humans.

Q: Would other civilizations be able to counter the possible Earth changes? Are the Orbs more positive to Humans?

The Oranges: Ask the Orbs if they are positive. They carry information to us. I do not think that the Oranges could alter or prevent any Earth changes. We just go to another location until these changes have happened and then come back.

Q: Regarding other controlling civilizations, what can we do as Humans to enter this chain of command?

The Oranges: If you mean the Confederation, you will have to wait until you are asked.

Q: Most religions of the world accept life after Earthly death. 96% of Humans accept this as fact. What is the alien concept and is there an equivalent life after death for them? Are there any races that believe in a God? What do the Reptilians believe?

The Oranges: Many questions again. We have already talked about God. We do not understand about living after you are dead. If we are damaged we stay in the Earth. There is no going on after we have stayed in the Earth. We do not know what the Reptilians believe.

Q: What mutual benefits are in place between different civilizations?

The Oranges: Most of the races that we know are working together. It is only Humans that are not working with the races.

Q: Why is this?

The Oranges. Perhaps, Humans will be accepted into the Confederation when they can work with the other races.

Q: What will help the Human race survive? Is the Human race expendable? Are we in danger of decimation some time in the future?

The Oranges: Humans are fragile. They prefer to live on the outside of the Earth and at constant risk. We live inside the Earth and our risk is less. Humans have more risk of decimation than the Oranges. We cannot see the future.

Q: Would there be a sharing of resources with different species in the future. This could affect the Earth financially. Would our leadership agree to share resources? How best can we manage our natural resources without destroying ourselves?

The Oranges: There is already a sharing and it has not harmed Humans or the Orange race. There have been some Humans in the past who have shared and interacted with us. There are some people you call the Mud People. They know about us and our lives in the Earth. Talk to them.

Q: Are some races hindering or helping us? Do they have a respect for intelligent life?

The Oranges: All races respect each other. We have a respect for all intelligent life and non-intelligent life also. The rest of the question we do not know about. Have these answers been sufficient.

Q: Yes, we may come back and ask some more. We thank and respect the Oranges. The next race to be interviewed is called the Angels by the other races.

9: The Exobiology Project: Talking With The Angels

Specific Questions for The Angels:

This current race, the Angels, has been called several different names by other races: some also call them the Lights or the Smooths. But I do not think we can confuse them with the Angels of Human history and mythology. I have chosen to retain the name of the Angels for this interview.

Q: Who are the Angels and where do they fit into the scheme of other races?

ANGELS: Angels are a gentle race of people who are intermingled with humans for a long, long time.

Q: Are you what humans call Angels?

ANGELS: Yes.

Q: You have referred to yourself as a people, rather than a race? Why is this?

ANGELS: We call ourselves a people because we are closest to humans than any of the other races. We consider ourselves a people. We fit in with the other races on a peripheral level. We do not act with the Grays or Nordics except to travel with them sometimes on their craft.

Q: What is the main purpose and intent of Angels? Do you have a group mind like the Grays?

ANGELS: Our purpose is to guide, to impart knowledge, to help and to direct. The intent is to provide humans with mental maps of how to become better humans. We have a group mind like some of the other races but on a different level. We can also interact on a mental level with many of the other races.

Q: How do the Angels benefit from interacting and guiding humans?

ANGELS: There is no benefit except that we guide and help. It is what we do. Humans always have to have something back for what they do, we do not have to have something back.

Q: How do Angels work with the Nordics, the Grays, the Orbs and any other race?

ANGELS: We work with the other races to access the location of humans. We work with many humans but not all humans. We interact with the Orbs to access information and we can send the Orbs with information. We can send Orbs to scout and see where humans are.

Q: Is there a Central Being, a Universal Source, which we refer to as God?

ANGELS: Yes, there is a central intelligence but it is everywhere. This intelligence is all knowing, all seeing, all acting, is forever and forever and does not fade.

Q: Have you ever seen or interacted with God?

ANGELS: We have never seen God but we have interacted with God.

Q: What was that interaction like?

ANGELS: It was not like anything, it was unique. There was total acceptance, total care, and total peace. There was total light, an absence of dark, everything was clear and shiny.

Q: Was this total light God?

ANGELS: No, this was where God was, we have not seen God.

Q: Are the Elementals a manifestation of what we call God?

ANGELS: All races are an expression of God. The Elementals and Orbs and the Angels are closest to the expression of God.

Q: Is the confederation God?

ANGELS: No. The confederation is not God.

Q: The other races have talked about other races such as the Darks, the Greens, the Propers, and the Roughs. Are there other races that are interacting with humans that we need to contact?

ANGELS: There are many other races that are interacting with humans. Humans are just discovering multi-dimensions outside of the common dimension, which is the Earth dimension. There are multitudes of these dimensions where other races are available to talk to. Most are very Earth-like and the people very human-like but there are differences.

Q: Are there dimensions that are mirrors of Earth, alternative dimensions?

ANGELS: Not exactly of Earth and there are no mirror people of people that exist on Earth today. But they are very similar.

Q: So someone doing a kind act on Earth, would not have a mirror person in another dimension doing a kind act or an unkind act?

ANGELS: No.

Q: Can we call on and interact with these other dimensions?

ANGELS: Yes. Just ask them.

Q: What percentage of humans is interacting telepathically with non-human races?

ANGELS: Most humans have some telepathic ability, most have just a little ability. Everyone is born with this ability but some maintain this to adulthood. It is a vital ability for an infant to have. It is a survival ability. As people age they do not need it and it atrophies. Some humans who are born with a strong ability, and who go through adversity in childhood, retain more of this ability. It is for survival.

Q: Why are other races at that specific location (Skinwalker Ranch)?

ANGELS: Another race that was present at the ranch was a being we call the father-being.

Q: What is the father-being?

ANGELS: It is an ancient race that lives in natural elements, like stones, and living entities such as trees. It is slow, ancient, wise, and can be accessed but it is very difficult to understand and interpret.

Q: Is there a similar mother-being?

ANGELS: Yes, in the sky. It is also difficult to comprehend the mother-being because her communications are difficult to catch and know.

Q: Why and how do these races interfere with humanity?

ANGELS: The only races that interfere with humans are those that collect humans for hybrid and other purposes.

Q: Would the Angels interactions with humans be seen as interfering?

ANGELS: No, we help and guide humans, we do not interfere.

Q: Do Angels understand the concept of free will?

ANGELS: Yes, we help and guide but the human does not have to follow what we say.

Q: Are there other locations where Angels are either working alone or with other races?

ANGELS: Angels are everywhere there are humans.

Q: Do Angels also work with hybrids that have a high percentage of human in them?

ANGELS: Yes.

Q: Were the entities that my brother and I encountered in Dorset in the 1960s Angels?

ANGELS: Yes, we were the beings that you saw after you saw the light. We came because you and your brother were talking about Angels.

Q: I do not remember that?

ANGELS: You asked each other if Angels existed, we came to show you that we did.

Q: My brother saw a craft first, before the beings came into the house, did you come by way of the craft? Or do you have wings and can fly?

ANGELS: Yes, we came as it was the quickest way to come. We do not fly, we do not have wings.

Q: Can you bilocate like the Nordics?

ANGELS: No, we cannot bilocate but we can *transpose*.

Q: What does that mean?

ANGELS: It is a way to get from one place to another with the original body. Nordics send a copy ahead. We can send the original body through transposing. Transposing takes energy and time so we are often carried by craft. The craft were coming to that location so we transposed to the craft and came to your location.

Q: Were the Grays there to collect my brother and me for their purposes?

ANGELS: Yes, but we spoke with you first. Then they took you to the craft for their purposes. We transposed elsewhere when that happened so we did not have any knowledge of the Grays work and what they do.

Q: What did we talk about?

ANGELS: We talked about the reality of Angels. We talked about the future roles of humans? We talked about certain humans that have roles to play in human history. We talked about how some humans are successful at this and others are not.

Q: Did we talk so we could hear each other or with our minds?

ANGELS: With the mind only.

Q: Was there important information given to us?

ANGELS: There was information shared but you have remembered most of it already.

Q: I do not remember specifics.

ANGELS: You have already remembered it and use it in your everyday life.

Q: Were we told anything about the future?

ANGELS: Yes, you were told about the future. How you would live in many places and meet many people. Not to be surprised when others recognized you and you did not recognize them. That you and your brother would retain many of your abilities.

Q: Were we told anything about the future of the Earth?

ANGELS: No, just about yourselves. But, you can ask.

Q: Do Angels have the ability to access information about the future?

ANGELS: In some respects but we have to ask too.

Q: Who do you ask?

ANGELS: The Record Keepers.

Q: Who are the Record Keepers?

ANGELS: They are a form of Elemental that keep the records.

Q: So the Elementals can tell us what will happen in the future?

ANGELS: Only some of them, the Record Keepers. The one that you spoke to before was not a Record Keeper.

Q: Why would that Elemental not refer me to the Record Keepers?

ANGELS: Because they did not know.

Questions Asked of all Races:

Q: How do the Angels cooperate? Is there a Confederation that is acting together? Who do they act as messengers for? Why cannot Humans access information that they are carrying? How best can humans communicate with the Orbs? Does the information that the Orbs carry, bubble-up into consciousness? Are the Orbs autonomous? What is their intent? How do they work? What can the Orbs tell us about the confederation?

ANGELS: We have answered some of these questions. We cooperate with all races but only work with humans. Yes, there is a Confederation and Angels are part of the confederation. We do not act as messengers except to humans, Orbs act as messengers. You have information about the Orbs that we do not need to add to.

Q: Can the different extraterrestrial races also manifest responses and are they positively oriented? Are there inherent conflicts detrimental to our interests?

ANGELS: Yes, there are conflicts between different races, more than you have learned already. Just because we do not stay all the time on Earth, does not mean that we have less conflict. There will be conflicts wherever there are races.

Q: Who are the good guys, who are the bad guys and what can we learn from them?

ANGELS: That is a totally odd question as you know so already. Humans sometimes know who are the good and bad guys but do not acknowledge it or act upon the knowledge.

Q: What and who are the Indigo Children? Is there a specific race that is producing the Indigo Children?

ANGELS: We like the Indigo Children. They are the easiest for us to talk to and to interact with. They have a natural ability to call us and interact with us. We are happy to interact with them. We light up with pleasure. The Indigo Children are a delight.

In addition the following philosophical questions were addressed to each of the accessed extraterrestrial races.

Q: They obviously find our human civilization to possess valuable galactic characteristics, some of which they probably lost eons ago, or they wouldn't be interbreeding with us. They certainly possess the ability to destroy our human civilization, but have not, why?

ANGELS: Our purpose is to help the human race not to destroy it. There are many races and none have destroyed the human race.

Q: Is this intergalactic ethics - being held to certain behavior by other ET civilizations? Or is it just that their self-interest benefits more by using us for their own needs rather than simply destroying us (a similar model of how things operate on Earth)?

ANGELS: There are rules that the confederation imposes. We do not need the rules because we have our own. We help humans and our purposes to not go against the confederation rules.

Q: Will there be a scenario like a "shock wave" from a distant part of the galaxy that will wipe out Earth? Will it hit the Earth and its oceans?

ANGELS: This we do not know about. If such an event occurred we would help the humans manage this. But they would have to call us for help. Most humans only call us when there is a catastrophe or crisis. We can help at other times too.

Q: Are there specific races that are influencing our leaders and the process of civilization? Does any one race or a combination control our civilizations? If so why is this permitted?

ANGELS: Yes, the Angels talk to the leaders but they do not always listen or act on how we guide them. Not all leaders listen to us or call us. Some do and we offer guidance. It is permitted because it always has been.

Q: Most religions of the world accept life after Earthly death. 96% of humans accept this as fact. What is the alien concept and is there an equivalent life after death for them? Are there any races that believe in a God? What do the reptilians believe?

ANGELS: Most of the races either go on forever or just stop being. Some are able to bilocate into other bodies. The Angels do not change and do not stop or transpose into other bodies. Most of the other races do not have a concept of God. We do. Reptilians? They belong on the other side

Q: Does that mean a dark side?

ANGELS: Yes.

Q: What will help the human race survive? Is the human race expendable? Are we in danger of decimation sometime in the future?

ANGELS: The human race is always trying to extinguish itself. Why is this? Humans are always doing things to end their lives by risk and danger. We do not understand this. Life is precious. Why would humans keep trying to end their own and other human's lives? We do not understand.

Q: Are some races hindering or helping us? Do they have a respect for intelligent life?

ANGELS: Many races are helping the human race, even the Grays and the reptilians in their own way, although they are helping themselves more. There is no race that is hindering humans. Humans hinder humans.

Q: What role do the Angels play in the lives of humans and in the lives of the other races?

ANGELS: We have told this already. We guide and help humans not the other races.

Q: What do people ask the Angels to do for them?

ANGELS: The humans ask that we intercede and help them in crises and with problems.

Q: How can the Angels help us run our lives? How have the Angels helped other humans or other races with their lives? How successful has this help been? How successful are the Angels in fulfilling requests from either humans or other races?

ANGELS: Angels are very successful in helping humans. There is no percentage but Angels are there wherever needed and helping. We have helped in major crises and in small everyday problems.

Q: What have been the ten most frequent ways that humans have asked for help from the Angels and how successfully have these requests been fulfilled? It would be helpful to give specific events.

ANGELS: Bridge collapsing, humans helped to shore: Baby very sick, life energy given to baby; Man has no money, opportunities given to man: Young person needs guidance for life, given: Young girl in specific sexual predicament, guidance to look for alternatives: Sad woman wanting to end life, woman shown light, love and compassion: Person at end of life wanting to know if all will be well, given: Sick person needing healing, healing energy given: Times of war, help and guidance given; Information given to humans to find a missing person. All have been successful.

Q: What keeps the Angels from successfully fulfilling requests?

ANGELS: Angels fulfill almost all requests. Only if the request would result in great tragedy for many people would the request not be met and the Angels would go away.

Q: What do they think that humans should be asking that would help them?

ANGELS: Anything. We help with anything if asked.

Q: In what way should humans be asking for help from the Angels?

ANGELS: Just ask or have an interest in the Angels. It is simple to ask.

Q: How are the Angels called by humans?

ANGELS: Just ask.

Q: What can we do for them that would help them?

ANGELS: We do not need anything from humans, we just help humans.

Q: What can the Angels learn from us?

ANGELS: We learn that humans are not always able to help themselves, that they have a very dark view of life, that they try to eliminate themselves and other humans, that humans are not satisfied with all that they have, that humans need the help of the Angels.

Q: Are there other groups or races that humans can call on for achieve certain needs?

ANGELS: Angels, Orbs and elementals are all available for different reasons.

Q: Are the Angels confined to Earth or can they go anywhere, as they previously stated? Can they go out to other universes, other galaxies?

ANGELS: Angels are mainly confined to Earth although there are other dimensions that we can visit and interact with other beings. We cannot travel the galaxies as other races do.

Follow Up Questions for Three Races: Orbs, Elementals, and Angels

(The Elementals are an Earth-bound race that has been interviewed but not included in these interviews.)

Q: The Orbs, The Elementals and the Angels have all indicated that they can be called to assist humans. They indicate that they can be called for different reasons. How do we specifically call each one? For what different purposes can they be called?

Orbs: We can be called by humans by calling our name: *Orbs*, in your mind or in words. That is the simplest explanation of how you call an orb. We are attracted by low frequencies and we are curious. If someone is calling out for spirits, say for a ghostly haunting, we will appear out of curiosity and are often mistaken for the deceased. We will also be close to a human if we have been instructed to act as a probe by one of the other races, particularly the Grays or the Nordics. Indicate that you have some information for us to convey and we will carry that information. You can also ask for information and we will find it for you. We deal in information and energy.

Q: How can a human send or receive energy?

Orbs: Humans do this already in carrying out healing. They call in energy, we come with the energy and it is conveyed to a sick human. Many healers do not know that they are calling Orbs this way. Humans can receive and send energy through an altered state of consciousness. To avoid interrupting an orb that is nearby but on a separate journey, indicate that you need an *empty orb*. The whole process is more complex than that but this is the best approximation.

Elementals: We can be called the same way as Orbs but we have a different process of carrying out requests. We are attracted by firelight, flickering candles or other lights. We can also come through a human making a wish or an affirmation. We deal with the practical and the mundane. We can act as one tiny unit or enmesh as a larger unit for a larger effect. Sometimes the Orbs will convey a request to us from a human although humans also can make their requests directly to us. We are everywhere and available until called. We are not like the Orbs that are on journeys. When we are called to enmesh, others crowd in to take out place, so there is never a void. We are always around.

ANGELS: Angels can be called with emotion. We are spiritual in nature and we respond to emotional calls where there is a need. If someone is in pain, in distress, or in crisis, we will come. We will usually hover nearby until a request is made. If the request is not made we go away. We specifically help humans. We can offer advice, guidance and even intervene physically if there is a need.

Q: The Angels said that "The only races that interfere with humans are those that collect humans for hybrid and other purposes." What other purposes would the other races collect humans apart from the hybrid program?

Orb: We have seen humans aboard the craft helping Grays and Nordics with the humans that have been collected. They are not being used in the hybrid program but helping the other races calm or move the other humans.

Q: Are the humans there voluntarily and consciously?

ANGELS: No, they have been collected like the ones used in the hybrid program.

Elemental: Sometimes humans have made a request to see other races, particularly if they, the humans, have not been involved in the collection process. We can assist the Grays in manifesting the other races in the vicinity of the humans or the humans may be collected out of curiosity to see why they are asking. This is usually just the one time. The humans usually only ask once or twice. Humans are also collected, other than for the hybrid program, to teach and test them. The races are learning a great deal about humans in this way. There is much teaching and testing and learning from the humans this way.

ANGELS: Humans are collected as the Grays know that another human will act compassionately to another human if they are in distress. This helps the Grays to carry out procedures on the humans. Humans are also strong and can lift or carry other humans when there is a need. It is a practical collection and use of humans.

Q: Why ask for the Angels help when we could ask God directly for help?

Orb: We do not know this concept.

Elemental: NR

ANGELS: Asking the Angels is the same as asking God. Except that we can be there and help as we are nearby already when we sense the need. Asking God directly is the same as asking the Angels, we are then sent to help. So, one is the same as the other.

Part 2

We would first like thank the Angels for this additional interview, for their responses and cooperation. We respect and honor the Angels for their compassion and help to Humans.

Q: What other races are comparable to the Angels? Are these comparable races terrestrial or not of Earth?

ANGELS: There are no races that are comparable with us although there are many that are like us in many aspects. If you are meaning are there other species that are in direct communication with Humans and help Humans as we are, then the Aldebarans are the race that is closest. They have been in contact with Humans and have helped Humans. If you mean being in contact with Humans on a long-term basis but not helping Humans as the Angels help Humans, then the Grays are like us. If you mean are there many other races that have the physical characteristics of Angels, such as having a discernable head and limbs, there are too many to count. There are many races that are terrestrial but not all help Humans, they are there either helping themselves or helping others who are not terrestrial. Otherwise, all of the other races, which are like us, are not terrestrial.

Q: Regarding looking into the future. Many entities can foresee the future by projecting the past and the present. Are there multiple layers of time? We assume that there are entities that can truly see ahead into the future, not just as a projection of the past and present? For example, non-steady states have cycles such as the Earth's environment, the nature of life itself, and other factors related to the environment.

ANGELS: Humans have a complex view of time. In the past Humans had no concept of time passing, except that they aged. Every day was the same day except that on some days interesting things happened: a large animal was overcome or a birth or death occurred. Most days events could be predicted depending on the previous day's events. As Humans evolved they understood that each day was not the same day come again but a different day each time. This is when the concept of a future developed. As Humans continued to evolve Humans decided that the future was a nebulous thing that could not be depended upon: anything could happen, and Humans became very superstitious. It was at this time that Humans began to become aware of Angels although we had always been around. Humans began to believe that if certain things were said or done that this could change what happened the next day and they were partially correct. The future became partially predictable. Humans also began to understand that there were cycles to the seasons and the weather and could begin to plan accordingly. They could plant, harvest and store food. The next step was that Humans began to understand that long term predictions could be made depending on cycles and an understanding of these cycles. These long-term predictions were not perfect but served well for everyday purposes. There has been a parallel process taking place over time: the more Humans evolved, the longer into the future they wished their predictions to be. But when we look at the concept of time, it is not what Humans have understood it. Time is solely a function of the place in which it takes place and the activity of the race at that place. As seen from our story of the Human development of time, Humans have developed a complex myth concerning time. Time has no substance and no measure of itself. There is no time and there can be no predictions that can take place! Humans have not yet understood that time is "plastic" and that Humans can make their own future. There are not alternative futures or layers of future as Humans understand it but many futures that individual Humans have set in place. For every Human there is a future that has been set in place by that Human. Sometimes individual futures can correlate and a common or consensual future can occur. Other times individual futures can collide and future events can become unpredictable. Humans are very much in control of their own future. If they agree to work with other Humans towards a planned future then that future has more likelihood of happening as predicted.

Q: Which entities can we contact who can tell us what lies ahead in the future? Will it be a continuation of what we are experiencing now or will it be different? For example, will severe weather patterns be a continuation of

Earth cycles or will these cycles become accelerated, at an unprecedented speed, through Human intervention?

ANGELS: The nature of the Earth itself predicts that the Earth will continue to have cycles of severe and less severe storms and good weather. It is redundant for Humans to ask other races for help with predicting Human futures because they have their own concepts of time and their own cycles to deal with. They will only predict Earth cycles based on their own understanding of their own cycles. Humans can work with Earth cycles that they already know and work towards planning their own future. Humans have the ability to intercede and are coming to the understanding that future events are totally within their own ability to predict and control.

Q: Humans are currently concerned about the adaptation of Human life on Earth in the short term only. How can we plan for and adapt to long-term changes?

ANGELS: This would be the next step in the evolution of Humans. In our previous story we communicated how Humans have developed a myth about time. Some Humans are now coming to understand the true nature of time: that it can be manipulated in ways that are totally different than previous myths of managing time. Time has been perceived to be concrete and non-plastic. Some Humans are beginning to see that time can be flexible and can be manipulated according to each Human's needs. The wonderful thing is that even if a Human manipulates time-space for themselves, this does not affect another Human's time-space. It does, though, affect the perception of each others' time-space; hence the concept that some Humans always appear to be late and others seem to manipulate their time better. It also explains why some Humans appear to have more time than other Humans. The Humans with more time are better manipulators of the time-space. Those Humans who can manage their time-space more effectively can better predict what is to happen as they can manipulate their future. Some Humans may become so adept at manipulating time that they can affect the time-space future of others so that certain events might occur more effectively.

Q: Sometime in the near or distant future a cosmic supernova could decimate life on Earth or even destroy it completely. It is possible that this could destroy the Human race? Is this a possibility? Did such an event occur in our solar system in our past? If so, did this affect life on other planets such as Mars and Venus? What happened to the races living there? How did such an event affect Earth and was Atlantis or parts of India affected by such an event?

ANGELS: There have been many such events taking place in the vicinity of Earth during the time that Humans have occupied the Earth. The solar environment that includes the Earth is still developing and events, while great in Human terms, are not as great as some of the early events that took place in this solar environment. Such events scorched the Earth and many of its neighbors. The Earth, its moon and many other planets suffered from these early events. We will not call them catastrophes because Human life was not involved and Humans only refer to catastrophes as events that include Humans. These very big events occurred before life came to these systems. They were natural events. No very large event has occurred since life came to this solar system.

Q: So life on Earth, on Mars or the Moon was not devastated by such an event?

ANGELS: No, these happened before life came to these systems. Humans now have the ability to physically perceive far into the Cosmos and see these events happening in other systems and make false predictions that they will happen to Earth.

Q: So what happened to the races that lived on Mars?

ANGELS: They were always there and are still there. They have chosen to live beneath the planet for their own purposes not because anything devastating happened to their planet that caused them to move underground.

Q: Thank you again for assisting us. What other entities would be helpful? So far, many of the entities that we have contacted have not been able to project themselves into the future, other than the Nordics and the Record Keepers. Are there any other races that we could contact? Our goal is to ensure that Humans persist on Earth in the long run.

ANGELS: You have already encountered helpful races such as us, the Angels, the Orbs, and the Elementals. Each of these races can help Humans in specific ways that you have already discovered. The Aldebarans are a race that would be helpful to humans: they are wise and gracious and would be a great asset to Humans.

Q: Are there spirit entities on Earth and how do they differ from non-Earth spirit entities? Are some non-corporeal and just exist as an intelligence?

ANGELS: We have already communicated about spirits that are Earth and non-Earth bound. Most of them exist in spirit only, as intelligence, although some can temporarily take on a body. Angels are one such type: we exist most of the time in spirit but we can take on Human form if needed, when help is needed in a physical way.

Q: Orbs seem to enjoy or create happiness for themselves by being in the presence of different energies. Does this happen because of curiosity, on the part of the Orbs, or is this just an experience for the, or just information to them?

ANGELS: Orbs are not happy in the sense that Humans use the word. Orbs have few needs and for them to be moving and carrying information is what makes them "happy". They do like to be around certain energies because this allows them to do their job more effectively. This is what makes them happy.

Q: Why are there so many Orbs on and around the Earth? If this is the case, are there as many Orbs in all the galaxies and all the planetary systems, as well? Or are they sent here as information gatherers by other life forms, which would account for there being so many?

ANGELS: Orbs, like Angels, are everywhere in the Cosmos and have no restrictions as to where they are sent. They do not usually travel without being sent with some information or to collect some information. There are as many Orbs here on Earth as there in other places although the number decreases or increases as needed. The Orbs are very special to the Angels. Angels work very closely with Orbs and they are what bring Human thoughts, wishes and prayers to us. Other times, they can communicate, as we are now communicating.

Q: All the entities talk about Humans as a race but we are not a cohesive race as we are all separate races with separate consciousness. Are there any races that could help specific individuals to better cope with their lives?

ANGELS: All Humans began as one single race but it is not so now. There can be no going back to the one race state. Each race is responsible for living their lives as best they can. The problem, as seen by the Angels and many other races, is that each group of Humans perceives their way of coping with life to be superior to how other Humans manage their life. This is a myth as each group of Humans has developed a way of managing their life that best suits their environment and living. Without interference from other groups each Human group can manage their life as well as they can. When Humans stop interfering with other groups and learn to manage their own lives, then Humans will learn to live as many groups on one planet.

Q: Could an individual establish a helpful relationship with another race that would benefit other Humans and other races? Humans are separate entities. Is such knowledge helpful or hindering to us? What information should we be seeking to help our own races and other races?

ANGELS: Humans and the other races, such as the Angels, have been working this way for as long as Humans have been on the Earth although it has not always been recognized. Even though Humans perceive the Gray races to be detrimental to Human ways, they are in some respects helping Humans rather than hindering them. We agree with some of the other races that the Grays are doing Humans a service by ensuring that Humans continue to grow by being sent as pioneers in hybrid bodies to all reaches of the Universe. Not everybody would agree with us but we see the long-term benefits and not the short term. The hybrids are definitely helping other races and working with other races. As they are part Human, then that means that Humans are developing a relationship with other races in many distant places. Humans are still evolving on Earth, as well as in many other places in the Universe. Humans are pioneers, even though they do not plan and carry out these travels and relocations throughout the Galaxies. Humans will eventually be in every part of the Galaxy although this will be a long time in the future, Even Angels can make predictions!

Q: What do the Angels think of our projects? Are we going about these projects in the right or the wrong way? When we are talking to the Angels are we talking to all other Angels? When we talk to the Angels do other races also hear the discussion? What other Humans have communicated with the Angels, other than those asking for help?

ANGELS: These are wonderful projects and we are happy to see this happening among Humans. For so long Humans have considered themselves alone in the Universe or have denied that there are other races. This is a great step for Humans to consider communicating with other races in the Universe. You consider yourselves pioneers and this is what you are. When you talk to the Angels we all hear you but we only share with other races if there is a need. If there is a call for help from a Human and the other races can help we call on them. All races have a tiny bit of Angel in them.

Q: How is this so?

ANGELS: Every race came from the Angel race, which is one of the oldest in the Universe. That is why we are close to God. Other Humans have contacted the Angels but usually also in request.

Q: Specifically who else, at this time is communicating with the Angels in the way that we are communicating?

ANGELS: There are too many to tell.

Q: Can you tell me about three?

ANGELS: One is a young monk who lives on the borders of India. He has been recommended by his Bishop to communicate with us. He is considered an adept and we have had some illuminating conversations with him. The second is a young man in Slovakia, one of the Slovakian countries, who is very much alone and only talks to us. He does not talk to other Humans, he has made that choice. He only talks to us. He is very lonely and we provide comfort for him. The third is an old Japanese man who has spent much of his life in communication with spirits and other races. We have been communicating with him for a very long time and we know a great deal about each other.

Q: Have any of them written about their experiences?

ANGELS: No, none have written about their experiences. We have found that those who write about the Angels write what they think the Angels would say and do, instead of what we really say and do.

Q: Do Humans have a personal Angel or do we draw from a group when we ask for help? To what extent can Angels help Humans and are there any limits?

ANGELS: From the many Angels Humans have a pick of Angels. When an individual first asks for help, sometimes in childhood, sometimes in adulthood, we assign one Angel. Many of us guard children and that is always a special task. However, as soon as the request has been met the Angel returns to the group and another is sent when there is a new request. It has always been this way and all Angels serve this way.

Q: There is an Earth belief that departed relatives become Guardian Angels over their relatives when they die?

ANGELS: This is not so. The spirits of departed relatives can visit those who remain on Earth but they do not become Angels. This is a Human belief only. Angels can help with anything that Humans ask and there are no limits, although we will ask other races to help if there are things they can do for the Human.

Q: The responses by the Sirian's (a parallel interview, with another race) sounded very Buddhist? Are there similarities in what the Dalai Lama teaches? Are there any similarities between what the Angels were saying, Buddhism, and what the Angels believe?

ANGELS: As we mentioned in the previous communication we are not like the Sirians. They exist in a steady state where they are almost non-existent. They persist but in a very hidden way. The Buddhist and the Dalai Lama would very much like to exist as a Sirian exists and they can do this because they have abandoned the usual Human ways of life. They live in seclusion, they have no relationships, and they have no need to labor daily, so they can exist in a way that the Sirian's exist. There is no connection between these ways of being and how the Angels exist.

Q: We would still like to understand the Angel's concept of God. Do the Angels interact with God, What is the nature of God? Is it different and how is it different from the Earthly concept of God? Some of the other races have no concept of God, why is that?

ANGELS: We have already communicated that: When you talk to us, you talk to God, we and God are one and the same. We exist in every race to some degree. This concept is very different from the concept of the Earthly God as a male figure. Every race, that has a concept of God, sees God in their own image. This is similar to Humans seeing God in their Human image. So, each race sees God as one of them, this makes it easier for each race to follow teachings of their God. Some races have no concept of a God because their image is so nebulous or insubstantial that they cannot conceive of a God in their own image. This is the basic reason.

Q: Thank you for your answers and cooperation. There are two more sessions to follow when the remainder of the questions we have will be put forward.

Part 4

This remaining fourth section– communication with the Angels - proposes some additional questions which focus on previous answers by the Sirians plus specific questions for the Angels. We would like to thank the Angels for this additional interview, for their responses and cooperation. We respect and honor the Angels for their compassion and help to Humans.

Q: Humans have difficulty in communicating with those who have passed from the corporeal world to the spirit world. How can Humans best communicate with those who are now spirits?

ANGELS: Humans are present on the Earth for a finite time. At the end of that finite time, however short or long that time is, they have had their opportunity to procreate and pass along their genes and knowledge.

Q: What about person such as myself who have never given birth to children?

ANGELS: Humans such as you have other opportunities to return to Earth and to procreate. There are others who have chosen to come back one last time to act for good in the World and perhaps you are one of those Humans.

Q: Perhaps, but I am not so sure of that. Is the decreasing fertility rate in the developing nations indicative that Humans may not have their chance to procreate and fulfill their role?

ANGELS: If they have not procreated then they will have other opportunities to return to Earth.

Q: I cannot believe that this is the main reason that Humans are here on Earth?

ANGELS: It is the main reason but not the only reason. Human procreation and bringing forth young is the most sacred of all the acts that a Human can achieve. Both males and females achieve sacredness by this act. Not all races can bring forth in this way and Humans are envied this act.

ANGELS: When Humans have completed what they needed to achieve, they leave the physical body and transfer into a spirit body. That is, the spirit body, that they are inside a Human, exits and becomes independent outside of the Human body. This spirit body can then travel and spends some time independent before deciding what next to do. Some travel around the Universe and then decide to re-enter Earth again as a Human. This completes a cycle and is a sacred act in itself. If they decide to stay outside Earth they can travel in spirit and learn many new things about the Universe. There is no demand that they return to Earth; it is a choice.

Q: One of the races that have been contacted are the Companions. They talked about how the hybrids (that the Grays are developing) are part of a "sacred act" Can the Angels talk more about this and why hybrid births are thought of as "sacred?" Is it to do the creation of life itself or the manipulation of life or the role of the hybrids?

ANGELS: Whether Humans or Grays give rise to life, all is sacred. The act of creating the spark of life is sacred. There is nothing more to say, it is sacred and needs to be accepted just as that, nothing more, nothing less.

Q: The Sirian's talk about there being alternative strata, which we can visit, explore and, perhaps, utilize? Can the Angels tell us more about the strata?

ANGELS: The strata exist as layers that enclose and, sometimes, permeate Human space. The layers can be seen as sometimes "dimpling", when another strata permeates Human space. At those times activities, objects and events can locate in a different space. Then, when the dimpling occurs again, they can return. Some races, such as the Sirians, have learned how to calculate when the dimpling occurs and when they can hop between the strata. Humans, too, can learn to move among the strata through intent.

ANGELS: All the strata have life and activities that can sometimes transfer to Earth for a short period, and then get taken back, the next time the dimpling occurs. Due to differences in wavelength and frequencies, these are not always perceived by Humans, who just observe that something is different in their environment. It is more common however, for Earth artifacts to go through the dimpling and to return to Earth at another time. Sirian's use the strata to hide when they do not want to experience something they do not like or to hide from the other races. Other races, including Humans, use the strata to explore and learn.

Q: The Grays continue to interact with Humans. Are the Grays also hybridizing other races and why? Please note that we are not denigrating the Grays but are interested in all races and how they function. Are the Grays hybridizing the Angels if not, why not?

ANGELS: The Grays have hybridized many races over the span of their history, but do not hybridize Angels because we do not have the physical qualities that they need. We understand that you are not denigrating the Grays but you do not understand them. They are not so different from Humans, that it is easier for them to hybridize Humans that any other race in this part of the Universe. Other races have tried to show you how it is a beneficial thing for Humans to spread their hybridized offspring throughout the Galaxies. Humans want to judge the Grays using Human values and ethics, but the Grays are not Human and work within their own justification and values. Nothing can change this.

Q: Have the Angels played a role in the Confederation? Are they the Confederation? Do they play a small role or a larger role in the Confederation? Were the Angels involved in the creation of the Galactic Confederations?

ANGELS: The Angels are not the Confederation, although Angels make up a large part of the Confederation, have been in the Confederation for a very long time, and have instituted many of the rules that the Confederations apply. The Angels have been present in the Galaxies for much longer than any of the other races, so we were an original part of many of the Confederations. The Angels would like to see Humans within the Confederation but it is not yet time.

Q: The Angels are said to be peacekeepers. Do Angels have any influence in the role of peacekeeping in the Universe or on Earth?

ANGELS: Peacekeeping is not our role. Helping is our role. There are many Humans who ask us for peace, on many different levels, but we cannot give this to Humans. We can show them how to be peaceful in their own lives and their own communities. Peace is a nebulous state, which fluctuates according to circumstance. All that the Angels can do is to show Humans that peace can be achieved and to help encourage a peaceful state.

Q: We would like to give the Angels an opportunity to add anything else that they feel is important for Humans to know. We have been asking a lot of questions but this is an opportunity for the Angels to tell us what they want us to know.

ANGELS: The Angels would like Humans to know that they, Humans, are unique in the Universe. There are other worlds with races similar to Humans but Earth Humans have a richness, a variety, a capacity for emotion, that many other races do not have. The other races admire Humans for their ability to experience humor, to experience emotion, and having the autonomy to be creative.

Q: Why is it that some people can physically perceive Angels? Under what circumstances do Angels come to Earth in physical form?

ANGELS: Angels can appear on Earth in a physical form, which resembles Humans, in special circumstances. We can appear at the moment of birth or at the moment of death. We can appear at the moment of great physical stress for a Human and we can appear during a very contemplative moment. We can appear if needed to carry out an act that will help a Human, especially if the Human is in distress. We can appear if there is a heightened sense of emotion from a large group of people, especially if the emotion is carried in prayers and song.

ANGELS: Not every Human in a group will see us in Human form but as lights, shimmering, and as shifts in perception. A very few will see us in the Human-mindset of the Angelic form with wings and long hair but that is very rare. We are often mistaken for spirits, Orbs, ghosts, and other non-Human entities. You will know that the Angels have visited because of the quietening of ambient noise and the calm that is felt in the location. That is all.

A: Thank you, Angels, for your patience with us, for your answers and your cooperation.

Dialog with the Angels

On re-reading the interviews, it appeared that the Light Beings only wanted to be companions to humans, not advisors. The Angels were more amenable to talking with humans and providing information and assistance. Other races that might be amenable to dialogue are Hybrids, Orbs, and Elementals. This session dialogues exclusively with the Angels. (Lighting a candle).

A: Welcome Angels and thank you for agreeing to dialogue with us.

ANGELS: We are here to help and assist and bring what we know into the dialogue. We understand all the conditions that humans are causing and suffering and wish to assist. We do not know how we can assist but it is possible that there is a way. We have been aware of the increases in human health problems for many decades. We have been aware that the quality of the air has been changing. We have seen many of the Earth changes that have been taking place. We will try and suggest some ways that might be helpful for humans to cope with these problems. If they cannot cope, then we have tried.

Q: Thank you. Are the Angels able to suggest ways that humans can cope with these changes in the atmosphere? I would like to keep this as a dialogue, rather than question and answer but will pose questions when needed. There is a definite agreement among humans (with some dissenters) that humans have real problems with the atmosphere deteriorating and global warming/cooling taking place. What puzzles me is that a few decades ago, scientists were saying that global warming was responsible for the increase in the hole in the ozone hole but that problem appears to have been solved. Now the environment and global warming are said to be inter-correlated and having an effect on each other. Are there solutions to these problems?

ANGELS: We see many children that die because of the air quality but it is little compared to the children who are dying of starvation and illness in the world. There is much ignorance and reluctance to learn. Humans know what they have to do to make the world live-able but they do not learn from generation to generation. It is as if each generation of humans has to relearn everything again. Angels have helped every generation but cannot understand why humans cannot learn and pass onto their children what they learn.

ANGELS: You ask for practical solutions. The practical solutions are to clean up the world. There is too much waste and dirt. Humans put waste into the air, into the water and into the land. They have not learned how to care for themselves. The answers are simple, clean the Earth. As soon as the cleaning begins, the Earth will begin to revert back to its original balance.

ANGELS: There is an excess of waste. Humans used to bury their deceased in the ground with little more than a box or cloth. Now humans bury their dead in the ground in metal boxes into stone-lined spaces in the ground. They fill their deceased with minerals, as if the very act of preservation of the body will preserve the mind and the soul. Humans complain that they are running out of room for the deceased. Some humans burn the deceased yet do not return them to nature but hold them close, as if they can hold onto the essence of the person. It does not make sense to the Angels. We know about these things because it is at these times that humans call on the Angels for support and care.

Q: Humans fear death and it is seen by the medical profession as a failure. Perhaps this fear of death has caused an increase in preserving the dead: much like the Egyptians preserved their dead. There is a great deal made, in the Western world, of preserving human youth-like status and decrying natural aging. Death is seen as the ultimate failure instead of a graduation from one life to the next.

ANGELS: But it is paradoxical. Humans fear death, yet they poison their world and bring on death sooner. It is a terrible condition. We do not know how to assist in this matter. We can suggest ways to clean the Earth and to assist in bringing balance back to the Earth, the skies and the seas. The key is water. There are many technologies that can use water. These must be pursued. They are clean and can help restore the Earth's balance.

ANGELS: The other assistance is the Earth's lower orders of life. They help humans to live and can help the Earth restore balance.

Q: Do you mean microbes?

ANGELS: Yes, all lower levels of life. They are abundant and everywhere. They do not have to be invented. They do not have to be taught. Just put them where they are needed and they will work for humans by being themselves and doing what they do.

Q: How can we clean the skies and the water? It seems such a large job to contemplate, all of the skies and waters of the Earth. The job seems overwhelming to many humans.

ANGELS: The skies and the water can be cleaned. The same as with the Earth: with lower orders of life. Many lower orders can clean the Earth, the skies, and the water on a large scale. They exist already but are overwhelmed. They need to be placed in clean areas where they can thrive, then placed in areas where they can work to clean the sky, Earth, and water. The lower orders are simple and hold an inherent balance within them. Together, in many numbers, they can restore balance to the Earth. That is what we know.

Q: How do we go about this? It seems such a huge job and, perhaps one that needs several generations to accomplish. It seems that the media are forever chiding people about waste and to recycle and to clean up but very little gets accomplished.

ANGELS: It will need generations of education of the young. If young humans receive this education very early, then it will carry on to new generations. There is a human saying about "the sins of the fathers being passed to the children." Well, the teachings of the fathers can be also perpetuated by the children. Rather than chiding other humans about what a mess they are leaving for their children and future generations, would not it be better to teach about the good things you are leaving for the next generations? Would not it be better to teach children that humans and their children are doing something about the mess? Rather than cry about it and chide each other, would not it be better to be doing something?

Q: Many human groups are doing active work to clean up the environment but it seems that it is too little, too late, and the point of no return may have been reached. Is it too late? It would be wonderful if there were a change in outlook and we could do something large scale and long term.

ANGELS: There are many things to do. It starts with the largest and works down to the lowest. That is, those who are making the most mess must be tackled first, rather than expecting the many, smaller groups to clean up the bigger messes. Find who is doing the most damage to the air, the water, and the land and confront them with alternatives. They do not make changes because they do not know about alternatives and if they will work for them. When smaller groups see the larger groups having success, the smaller groups will follow. Then, many of the individual humans will also follow and clean up their individual messes. Soon, it will become a new paradigm to follow. It can start in one place and then many places and people will follow. There is nothing magical or special about this. It can happen and the Angels will help it happen.

Q: It sounds wonderful. I see the major problem of persuading the large offenders to adopt new technologies and procedures. Start at the top, sounds, ideal, and I can see the common sense in this.

ANGELS: It is common sense but humans have lost their common sense. They have become complacent. They expect other people to clean up their messes instead of cleaning up their own messes. Everything can be cleaned: the air, the water and the land. All of these elements are self-sustaining without human help but with human interference they cannot sustain themselves. Humans think that they have to manage everything: the air, the water, the animals, and the land, but they are self-managing. They were self-managing before humans and can do so again. Managing is control and control is not needed when an element is independent and self-sustaining. Leave them alone once they have regained balance. Humans have become overwhelmed with trying to manage.

Q: How long would it take to get everything back into balance? It seems as if the imbalance has taken place over the past few generations, perhaps it will take many more generations for the Earth to get back into balance.

ANGELS: It would be surprisingly sooner. The Earth has great recuperative powers. It is not a living, sentient organism, as some think, but it is a self-sustaining one. Once it is put back on a path to self-sustaining it will take less time than imagined. It will start slow but will quicken as time goes on. It could even happen in one or two generations. That is all we can do to help.

Q: Thank you for the dialogue. We are hoping that there can be mutual help and we ask how we can assist the Angels? Are there other races that we can also ask for assistance?

ANGELS: You can assist the Angels by continuing to ask for our help. We cannot tell you any other races to ask for help. You must ask those that you know.

Q: Thank you.

Asking Angels about the Orbs

We would like to thank the Angels for their patience with us, their help, and their contributions to our knowledge. We respect and appreciate the Angels. In this session we would like to ask the Angels some questions about the Orbs. We have had many experiences with Orbs and have worked with them to acquire information. We also respect the Orbs for their interest in our work and for the information that they have brought us. However, we are intrigued by them and how they function and their appearance.

We are concerned about potential problems in the world: Earthquakes, the ozone holes, the depletion of fish in the oceans, deforestation and depletion of oxygen, the heating of the oceans, drought and floods, toxicity and waste dumps, dangers from nuclear reactors, economic collapse and debt of the nation, and fault lines in the Middle East that could impact oil supplies and prices over the next 10-20 years. All of these issues could relate to a social and economic collapse of both the United States and relay to the rest of the world.

Q: Can the Angels and the Orbs tell us about potential problems in the world: Earthquakes, the ozone holes, the depletion of fish in the oceans, deforestation and depletion of oxygen, the heating of the oceans, drought and floods, toxicity and waste dumps, dangers from nuclear reactors, economic collapse and debt of the nation, and fault lines in the Middle East that could impact oil supplies and prices over the next 10-20 years. All of these issues could relate to a social and economic collapse of both the United States and relay to the rest of the world.

Angels: During the next three years, Humans will see a big increase in all of these problems, particularly the environmental issues that they are so worried about. After that, there will be a plateau, for another two years, then more serious problems with the environment that will have Humans moving between countries. After another two years, there will be a lull for another six years. The Angels will be there to protect and help. All of the other problems are Human in design and can be predicted and managed through Human intervention. Many of the problems are caused by Human fear itself and wasteful and inadequate Human management. The Angels cannot predict for Humans but can make guesses at what will happen. We, the Angels, can only be there to assist.

Orbs: As the Record Keepers have already told you, we do not keep records of past events and have to go to the record Keepers for all of this information. We know, from ferrying information back and forth, that all of the preceding questions have already been asked of and answered by the Record Keepers. However, from what we observe, Humans are doing a good job of mismanaging their resources and, until this changes, Humans cannot expect a positive outcome.

Questions to the Angels about the Orbs:

Q: One of the answers given us by the Orbs, at one time, was that the faces in the Orbs reflected the faces of the individuals giving the Orbs information or tasks. Is this so?

Angels: This is so, in some cases. In other cases, the Orbs carry what Humans call the "soul" of a deceased Human who has not passed to the next level of existence.

Q: Some Orbs show up when people dance. Are these attracted by the dance or are they always there? Why do the Orbs show up? Are they sent? Are they observing Human behavior for other races?

Angels: Again, it all depends. Orbs are everywhere, so when someone begins to dance, some may be attracted to the movements and the frequency of the music. Others are nearby and, again, are attracted by the movement and music. Sometimes, Orbs are called by the dancer, so that when they dance there are many Orbs. Orbs are very curious and will appear when there is something of interest to observe and carry to the Record Keepers.

Q: Can Orbs carry people? I have been reading a book where Orbs appeared in conjunction with a beam from a Gray craft, which levitated Humans to the craft. Were the Orbs involved in the levitation of the Humans and how? Can the Orbs carry or pull up a grown person?

Angels: No, the Orbs cannot carry people or animals but they can assist and observe when people are being lifted, for example by the Grays. They are often observed by Humans to be around when this type of levitation takes place.

Q: Orbs have been seen around volcanoes and prior to eruptions and Earthquakes. Why is this? Are they sent to record the event and who sends them?

Angels: Yes, they are around to observe and record. Some are already in the area and some are attracted to the energy and the movement of the volcano. Anything that generates noise, energy, heat, or movement attracts the Orbs.

Q: Can the Orbs act in an independent manner and acquire information without instruction from another race?

Angels: Orbs have a small amount of autonomy and can travel a short distance of their own accord to observe and record. They can be called from a great distance, too. They cannot travel a great distance of their own volition, but need to be called or sent.

Q: Are they attracted by low frequency and is that why they are drawn to music, dance, pre-Earthquake rumblings?

Angels: Yes, they are attracted by frequencies such as music, light, movement and other energies. However, some music and frequencies sends them away, such as discordant sounds, metal screeching, and loud banging.

Q: Orbs are often seen and photographed at "ghost hunting" events and are presumed to be the energies or spirits of dead Humans. Is this so?

Angels: Sometimes, this is so. As mentioned previously, some Orbs carry the "soul" of a deceased person until they have decided where they want to go, and then the Orb will take them there.

Q: Regarding Human history, can the Angels tell us who or what assisted Humans to levitate great blocks of stone for constructions such as that at Mesa Verde, Chaco Canyon and Macho Pichu? How did this affect the beliefs of the people at that time? How was this knowledge acquired and how did it become lost? Where did the people at these sites come from? Where did the people at these sites go to? Why did they build where they did, why did they live there and why did they leave?

Angels: Orbs cannot lift animals or Humans, and they cannot lift stone or other immaterial objects. Some stones were lifted both by Earthly forces and by non-Earthy forces. That is, water and landslide carried some very large stones and the stones were levered into place. Sometimes, the Races helped, but this was rare. What some do not know is that many of these blocks were not cut from stone but were mixed, as a form of concrete, and poured in place. The ancients had many such recipes and formulas, which have since been lost. When in place, they were then shaped with tools, giving the appearance of being great blocks lifted into place. The ancient ones used a mixture of Earth, rock, plants, and water to create these blocks. The people who had this knowledge were gradually eroded by disease, famine and lack of sufficient water. Some have survived but the knowledge has been lost except to a small few.

Q: Where can people live on the Earth peacefully and healthily? Thinking about all the problems that beset Humans as outlined in the Introduction, where can Humans live where they can be safe and live healthily?

Angels: There are two narrow, regions of the Earth that circle the globe below the poles. These include the colder countries of the North and South. The colder countries have milder disturbances of the surface of the Earth, than do the warmer countries, so colder is safer and healthier for Humans. There is less disease, less stress, and less cause to move from place to place.

Q: Thank you Angels for your patience and information.

10: The Exobiology Project: Talking With The Light Beings

"We have no need of musical instruments, we are the instruments."
—Light Beings"

During the spring of 2006, additional projects were conducted that interviewed several Earth-based races: the Elementals and another called the Record-Keepers. As these were not strictly extraterrestrial but were bound up with Human history and mythology, they are not included in this series. However, their contributions are included in later dialogues with the other races.

As a beginning to the next stage of the Exobiology project, alternative questions were suggested to ask of the Exobiology contacts. The first entity interviewed in this new phase was a Light Being that had been encountered by a friend of a colleague. The friend has been abducted many times and escorted by "Light Beings" who she had described as "milky, glowing, luminous, with very loving emotions." She felt totally safe with them and cared for by them. Who were they?

Additional races be interviewed, would be the Greens, the Propers, the Roughs, and the Darks. It was felt that the Tall Oranges might be akin to the Skin Walker, seen at the Sherman/Gorman Ranch, and to be a different race than the Oranges previously interviewed.

New Questions:

Q: How does this race, the Light Beings", describe themselves? How do they travel and interact across the galaxy. How often do they travel and interact?

LB: We call ourselves the Companions and we think of ourselves as companions to many races. We have very little substance and many do not see us. When another race needs another presence, we can be there. There is no limit to our travel and interactions.

Q: Do you have such concepts as space and time?

LB: No.

Q: Am I interacting with one Light Being or many?

LB: Many, at one time.

Q: In interacting with the many, am I interacting with all Light Beings?

LB: No.

Q: Why? We are interacting as a group but not with the whole?

LB: We are a group. There are many groups. We companion with the group where we travel.

Q: How did the colleague's friend perceive you?
LB: She saw our form and perceived our caring.
Q: Should I refer to you as Light Beings or Companions?
LB: It does not matter.
Q: I will refer to you as Light Beings.
Q: The colleague's friend perceived you when she was returning from an abduction. Do you work with the Grays?
LB: Only when asked to companion.
Q: Is this often?
LB: Not very often.
Q: Under what circumstances do the Grays ask you to accompany a Human?
LB: When there are two being returned.
Q: What does that mean?
LB: The Human and a Hybrid.
Q: So, if a Human has a Hybrid fetus, you accompany the Human?
LB: Yes, it is a sacred thing to accompany such a Human.
Q: Are you the same race as the Angels or Nordics?
LB: No.
Q: The Light Beings are perceived as very gentle, very quiet, and very unobtrusive. They appear to have knowledge and advanced physics that include levitation and the ability to move through solid objects, like the Grays.
Q: In their interactions with Humans, how often does this happen and why is this interaction carried out? For observation? Are they monitors for the Confederation?
LB: We interact whenever needed. Sometimes this is often, but sometimes not very often. The interactions are because we have been asked. There is a sacred event that needs special care that the other races cannot complete.
Q: What special care do you provide that the Grays cannot provide?
LB: We soothe when Humans are frightened. We company where there are two.
Q: Some Humans have perceived a Tall Gray that comforts them during an abduction. Can you change shape or is that your real shape?
LB: We can take many shapes. We comfort Humans.
Q: Is your shape something like the ectoplasm that has been seen on photos?
LB: Something similar but we are not ectoplasm. We are not monitors for the Confederation although we are part of the Confederation. The Orbs and other races monitor for the Confederation.
Q: Which other races monitor for the Confederation?
LB: All races that belong to the Confederation can monitor for the Confederation.

Q: Can Light Beings help Humans if the entities are asked? How can Humans ask for help? If they can help us, in what way can we ask for this help?
LB: No, we cannot help Humans. Only those other races that ask for our help.
Q: Why cannot the Light Beings be asked for help by Humans?
LB: They are not part of the Confederation.
Q: The Grays are not part of the Confederation either?
LB: Other races, not the Grays, ask us to help the Grays.
Q: That sounds complex.
LB: It is not complex to us.
Q: Can we ask other Confederation races for you to help us?
LB: That has not been done.
Q: What use do the Light Beings make for natural Earth resources? Do they need these for survival etc?
LB: We are "electrical" in nature.
Q: I am assuming that "electrical" means some sort of energy?
LB: Yes, "electrical" is the nearest equivalent. We do not need Earth resources for survival. We are very simple.
Q: Are Light Beings positively or negatively oriented towards Humans?
LB: Neither positive nor negative about Humans. We do not care. We are companions when asked, nothing more.
Q: So you would consider yourselves neutral?
LB: Yes.
Q: If another race asked you to act negatively to Humans, would you do so?
LB: No. It is against the Confederation to do so.
Q: Why are Grays interacting with us on a conscious level and not others?
LB: This is because the Grays have been interacting with Humans for centuries and a recognition bond has developed between the two races. There are others such as Hybrids and Nordics that can be perceived by Humans on a conscious level. Humans can also perceive us when we take the shape of a bonded entity.
Q: Are there other entities out in the Universe? Why, how, and what?
LB: There are many entities belonging to many families in the Universe. We do not know all of them. We know some of them. Some you have already interacted with.
Q: How do you know which others I have interacted with?
LB: When you interact with us we know which other groups you have also interacted with.
Q: OK.
Q: Can you tell me about some of the other entities out in the Universe?
LB: Yes, but at the right time.

Q: Can you give me some idea now?

LB: No.

Q: Does this race, the Light Beings, have the ability to look into the future?

LB: We do not have the ability to look into the future. We have the ability to logically deduce things about the future but not to predict on a non-logical level. We are logical, not non-logical.

Q: Is this race helping, hindering or ignoring us?

LB: We do nothing more than assist other races to accompany and assist. We only do what other races ask us to do.

Q: Do you ever do anything for yourselves that is not asked of you by other races?

LB: NR (No Response).

Q: I have the idea that the Light Beings are frail and tire easily, and I have had to give them many breaks. They are not prepared to answer all questions.

Q: Is the Confederation just of our Galaxy or of the Universe?

LB: We only know the Confederation of this Galaxy. We do not know any other Confederation.

Q: Are there other Confederations?

LB: We do not know.

Q: Is this entity, the Light Beings, a Galactic or Universal entity?

LB: We are of the Confederation that belongs to this Galaxy. That is all we know.

Q: Regarding the Rules of the Confederation – are these also applicable to non-members, such as the need to respect and cooperate with other races?

LB: The rules of the Confederation apply to everyone regardless of whether they belong to the Confederation. They are basic rules for the Galaxy.

Q: Are there other rules?

LB: Yes. There are rules about fair trade and about giving fair measure.

Q: Concerning the abduction by Grays of Humans how does this constitute fair trade or fair measure?

LB: In the long run it is fair trade. It is a process of reciprocal trade: the Humans provide Hybrids, the Grays prepare the Hybrids for space exploration, and Hybrids prolong Human life into other galaxies. That is a fair trade and fair measure.

Q: Do Light Beings have a sense of who people are? Do they have autonomy or are they on a mission for others, or for another group?

LB: We have autonomy but this is private. We assist and accompany others.

Q: Regarding fair trade and fair measure, what do you receive in return for your assistance and company?

LB: NR

Q: What questions should Humans ask of the Exobiology entities?
LB: The Humans should not be asking any questions.
Q: !? (Questioner's surprise at answer).
Q: What should the Exobiology entities be asking of us or want to ask us?
LB: There are many questions. What is emotion? It is an energy that can raise physical objects. How do the Humans not know this and use it? Why do Humans not manage emotion well? Why do they not realize its potential? Why do they waste emotion? Do Humans see emotion as a waste product?
Q: Some parapsychologists realize the role of emotion in psychokinesis. Is that a beginning?
LB: It is only a beginning.
Q: Are there Exobiology entities that are detrimental to Human interests? Are there entities that we should not interact with?
LB: There are many entities that Humans should not interact with and that are dangerous to Humans. There are energy entities in the Galaxy, that are perceived as sheets of energy that will deactivate Humans and all of their devices. These are not near Earth but roam the Galaxy. Other groups that have been in the Galaxy for a longer time know how to interact with them. There are also entity groups that appear benign but can become dangerous. They have the ability to reverse their affect and become dangerous.
Q: Is this similar to someone on Earth with manic-depression?
LB: Much more dangerous.
Q: Are the Light Beings dangerous to Humans?
LB: No.
Q: Does this entity group have a concept of God – of a Universal source?
LB: We do not know such a concept. There have been over-hearings of Humans who say that we act as if we know God but we do not know God. We act as we act not because we belong to such another race. Is God a race?
Q: No, God is conceived to be a supreme power, the creator of the Universe, a divine Being.
LB: We do not know this entity.
Q: Do Light Beings need two genders to reproduce like we do? Do they manipulate DNA to reproduce, how?
LB: No, we do not reproduce. There is no need. There are enough of us.
Q: Is Earth toxic to these entities, Light Beings, i.e. ultraviolet is toxic to Grays?
LB: Earth is not toxic to us. We can come and go with no ill effects. It is good of you to be concerned about us.
Q: We are curious about how our environment affects us, so we are also concerned about how it affects other races that visit us.

Q: How do they sustain themselves, nutrient baths etc? All entities have the need to survive. Humans need food, water, air, sunshine to exist. Do Entities need these same things or something different? Do they need warmth, shelter, etc., like we do to survive?

LB: We do not have the same needs except the need to survive. We can garner energy from our environment for movement and for repair. We do not have the needs of some other races.

Q: Are the Beings surprised by the way that our species is socially organized? How does this differ from their social organization? It is hard for us to conceive of a species that is not centrally controlled. We conceive of centralized control as a means to prevent destruction within and between people. Is this process in place in the Exobiology Being's worlds? Within species? Between species?

LB: We do not have a social organization except to be in a group. We are also part of the Confederation and abide by their rules. Otherwise, we are unique and alone in our decisions, and logic, and living. Other species, such as the Grays and their like, are centrally controlled and all work together. Their control is the control of the all thinking as one.

Q: Is there anything, within the next 25 Earth years (rotations around our Sun) that Humans should be concerned about?

LB: We do not perceive non-logically into the future. We can do elaborate calculations, based on what has happened in the past to predict what will happen in the future. What is predicted for Earth? More fighting, more territoriality, and more wars. It does not take non-logical prediction to know that. Humans should be concerned that they do not learn from their mistakes.

Q: Do Light Beings make mistakes and learn from them?

LB: We make mistakes only when we come across a new situation and we can learn from our mistakes.

Q: Do the different Exobiology races manifest a sense of creativity? Do Light Beings manufacture anything? Do Light Beings have writing, music, or art?

LB: We do not manufacture, we only repair ourselves and others. We have no need for writing or art that are physical constructs. We do have "music": we have frequencies and vibrations. Some of us meet in the *void* and create frequencies that please us and cause our energy to increase. We have no need of musical instruments, we are the instruments.

Q: Do they get sick or have illnesses? Do they have any internal or external threats? Do they die? How do they deal with death?

LB: Light Beings do not have a concept of death but we understand that Humans and some other beings' physical bodies can finish. We do not have to deal with death either; our own or that of others. We have no threats and are not a threat to others.

Q: Are they surprised that Humans can reach out and communicate with them and how often does this happen? When does this happen and from where? Is this contact carried out telepathically?

LB: Yes, we are very surprised that Humans can reach out and communicate with us. Sometimes a Human will try and communicate with us when we are accompanying them but they cannot understand us. We do not try and communicate with them except for the essentials need to comfort and accompany them. It is always telepathically as we have no voice. We are surprised that some Humans can hear us, even when we do not start the communication. We are happy for this communication.

Q: Native American people's, such as the Hopi and other races, have described how their ancestors had a connection to Beings from Sirius and the Pleiades. They claim that these Beings were their ancestors and that they are still interacting. There is some folklore that these Beings were escaping from Sirius and the Pleiades. How did they come to Earth and are they still able to communicate?

LB: Those were some other Beings, not us. There is information that this is so but it was not us. We have no knowledge of this information except that it is so.

Q: What potential does Earth have for Light Beings?

LB: Earth has great potential for many races but not for us, we do not need what Earth offers. We do not have the needs that other races have. Earth is for others, not for us.

Q: Is there any further information about the other races outlined above that will soon be interviewed? Who can we talk to? Are there dangerous entities?

LB: We cannot give you any other information than we have already.

Q: The Dark Ones are on the list of entities to be interviewed. Are they dangerous? Should I be careful?

LB: Yes, they have ways of insinuating into Human lives. Clear them away after interacting with them.

Q: What does that mean, clear them away?

LB: Make sure that they have not stayed behind.

Q: We thank and respect the Light Beings for this interview. The next race to be interviewed is the "Dark Ones".

11: The Exobiology Project: Talking With The Dark Ones

"Earth is not toxic to us but some Humans are toxic to us."
—The Dark Ones

The second race to be interviewed is the group known as the Dark Ones (DO). Care is being taken in interviewing the Dark Ones in view of the information given by the Light Beings. They noted that the Dark Ones have a way of insinuating themselves into Human lives and to "clear them away" after interacting with them, to make sure that they have not stayed behind. Therefore, I am invoking the Light Beings and any other helpful races to be on-hand to assist if this should prove to be a difficult project and to help me clear away all vestiges of the Dark Ones, if they should try and persist in my personal space.

Q: How does this race, the "Dark Ones" describe themselves? How do they travel and interact across the galaxy. How often do they travel and interact?

DO: We are great and horrible to some people but that is on the outside only. It is a perception. Why have you taken so long from your original intention to talk to us?

Q: I had some trepidation about talking to you. I wanted to protect myself.

DO: That is a misconception that people need protection from us. We are not dangerous.

Q: The Light beings felt that you are dangerous and warned me about you.

DO: The Light Beings are very different from us and do not understand us. We were getting impatient to talk to you.

Q: I am here now. Can you please describe yourselves and which race you are closest to?

DO: We are closest to the Nordics.

Q: That is surprising.

DO: We are darker than them and we cannot bi-locate into new bodies. When we dissolve from our physical bodies to travel, we become a shadow or shade that can go anywhere.

Q: What do you look like in your physical body?

DO: We look like the Nordics but with dark hair and features. We are not frightening but do not appear to be like the other races.

Q: Are you part of the Confederation and do you abide by the rules of the Confederation such as having respect and cooperation for and with the other races?

DO: No we are set apart.
Q: What does that mean?
DO: We have set ourselves apart and live by our own rules.
Q: Are there other races that have set themselves apart?
DO: Yes, there are some. We pass them by sometimes but we do not interact.
Q: Have Humans interacted with them?
DO: Sometimes.
Q: Are the Dark Ones similar to the entities that have been seen recently in Mexico, which can fly in the air, and have attacked policemen, etc.
DO: No, they are not us but some other race.
Q: Have you met them?
DO: No.
Q: How do you travel?
DO: We bi-locate and travel as Shadows or Shades.
Q: How often do you travel?
DO: Whenever it is necessary.
Q: Why do you travel and what is your purpose?
DO: We travel to visit and inquire.
Q: What does that mean?
DO: We like to know what is happening. We are inquisitive.
Q: Are you destructive, aggressive, or malevolent?
DO: No. We travel and attach to learn.
Q: Just so that you know, ahead of time, you cannot attach to me. I am independent and cannot work with anything attached. So please do not attach to me.
DO: That is as requested.
Q: In their interactions with Humans, how often does this happen and why is this interaction carried out? For observation? Are they monitors for the Confederation?
DO: We are not monitors for anybody except ourselves. We are also independent but can attach to other entities and races to learn.
Q: What is the point of learning from other races? How does this benefit you?
DO: We learn where the energy sources are.
Q: Are these energy sources that you need to grow and develop, to live?
DO: Yes.
Q: Can you describe an energy source that I would know about?
DO: Inside the Earth are *wells* of energy, due to the Earth rotating, the waters running, and the air moving. We do not need physical structures to make and harvest this energy; we can do so with our *being*.
Q: Then you access other races and entities to try and locate these resources?

DO: Yes.

Q: The Light Beings and some Humans have said that traces of Shades and Shadows can linger around and attach themselves to Humans. Is that true?

DO: Yes, these are our *children.* We can bi-locate and we can subdivide into smaller pieces.

Q: Is that on a holographic scale i.e. each piece retains information about the whole?

DO: Yes, and we can continue to perceive and store information.

Q: Do you work with the other races?

DO: No, we act and live alone.

Q: How often are Humans accessed for information?

Q: Very often. Most often, the Human does not know we are there, they only see an occasional shadow of us. We stay for varying lengths of time then travel on.

Q: Are you the same as what we describe as a ghost?

DO: Sometimes we are wrongly identified as a ghost but we are not a ghost, we are a living race of beings.

Q: Can Dark Ones help Humans if the entities are asked? How can Humans ask for help? If they can help us, in what way can we ask for this help?

DO: No, we do not help Humans or any other race. We are by ourselves and only live by ourselves. We cannot look at the future: we do not look at the past, except to compare new information with old. We have no limitations.

Q: Some Humans would say that having no ability to see past and future is limiting?

DO: We have no limitations. Humans and other races have limitations as they cannot be strongly present in the moment.

Q: That sounds a lot like Buddhism.

DO: We do not know Buddhism.

Q: It is a Human religious movement that began with a spiritual Human called Buddha, who taught that Humans should live in the present moment.

DO: We do not know Buddha but it describes what we do.

Q: Would you call yourselves Enlightened?

DO: What is Enlightened?

DO: Having spiritual knowledge and being at-one with the universe?

DO: No, we are not Enlightened. We are not at-one with the universe. We are alone and live alone. We would not help Humans or any other race. We do not have spiritual knowledge, only of energy sources.

Q: What use do the Dark Ones make for natural Earth resources? Do they need these for survival etc?

DO: Yes, this is what we do. We need energy sources that reside in the Earth.

Q: Do you sometimes drain Human energy?

DO: Yes, if needed.

Q: That is why Humans do not like you and have developed stories about you, which sound like they are true.

DO: We do not take much.

Q: But it is enough that it harms or hurts the Human.

DO: We take what we need. We take what our *children* need.

Q: Has it always been this way?

DO: Yes.

Q: Is there not enough energy within the Earth that you need not take Human energy?

DO: There may be but Human energy is special. Our *children* need it to grow.

Q: Are you in communication with other Dark Ones?

DO: Yes.

Q: Can you indicate that the taking of Human energy hurts Humans?

DO: Yes but it will make no difference. We need Human energy for our *children* to grow. We will always need Human energy.

Q: Can Humans refuse to have the Shades attach to them, as I have done?

DO: Yes, all they have to do is say so. We will leave and find another Human.

Q: Many Humans do not know this.

DO: Do not tell them. (!)

Q: Are Dark Ones positively or negatively oriented towards Humans?

DO: We have no knowledge of these words. We do what we do. We look for energy sources. We take what we need. That is not positive or negative. We take what we need for us and our *children*. If your children needed energy you would find it for them?

Q: Some Humans would look at you as parasites.

DO: Humans already have many parasites, some that they cannot see. We are only one of many. Humans have been living with these things for ever. This is nothing new.

Q: Why are Grays interacting with us on a conscious level and not others?

DO: We do not work with the Grays. We do not know what they are doing or why.

Q: Are there other entities out in the Universe? Why, how, and what?

DO: You do not know about the other entities? You are limited.

Q: As Humans we have interacted with many races including the Grays, the Nordics, and the Reptilians. Your use of the word *limited* is also used by the Reptilians and others. Is this a common perception of Humans by some entities?

DO: Yes. Humans are limited.

Q: Do you know the Reptilians?

DO: Yes, we know of them.

Q: Have you interacted with them?

DO: NR (No Response).

Q: Does this race, the Dark Ones, have the ability to look into the future?

DO: No. we do not look into the future. Comparing – you have already asked us this question.

Q: Is this race, the Dark Ones, helping, hindering, or ignoring us?

DO: We do none of these things. We take what we need. If it hinders Humans, that is not our concern. Mostly we ignore Humans and other races.

Q: Is the Confederation just of our Galaxy or of the Universe?

DO: We do not know about the Confederation or other Confederations. We do not live by their rules.

Q: So you are aware that some races live by the Confederation rules?

DO: Yes.

Q: When was the decision made that the Dark Ones would not abide by Confederation rules?

DO: NR

Q: Is this entity, the Dark Ones, a Galactic or Universal entity?

DO: What does that mean?

Q: Are you resident just in this Galaxy or can you go everywhere?

DO: We can go everywhere.

Q: Regarding the Rules of the Confederation – are these also applicable to non-members, such as the need to respect and cooperate with other races?

DO: The rules of the Confederation do not apply to us. They know this. We do what we want and what we have always done.

Q: So you do not respect or cooperate with other races?

DO: No.

Q: Do Dark Ones have a sense of who people are? Do they have autonomy or are they on a mission for others, or for another group?

DO: Yes, we have a sense of Humans. We use Humans for energy. That is all we need to know. We do not need to know other things about Humans. It is not necessary. We are not on a mission for other races. We are alone with our own mission. That is to help ourselves.

Q: What questions should Humans be asking of the Exobiology entities?

DO: If Humans ask, we do not answer.

Q: You are listening to me and answering my questions. You listen when Humans ask you to go away.

DO: These are special circumstances and will be forgotten very quickly. The *askings* and questions will go away and we will continue as we have always done so.

Q: What should the Exobiology entities be asking of us or want to ask us?

DO: We do not want to know anything about the Humans except are they good sources of energy.

Q: What makes a person a source of good energy?

DO: When they are red.

Q: What does that mean?

DO: When they have a red face, when they are breathing hard, when they have emotions.

Q: Do the emotions have to be negative or positive?

DO: We prefer it when the emotions are focused against another person. We do not know what it is called: when one Human voices loudly at another or voices loudly at another in their head. That is when the energy is strongest. That is what we like. That is what we need.

Q: Are there Exobiology entities that are detrimental to Human interests? Are there entities that we should not interact with?

DO: We do not care which other entities the Humans interact with as long as they are available when we need them for energy. We do not care what other entities there are.

Q: Does this entity group have a concept of God – of a Universal source?

DO: We are the universal source. We know where all the energy sources are. We are God.

Q: Humans do not consider you as God. They have a different conception of God.

DO: We consider ourselves God. We do not know anything else but ourselves.

Q: Do Dark Ones need two genders to reproduce like we do? Do they manipulate DNA to reproduce, how?

DO: We do not need two genders, like Humans. We bi-locate and separate to provide *children*. The *children* are nurtured by the energy that we find for them. They do not know DNA.

Q: Is Earth toxic to these entities, Dark Ones, i.e. ultraviolet toxic to Grays?

DO: Earth is not toxic to us but some Humans are toxic to us.

Q: Which Humans are toxic to you?

DO: There are Humans who set themselves apart and wear the same clothes. We avoid them. They make a ritual of keeping us away.

Q: Are you talking about spiritual people, such as monks and nuns?

DO: We do not know what they are called. They collect themselves in one place, wear the same clothes, think the same things, and keep us away from them. If there are too many of them we may not find energy and we cannot provide energy for our *children.* We stay away from these Humans. We do not like them.

20. How do they sustain themselves, nutrient baths etc? All entities have the need to survive. Humans need food, water, air, sunshine to exist. Do Entities need these same things or something different? Do they need warmth, shelter, etc like we do to survive?

DO: Our race only needs energy. We find energy in many places, including the Earth and Humans.

Q: Do you find other planets, other races that can provide food for your children?

DO: Yes, there are many places and many races. We do not need shelter or other Human needs. Humans are limited in these needs.

Q: When Humans die, they believe that they are also spirits that have no need of these Earth resources. Do you know about this?

DO: Yes, then they are unlimited.

Q: Are the Beings surprised by the way that our species is socially organized? How does this differ from their social organization? It is hard for us to conceive of a species that is not centrally controlled. We conceive of centralized control as a means to prevent destruction within and between people. Is this process in place in the Exobiology Being's worlds? Within species? Between species?

DO: We do not have a central organization. We all act alone. We are aware of others of our race but do not interact except to share information about energy sources. We control ourselves. There is no need for others to control us or for us to control others. That does not make sense to us. We are aware of other races. They do not control us and we do not control them. There is no need.

Q: Is there anything, within the next 25 Earth years (rotations around our Sun) that Humans should be concerned about?

DO: We do not see that far. All we need are energy resources, including Humans.

Q: If a catastrophe were to occur that caused all the Humans to disappear, how would that affect the Dark Ones?

DO: We would go elsewhere for energy for our *children.* There are other races that we would visit.

Q: Are you aware of the Hybrids?

DO: What are the hybrids?

Q: No matter, it does not matter.

Q: Do the different Exobiology races manifest a sense of creativity? Do Dark Ones manufacture anything? Do Dark Ones have writing, music, or art?

DO: We have nothing like that. We do have a sense of completion when we produce our *children.* They could be said to be our art, our music but we do not know these terms.

Q: Music is a vibration that Humans make with devices, that is usually pleasant to our senses. Is there any special music that attracts the Dark Ones?

DO: No.

Q: That surprises me. I thought that some music, that generates negative emotion in some people, such as rap, would attract the Dark Ones.

DO: We are not attracted by frequencies, only Human energy. If the energy is red, then we know that is energy for us.

Q: Do they get sick or have illnesses? Do they have any internal or external threats? Do they die? How do they deal with death?

DO: The only Humans that we do not interact with are the ones that get together, wear the same clothes, eat the same foods, and keep us away with the same thoughts. We also go away from Humans that ask us to and keep their energy away from being red.

Q: Are they surprised that Humans can reach out and communicate with them and how often does this happen? When does this happen and from where? Is this contact carried out telepathically?

DO: We can hear you and communicate with you but we do not know if there have been others. We know that we can communicate with you and it is race to race. We can interact with Humans who ask us to go away or get together as a group to keep us away. So, there is some communication. So we are not surprised.

Q: Native American people, such as the Hopi's and other races, have described how their ancestors had a connection to Beings from Sirius and the Pleiades. They claim that these Beings were their ancestors and that they are still interacting. There is some folklore that these beings were escaping from Sirius and the Pleiades. How did they come to Earth and are they still able to communicate?

DO: We do not know about this.

Q: What potential does Earth have for Dark Ones?

DO: Earth and Humans are a source of energy for us and for our *children.* Nothing more.

Q: Regarding the supermarket cart incident and my friend's sunglasses, please know that we need respect and give respect and do not appreciate poltergeist behavior. If the entities are interested in our technology, personal items, please do not take them.

DO: We do not know about this. We do not need technology and other Human things unless they cause the Human to have red energy, which we can use.

Q: Is there any further information about the other races outlined above that will soon be interviewed? Who can we talk to? Are there dangerous entities?

DO: We do not know about the other entities, we do not know about dangerous entities. We do not know who you can talk to.

Q: I am asking now that the Dark Ones leave me, that my energy is not red, that they can leave and not cause any *children* to be left behind in my body, my mind, or my home: that they leave and go somewhere else. There is nothing here for them. I am also asking that they do not attach themselves to others who will read this interview. Thank you.

12: The Exobiology Project: Talking With The Anaka

"We are the Anaka people and we have been here forever."

—The Anaka

Another previous interview identified the Anaka as the race of beings that had interacted with Native American tribes in history. It was related that the Anaka were still interacting with Humans. It was decided to include them in the Exobiology series.

Q: How does this race, the Anaka, describe themselves? How do they travel and interact across the galaxy. How often do they travel and interact?

AK: We are the Anaka. We do not travel. We are here on the Earth and have always been here on the Earth. We are the Anaka people and we have been here forever. We travel as Humans travel. We are a modern people.

Q: I am surprised, as I thought you would be the same as the other races we have encountered.

AK: We are not like any other race as we are here and have always been here.

Q: Please tell me how you travel?

AK: We travel the same as you, by foot, by car, by public transportation.

Q: That is surprising to me!

Q: How would you describe yourselves physically?

AK: We are of two types. One type is short and stocky; the other is tall and slender. We fall into these two groups. There is nothing in between. We have straight black hair, and dark eyes, with a darker complexion.

Q: Are you the same as the North Americans?

AK: No. We are a separate race.

Q: Are you just found in North America?

AK: No, we are in South America, Japan, the Russias, the Pacific Islands, everywhere on Earth.

Q: How long have you been here?

AK: We have been here before Humans.

Q: Have you interbred with other races?

AK: No. We are a separate race.

Q: If we were to meet you, how would we know that you are Anaka and not Native American or some other race?

AK: You would not know because we would not tell you.

Q: Would an intuitive person be able to tell?

AK: Maybe, yes.

Q: Is it something about the eyes?

AK: No.

Q: What is your role on Earth?

AK: The same as it always has been, to teach.

Q: Can you speak all languages?

AK: Some of us speak different languages, usually of the area where we are. We have an affinity for language.

Q: What professions would we find you in?

AK: All professions.

Q: On census forms, what race do you put down?

AK: We put the race closest to that which we resemble and where we live. We have all the privileges of each culture and travel and move with them as they do.

Q: So you would have a passport, Social Security card, what about a birth certificate?

AK: Yes, we have all of those as we have been here forever, so we were here at the beginning of these documents and so acquired them. We give birth to children and so perpetuate our race.

Q: So, what is to differentiate you from Humans?

AK: We know; we are the Anaka.

Q: In their interactions with Humans, how often does this happen and why is this interaction carried out? For observation? Are they monitors for the Confederation?

AK: We are always in communication with Humans and have always interacted.

Q: Was it the Anaka that gave rise to the "Wise Indian" myth?

AK: Probably, we have taught all races for all time. There are wise Anaka among all races but there have also been wise Humans too, that we have taught.

Q: I do not think that I have met any Anaka?

AK: Yes, you have but you did not know it was us. You are not Anaka.

Q: Can the Anaka help Humans if the entities are asked? How can Humans ask for help? If they can help us, in what way can we ask for this help?

AK: Yes, the Anaka can help with knowledge. We can assist when needed but we do not have Human paranormal abilities except to be able to communicate between ourselves without speech. We can assist with knowledge. The Humans can ask us for help, as you are doing now, or by asking us in person.

Q: If we do not know which people are the Anaka, if we cannot identify them, then how can we ask?

AK: Just ask and if we hear we will provide the information.

Q: What use does the Anaka make of natural Earth resources? Do they need these for survival etc?

AK: We need everything for survival that Humans need for survival. We are the closest of all the races in our needs.

Q: Do you know about all the other races?

AK: Yes, of course.

Q: Is the Anaka race positively or negatively oriented towards Humans?

AK: We are neither positive nor negative about the Human race. Whether they succeed is of no importance to our survival. We will be here when the Humans are gone.

Q: Then why try to help Humans with knowledge?

AK: Because we want the Earth to survive, so that we can survive. Without the Earth, we will not survive.

Q: Are the Humans considered superfluous to the Anaka?

AK: No, we also abide by the rules of respect and cooperation, that the other races abide by.

Q: So are you members of the Confederation?

AK: Yes, of course.

Q: Will you give us inside information about the Confederation?

AK: No.

Q: Why are Grays interacting with us on a conscious level and not others?

AK: Grays are not the only race interacting with Humans on a conscious level. Many others do so, including Nordics, the Hybrids and, of course, us. Others are not able to consciously interact with Humans, so that they can perceive them.

Q: I had a fleeting perception that, in the future, we would have technology, that could detect some of these other races, is that so?

AK: Yes, the beginning is with digital cameras, as these become more sophisticated, holographic, and different wavelengths, other races will be able to be perceived. This will become Big Business and everybody with the technology will be able to perceive other races.

Q: Will that be welcomed by the other races?

AK: Yes and no. Some races prefer not to be noticed. For others it will open a new wave of communication with Humans. It will be shocking for many Humans.

Q: Are there other entities out in the Universe? Why, how, and what?

AK: Of course, and you have communicated with many of them already. There are many more. You have a drawing of the world in relation to the other planets and to our solar system, how tiny the Earth is compared to them. It is foolishness to think that there are not multitudes of other people in the universe. It is arrogant of Humans to think so.

Q: Does this race, the Anaka, have the ability to look into the future?

AK: We do not have that ability. However, everything is cyclic and future events can be predicted from events that have already happened. Also the outcome of Human actions can be predicted quite accurately, we have known Humans forever and found that this is so and does not change.

Q: Is this race helping, hindering or ignoring us?

AK: We have always been helping Humans. There has never been a time when we did not help Humans. However, it amazes us that Humans take such a long time to learn basis things, like respect and cooperation. Just when we think that Humans understand, they do something that makes us think that they do not understand and, perhaps, will never understand.

Q: Is the Confederation just of our Galaxy or of the Universe?

AK: Every Galaxy has its Confederation and each Confederation has a Confederation. We only know about this Galaxy's Confederation.

Q: Will you tell me about the Confederation?

AK: NR: No Response.

Q: Is this race, the Anaka, a Galactic or Universal entity?

AK: We are of the Earth and of this Galaxy, and as the Galaxy is in the Universe, we are Universal.

Q: But you cannot travel outside of this Earth?

AK: We did not say that. We do not travel but we could travel. We are not traveling now but we can.

Q: How do you travel?

AK: NR

Q: I understand that you give teaching and have knowledge but do not share everything with Humans?

AK: Yes, that is right.

Q: Regarding the Rules of the Confederation – are these also applicable to non-members, such as the need to respect and cooperate with other races?

AK: All of the rules of the Confederation apply to all, members and non-members but some choose not to follow the rules – like Humans.

Q: Do the Anaka have a sense of who people are? Do they have autonomy or are they on a mission for others, or for another group?

AK: We have a very good sense of who people are. We have autonomy but follow Human rules as long as they do not conflict with our rules. For example, we would not kill a Human or one of our own, unless there was some very necessary reason. We are not on a mission for any other group or race.

Q: What questions should Humans ask of the Exobiology entities?

AK: What should be asked is how Humans can better follow the rules of the Confederation. That would be a good start. It is very interesting to find out about other races but without following the rules of the Confederation, this knowledge of other races is meaningless.

Q: There are some of us already who follow these rules, but we understand that not everybody follows these rules.

AK: That is correct.

Q: What should the Exobiology entities be asking of us or want to ask us?

AK: Follow the rules!

Q: Are there Exobiology entities that are detrimental to Human interests? Are there entities that we should not interact with?

AK: Many races are detrimental to Humans. Some are detrimental because their lifestyle is dangerous to Humans and it is better for Humans to stay away. Other races, such as the Reptile, can be aggressive to Humans if they get in its way.

Q: I have interviewed the Reptilians and Dark Ones, and found this to be true.

Q: Does this entity group have a concept of God – of a Universal source?

AK: Yes, there is a God but it is not what Humans worship. It is a central origin of the Universe, where all life springs from.

Q: Are the Hubble photographs of new solar systems and stars being born, the central origin of the universe?

AK: No, it is much further away, further away than Humans can comprehend. It is the source of all life, Human, Anaka, and all races and life. It can be called a Universal Source. Humans humanize this as an Earthly God with an Earthly appearance so that they can better understand God but this is not so. God does not have a Human face.

Q: Does the Anaka race need two genders to reproduce like we do? Do they manipulate DNA to reproduce, how?

AK: Yes, we replicate like Humans but we do not replicate with Humans.

Q: Is this the source of the 12 strand DNA that we keep hearing about in the literature?

AK: No, this 12 strand DNA is a fabrication and is not true. If it were true, Humans would be monsters and not Human.

Q: Do you have DNA?

AK: Yes, we have DNA. It is indistinguishable from Humans on tests.
Q: How would you test (on DNA tests)?
AK: We would test as if our lineage is the very oldest on the Earth.
Q: Is Earth toxic to these entities, the Anaka, i.e. ultraviolet toxic to Grays?
AK: No, Earth is not toxic to the Anaka.
Q: How do they sustain themselves, nutrient baths etc? All entities have the need to survive. Humans need food, water, air, sunshine to exist. Do Entities need these same things or something different? Do they need warmth, shelter, etc like we do to survive?
AK: The Anaka have the same physical needs as Humans.
Q: Did the Anaka and Humans come from the same root race?
AK: No. We came from another place.
Q: Where?
AK: NR
Q: I am very interested.
AK: We came from multiple places in the universe and we cannot tell you all the places.
Q: Are the Beings (Anaka) surprised by the way that our species is socially organized? How does this differ from their social organization? It is hard for us to conceive of a species that is not centrally controlled. We conceive of centralized control as a means to prevent destruction within and between people. Is this process in place in the Exobiology Being's worlds? Within species? Between species?
AK: The Anaka live within the socialized world of Humans and abide by their rules as much as possible but the Anaka also have their own rules and socialization that we keep secret, often only in thought. We do not interact socially with other species except Humans. We live on the Earth with Humans, so have to follow Earth society.
Q: Is there anything, within the next 25 Earth years (rotations around our Sun) that Humans should be concerned about?
AK: Just more of the same as happened the last 25 rotations. Everything is cyclic.
Q: Do the different Exobiology races manifest a sense of creativity? Does the Anaka manufacture anything? Does the Anaka race have writing, music, or art?
AK: The Anaka are a very creative people: you will find us as artists, musicians, poets, writers as well as in everyday lives. One of the features of the Anaka is that we are very emotional and very creative. We love to dance, to sing, to laugh, to be happy.
Q: Do they get sick or have illnesses? Do they have any internal or external threats? Do they die? How do they deal with death?

AK: The Anaka have the same illnesses, diseases, threats as Humans and we also die. In all of these respects we are the same as Humans. We deal with death as inevitable.

Q: Are they surprised that Humans can reach out and communicate with them and how often does this happen? When does this happen and from where? Is this contact carried out telepathically?

AK: No, we are not surprised. There are many Humans that can reach out in this telepathic way. We are always open to all types of communication, verbal and telepathic. Just do not make us gods. We will teach but we do not do miracles.

Q: Native American people's, such as the Hopi's and other races, have described how their ancestors had a connection to Beings from Sirius and the Pleiades. They claim that these Beings were their ancestors and that they are still interacting. There is some folklore that these beings were escaping from Sirius and the Pleiades. How did they come to Earth and are they still able to communicate?

AK: Yes, these were two of the places that the Anaka came from but we came from many other places, too. Yes, we taught the early Humans and, yes, we are still interacting and teaching all Humans. As you can see, we are still able to communicate.

Q: What potential does Earth have for the Anaka race?

AK: The Earth is our home and we survive on the Earth so it is in our interest to keep its potential positive for us.

Q: Would there come a time when the Anaka would be the only race on Earth?

AK: We do not see that happening. Events are cyclic, Human civilizations and populations wax and wane, and so do Anaka, there will always be a balance.

Q: Regarding the supermarket cart incident and my friend's sunglasses, please know that we need respect and give respect and do not appreciate poltergeist behavior. If the entities are interested in our technology, personal items, please do not take them.

AK: We are not able to do this, to take things under stealth. Anaka do not steal.

Q: Is there any further information about the other races outlined above that will soon be interviewed? Who can we talk to? Are there dangerous entities?

AK: Yes, there are dangerous entities. Some we do no talk about because talking about them attracts them, so we do not even mention them. They live far away, in Human terms, but they will come if called. Do not call them.

Q: Is there a race referred to as the "White Brotherhood"? Were they linked at some point in evolution to the Sumerian culture? Did they sire other descendants on the Earth? Why, are they still here, and are they still interconnected with their planets?

AK: There is not race that we know about, and we know many, that is called the "White Brotherhood." This is a name, perhaps made up, that describes another race? Many races interacted to help evolve the Sumerians including the Anaka. Neither the Anaka nor other races sired the Sumerians, we do not sire with other races, including Humans.

Q: Were the people-control networks on Earth a natural evolvement all over the planet, or were they due to influences of specific ET races competing for dominance and are, perhaps, still competing today?

AK: There are races in the galaxy and in the universe competing for dominance but they are the ones that do not follow the rules. Humans are included in the races that do not follow the rules. The rules are not for control or domination but a natural consequence of working together. Not following the rules has always been a Human trait and did not come from any other race.

Q: Is it important to ask permission of the races before interviewing them? Also, we need to know what is acceptable to know and not know. These interviews are carried out with respect and with no intent to harm the interviewed races.

AK: Yes, it is important to ask permission and this is part of the respect paid to another race. It is acknowledged that these interviews are carried out with respect and it is appreciated. What is acceptable to one race may not be acceptable to another, so please ask. If it is not known or a race cannot answer they will let you know. Most everything can be asked.

Q: Thank you.

Anaka Follow-Up

Q: Why did the Anaka leave Sirius and the Pleiades (if that is where they are from) and chose Earth to migrate too, and of course how did they get here?

AK: This was done in the spirit of discovery. Like all advanced races we, too, felt the need to explore and expand our race. We have visited Earth many times before we came here to stay, long before Humans were here.

Q: Did you help evolve Humans from other Earth species?

AK: No. That was another race: we do not have a name for them.

Q: You seem to have names for other races, why not this one?

AK: Because they came and went so quickly that we did not give them a name. We did not know much about them, they came, and went and the Humans began to evolve. Perhaps it was an accident.

Q: Are you suggesting that this race made an error in causing Humans to develop?

AK: Yes, that could have been the case.

Q: Some believe that Humans were evolved from an ape-like ancestor and that this was done to create a breeding stock or something similar to farm animals. Do you think this was the case?

AK: No, if that was the case, the other race would have been back by now.

Q: What did this other race look like?

AK: They looked like Humans.

Q: Could they have been the blond Nordics?

AK: No, they were not the Nordics; they were another race that has never come back to Earth. They are not here now and we have no knowledge of them.

Q: How did the Anaka get to Earth?

AK: We had craft.

Q: Are the craft still on Earth?

AK: Perhaps some but most have long since gone, they had many biological components which would have disappeared. Only some non-biological elements would remain and these would now be useless to the Anaka.

Q: Why was Earth chosen as a destination?

AK: Because it resembles our own world very much with air to breathe and water to drink. It was very like our own world.

Q: Were you from the Pleiades or from Sirius?

AK: Both systems are very large and it is an oversimplification to say that we came from those places. It would be similar to saying that a Human came from the Milky Way, this solar system, or this galaxy. We originated from small planets that are in the Pleiades and Sirius systems. You have no coordinates to perceive these places so we will not produce them.

Q: Do the Anaka plan to return to these places of origination?

AK: No, we have been here too long.

Q: I want to call you the Anakim, too. Are you the same as this race, which has been talked about by Humans?

AK: No, that is a Human term that we do not know.

Q: Is their race still living there and where else did they go?

AK: We do not know if our race is still living within the Pleiades or Sirius systems as we have no communication. Our race went out to many different locations. Those that went out before us traveled everywhere. We do not know where they went and if others went out after us.

Q: Did you have a prearranged destination? Was Earth a definite designation for you?

AK: Yes.

Q: How did you know about Earth?

AK: There were others who went out and returned.

Q: But you cannot return?

AK: No, we had a different journey.

Q: Where else did they go?

AK: The first designators went everywhere until they had found non-hostile places, then the races were sent to stay at those places.

Q: So, you do not know if there are people of your race still living in those systems?

AK: No.

Q: Did you leave because of some disaster, famine, or cataclysm?

AK: No.

Q: Are new Anaka continuing to visit Earth?

AK: We do not know of any.

Q: How many other Human-like entities live on Earth?

Q: Here I perceived what could be a chortle.

AK: There are multitudes of other races.

Q: Does that mean there are multitudes of a few races or multitudes of many races?

AK: It means that there are multitudes of a few races, like the Anaka.

Q: Can you tell me about some of them?

AK: There is another race of tall, thin men, mostly men, called the Goroth, who are an ancient race. They have interbred with Humans but retain their characteristics. It is only the men of the lineage that retain the characteristics of the Goroth.

Q: Do those descendents of the Goroth know that they are Goroth?

AK: No. But they are not completely Human.

Q: Are there other races?

AK: Yes, many.

Q: Can you tell me about others?

AK: No, not at this time.

Q: You know that we are interviewing many of the non-Human races, trying to understand them, their lifestyles, and their characteristics. This is being done with respect and compassion and understanding. Why can't you tell us more at this point?

AK: It is too much. It is too soon, more at a later time.

Q: Who else taught the Sumerians besides the Anaka, and what did they teach them?

AK: The Anaka did not teach the Sumerians, they stole ideas from us. We are not teachers; we would prefer to keep ourselves apart from Humans. The Sumerians were thieves and stole ideas and designs from us. We had no way and no reason to stop them. They were very primitive and the first ideas that they stole did not work, they could not make them work. But there were a few clever ones that made the ideas and the designs work, so we let them. The Anaka are not thieves and we do not understand the need to do this. The Sumerians were thieves but we did not understand them. No-one else taught the Sumerians. Everything new that they developed they stole from us.

Q: Are Humans still stealing ideas and designs from the Anaka?

AK: No, we do not have any new ideas or designs. So there is nothing to steal.

Q: If the Anaka did get any new ideas or designs would they share them with Humans?

AK: No.

Q: Other than values of how Humans need to live together more in line with the Confederation's rules, is there anything else you can teach us? If so what?

AK: The Anaka are not teachers. If we were, perhaps we could teach Humans not to steal ideas and designs. The Confederation rules are available to everyone and it is not to the Anaka to teach Humans how to live with these rules. Humans have to teach themselves to live by the Confederation rules.

Q: So there is nothing that you can teach us Humans?

AK: No.

Q: You said in the previous interview that you are here to teach. Yet, now you say that you are not here to teach Humans?

Q: These comments indicated to me that perhaps this second Anaka interview was with a different individual .

AK: We teach others, not Humans. Humans steal from us.

Q: Has there been interbreeding or DNA manipulations that have resulted in the evolution of Man, and or animals?

AK: Mentioned before was another race that interbred with earlier species and produced Humans as a result. As mentioned before, this was an accident or an error. The Anaka have not interbred with Humans, we do not want to interbreed with Humans! There has been no genetic manipulation by the Anaka of Humans.

Q: Why do they live here on Earth, and not elsewhere where Human-like entities are more evolved, live peacefully, and are not so suppressed?

AK: This is our home as it always has been. The Anaka are everywhere but this is home for this Anaka. We are not suppressed. We live our life as we choose to live it. We live peacefully and are already evolved. We do not need to evolve more. It is Humans that need to evolve more. Why do you think that we are suppressed? We are not suppressed.

Q: We know the rules of the Confederation are to cooperate with other entities, not to harm them, to show respect to other entities, Are there any other rules we need to learn and follow?

AK: There is a long list of rules including the rules to cooperate and respect, to live fairly and equitably. There are rules to honor those who came before and those who come after. The Confederation rules are already known by Humans but they choose not to follow them.

Q: Are the rules ones that we have already included in the World's religions and philosophies?

AK: Yes, to some extent except that they have been modified by Humans for their own need.

Q: Can you give me one more rule?

AK: Yes, respect the animals.

Q: I know what that means in Human terms, what does it mean in Confederation terms?

AK: Animals have form and beauty and thought. Respect is due them as it is for Humans.

Q: How can we do this?

AK: Many do so but many do not do so. More need to do so.

Q: OK.

Q: We believe life on Earth is at risk, or at a minimum, Humans will be decimated, which implies your race here on Earth is either at risk of extinction or decimation -mostly from major changes in the environment (many, many changes and degradations not conducive to sustaining life) and nuclear or bio-terrorism wars. What can you do to help us avoid this? Is this coming disaster of only Human origin, or are there extraterrestrial controlling Earth and creating this for their own needs (is it too dangerous for us to know this information?) Would you just leave Earth and go elsewhere. Where could you go? This seems inevitable as those few Humans who control the mass of Humanity are either oblivious to the extent of the risks, or are too confident in their own abilities to control things, or are too old to care about the future in which they will not be alive.

AK: Anaka have been here for many eons and have seen many disasters and wars. Everything is escalating and there is a danger that many Humans will die and not produce. The Anaka will survive as we are everywhere. Humans will survive as they are everywhere. There will be Anaka and Humans that are not destroyed and they will survive. They will continue. They will not continue in the same way but they will continue. Humans fear change more than they fear death. Anything that causes war, famine, catastrophe for Humans creates change and it is this change that is feared not the death. Humans have an interest in maintaining their way of life so that there are few changes. Yet they live on an Earth that is constantly changing. They fear these changes, they do not fear death. They do not want to live when great changes are taking place or after. The Anaka do not fear change as we have seen many changes. We would not go anywhere.

Q: Does that mean that Anaka and Humans will face extinction?

AK: No, none will face extinction, just change.

Q: Are there specific Humans that you feel comfortable sharing your wisdom and knowledge with, and therefore help yourselves survive here on Earth? Are there certain areas of knowledge that you feel more comfortable in sharing with us?

AK: Yes, there are certain Humans who have intelligence, understanding, compassion and the ability to hear and understand us that we feel comfortable sharing information. There are many areas of knowledge that we feel comfortable sharing information about. There are very few areas that we would not feel comfortable sharing information. We do not need to share knowledge to help us survive on the Earth; we will survive without sharing knowledge.

Q: You understand that I am an ambassador and share the questions of others with you for your answers?

AK: Yes, we know that.

1Q: If you are so Human-like in your DNA, why don't the Grays hybridize you too, or are they?

AK: We do not interact with the Grays and we do not interbreed with them. They do not make hybrids of us. There is no need. The Anaka have their explorers. The Grays have their explorers. The Grays and the Anaka have no need of each other.

Q: Does it bother you that the Grays abduct Humans and create Hybrids?

AK: No, that is their plan not ours. We do not interfere, although they interfere with us.

Q: How is that?

AK: They bother us, thinking we are Human until they discover that we are not Human.

Q: Gray Hybrids are tall and thin, too. How do we differentiate you from them?

AK: There are many differences. We do not have the Gray facial features, our facial features look Human. Gray hybrids have some Gray characteristics such as thin hair, we have thick, dark hair. We have Human-looking, narrow eyes; hybrids eyes are usually larger. There are many different facial characteristics. We know the difference. Humans may not know the difference.

Q: Is helping Humans an issue of only self-survival for your race, or is it your nature to do so, or is it the rule of the Confederation?

AK: Anaka do not help Humans. We do not teach.

Q: This goes against what you said in a previous interview. Did I misunderstand you?

AK: Yes, you misunderstood.

Q: So that I do not misunderstand, will you explain what you mean.

AK: We teach in a different sense. We live as the Anaka; others learn from us.

Q: Who are the others?

AK: Other races.

Q: Are there other extraterrestrials or Human spirits or Anaka spirits that you turn to when you need help or advice?

AK: The Anaka do not seek help or advice. We provide help to each other. We give examples to other races.

Q: Would you say that you are a perfect race?

AK: No, we are not perfect but we have had many years to become close to what Humans would call perfect. There is no true perfection. Perfection changes as the race changes, as demands change as change happens. There is no true perfection, only changing aspects of perfection.

Q: How do you avoid getting in the way of the Reptilians, and other potentially harmful entities?

AK: We stay away from the Reptilians. We have no need of the Reptilians and they have no need for us.

Q: Could the Anaka use the Reptilians to return to the Pleiades?

AK: That is something that is not considered and would not be considered.

Q: What is life after death like for an Anaka?

AK: There is a special place that we go to. It is a joining with other Anaka. We do not talk about it.

Q: I would be interested in hearing about it?

AK: It is a place that you would call mythical. We have not seen it but will see it when we have finished living. We are living with Humans so we abide by the customs of the community in which we live. But we have special beliefs that we are taken to a special place when we die.

Q: Is this similar to a Human Heaven?

AK: No, it is different. It is similar to the Human myth of Valhalla.

Q: That is a northern tradition.

AK: Yes, but it was our tradition before it was an Earth tradition.

Q: Do you have a concept for Hell?

AK: We have no concept for Hell. This Earth is difficult enough without adding to it.

Q: Is there anything else that you want to tell Humans about the Anaka?

AK: The Anaka are aware of their long heritage and of their place on the Earth. The Anaka would appreciate respect from Humans of this long heritage. Anaka and Humans will continue alongside each other for a long time more. Humans should not fear change.

Q: Is there anything else you would like to know about us?

AK: The Anaka know most everything about Humans. There is one thing that Humans have, that Anaka do not have and that is anger, we do not understand anger.

Q: Anger comes from fear. It is usually a reaction to fear. Perhaps it is also a reaction to change.

AK: That we understand.

Q: Thank you for your interview.

13: The Exobiology Project: Dialog With The Nordic

"If the human race is not ready for an idea then it will not be accepted. The inventor becomes disillusioned and goes away."

—The Nordic

Q: I am opening up dialog with the Nordics and invite one or more Nordics to come and converse with me.

N: This is the Nordic.

Q: Thank you. Would you please consider what is written before to the other races about potential Earth events and we can dialog on this topic?

N: Yes, we are aware of this material.

Q: How would you prefer to begin?

N: We have begun.

Q: The discussion is open to you.

N: When we were first approached by Humans to help them with this problem we refused. We now see that mutual assistance could be beneficial to both races.

We need to come to a place where Humans are aware and concerned about their surroundings. We do not care to come and be where people are not aware of their surroundings. There are many places where Humans do not care for their surroundings.

Q: So, from what you know about Humans and what you know about the Nordics, and what you know about our environment, can you please give us a picture on what is happening and how we can preserve our surroundings. I do not want this to revert to the previous format of question and answer but wish to create a dialog.

N: Understood. We, as the Nordics have no fears that global change will affect us: we can come and go as needed. However, we have a concern for Humans who do not have the abilities that we have and the inborn instinct to travel as we do. There are concerns among Humans that the human race will die out as a result of global warming, in the long run. This is not so. Humans will not die out. Over a long time, many of them will cease but the race will not perish. We understand the melting of the southern and northern ices and we understand the deterioration in air quality, both are unconnected. But Humans forget about the vastness of the Earth. They think only of the small piece of Earth that they occupy. They worry about their limited lives and how these global changes will affect them. They only worry about their own people, their own families, and their own buildings. They do not worry about the remainder of the world.

Q: Some of them do. We are concerned about tsunamis, we are concerned about Earthquakes, and volcanic eruptions that occur in other countries and create disaster. Our country sends aid each time there is a disaster, in the form of monetary and physical assistance. Many of these disasters are closely linked to global warming.

N: We have seen an increase in these events, too, but no greater than they have been in the distant past. There is a natural cyclic order to these events that are evident and Humans know about these events. Humans know that the arctic was once a green land of meadows, birds, and flowers. It was a paradise when the rest of the world was under water. The great lakes that flooded the world remained for a longer period of history than Humans have memory for. As the great seas diminished, the ice returned again to the south and north regions of the Earth. Humans believe, and we have heard them say this, that the melting of the ice will bring great flooding to the land. That is not the case here as the melting is not so severe or over such a long time as the previous melts. Most of the melting will be absorbed by the oceans before the land floods. The oceans are so vast that it will be a long time before the Earth is in danger of flooding.

Q: So, the melting is inevitable but will be absorbed by the oceans. Then why are people so intent on predicting a great flooding of land. Some of the scenarios are that the Gulf Stream will become diverted, that masses of people will first drift south, then north until the north once again become frigid and the south is a desert wasteland.

N: These are extreme predictions from a frightened people. These changes have happened before and look where these changes have taken people. They have lived where they would never have lived before, explored places that they would never have explored, changed in many ways that have made them more intelligent, creative, resourceful and spiritual. No race, whether it is Nordic or Human ever progressed by standing still. Every race progresses by overcoming challenges and obstacles. They learn how to live in different climates, with different wealth, with different tools and possessions. There can be no progress without challenge. Humans often challenge themselves but, from time to time, the climate and the Earth challenge humanity. Look at these challenges as an opportunity to grow as a human race.

Q: How can human races learn to live with these disasters and the events that Global Warming will bring? My perspective is that Humans should learn from previous generations that had a long civilization and survived major upheavals. For example, the industrialization of the United States brought the vast majority of Humans to the coastal regions where there is most danger. My feeling is that there should be a spreading out of these huge, industrialized areas to the safer, inland areas where they can experience less danger from tsunami, hurricanes, flooding, and Earthquake. My other feeling is that Humans need to get back in touch with their intuitive side that would warn them of great danger so that they could avoid such areas. For example, indigenous people and animals know when a tsunami is about to strike and go to higher ground. Teaching people how to intuitively recognize these dangers, and how to react to them, would be beneficial.

N: This would only be beneficial in the short term. There has to be a long term plan for humanity. A plan that would create a mobile, nomadic, race of Humans that would be comfortable in many different environments. It would be these Humans that would survive. They would have instinctual, intuitive abilities to warn of danger but these would only be needed long term, rather than short term. Humans have given up their own sense of danger, alertness, and preparedness by allowing other Humans to tell them when danger is evident and what to do about it. Humans need to take back the responsibility for understanding danger. By giving up this responsibility Humans have only themselves to blame when they get stuck in the middle of a cyclone, or hurricane, or Earthquake.

Q: That sounds a little heavy-handed but it also sounds correct. Humans have given up their responsibility to radio and TV news that tells them how things are. For example, the other day I tried to find a TV news program or computer site that would tell me the current temperature in my town, when I could have set foot outside my front door, experienced the temperature for myself, or read the outdoor thermometer. I became quite frustrated when I could not find a current news program or computer program. Humans have become conditioned to relying on others to tell them the state of the world instead of finding out for themselves.

N: Again, we will say that the air quality and warming are unconnected. There are different mechanisms for both. Both can interact with each other but they are not the cause of each other: air quality does not affect warming and warming does not affect air quality. One hundred years ago, in human history, air quality was much worse and warming was not yet apparent. Warming has continued on a gradual basis but air quality has improved over the hundred years. Air quality is closely related to the use of travel through the air, for the quest to reach the stars. Many human cities are built near air departures and terminals and no account is taken of the amount of Earth's air that is used by these multiple resources. It is a huge amount and deprives the surrounding areas with depleted air and produces dirty air. Nobody is thinking about this or if they do they do not talk about it. The Nordics do not need air travel and do not provide this depletion of air or dirtying of the air.

Q: That is true. In our area we have a commercial airport with planes arriving and leaving at around one-per-minute, there is an air base and at least three private airports. These airports surround the city which lies in a deep valley. I understand that plans to rebuild the airports have been suggested, out in more open areas, but people have resisted this. It would not be convenient or financially sound for people to build these airports away from the big cities.

N: Humans have become lazy and irritable with anything that makes them exert an effort. Humans are physical beings and have to think in physical terms. So, the value of something close by is weighted out to the quality of the air. It would take a special group of Humans to become nomads, to move where optimal conditions would create the most favorable living for Humans. Humans would be able to settle for perhaps two or three generations, then would move on when a consensus indicated that living conditions were not amenable to an excellent way of life. It would take many such groups to create a continuation of existence for Humans once conditions became non-livable in disaster areas. There are plenty of such places on the Earth.

Q: This way of living would be resisted by many people, not only Americans but from other countries. There would be disagreements about traditions and heritage, about usurping others' lands, about land rights and titles. However, I can see how this would work with groups moving away from disaster prone areas such as the Gulf Coast, from flooded coastal areas, from Earthquake prone areas of California and the path of volcanoes. This might be an idea that would be attractive to youth, to a new breed of adventurers and travelers who seek adventure and excitement.

N: There is nothing exciting and adventurous about deciding to live in an area that is safe from disaster. Youth would not be advantageous to do this because of their lack of qualifications and experience. This would have to be undertaken on a scale of a whole town moving to a new location. There would be difficulties but none that could not be overcome. This would save human lives: it would be the correct way to go.

Q: It seems to me that the early American settlers were nomads of this type. Do you advocate modern Americans doing treks like the settlers? It seems like reinventing the wheel. I don't think that becoming neo-nomads would create any better living conditions than we have now, although it would take people out of the way of danger.

N: There is no comparison with the suggested nomad concept and the settlers. The old settlers had no support, such as water and light. Modern nomads would have everything available. And amenities would travel with them. They would be more likely to work with natural amenities such as air, wind, sun, and water.

Q: What about ideas to market environmentally sound business ideas? Would that go a ways to providing answers to some of our current environmental problems? Some of our greatest innovators, such as Dean Kamen, have invented items like gyroscopic scooters and wheelchairs, and simple water filters for developing countries. Yet, none of these inventions seems to have been incorporated into modern American life or abroad. These ideas were lauded as "breakthroughs" when they became known. Now, nobody seems to know much about them. Would the same happen again?

N: Yes, if the human race is not ready for an idea then it will not be accepted. The inventor becomes disillusioned and goes away. Or the ideas are swallowed up into larger ideas by bigger inventors. But that should not stop Humans from creating new things. Humans are creative and imaginative and will always be inventing. But all the inventions will have only a very, very small effect in the bigger picture of global warming. Global warming is a very large effect and the small efforts that Humans make will have very little impact. Global warming may be slowed but not stopped. It is a natural process, a cyclic process and, once, started, cannot be stopped.

Q: Thank you for the dialog.

14: The Exobiology Project: Dialog With The Orbs

"Humans create many solutions but it is not always the most efficient solution that is used to mend a problem."

—The Orbs

Another race that was thought to be amenable to a dialogue was the Orbs. They were found, during their interview, to be able to carry information. This project accesses an available Orb in order to dialogue on the general concerns below, as well as some additional questions specifically for the Orb. These questions concern where the Orbs receive their information, who would we be able to talk to directly, and questions regarding the races from the Pleiades, Sirius and Andromeda, and other races that have interacted with Humans. It would be fascinating to include these and other races, mentioned earlier, in future writing. Lastly, some philosophical questions regarding the evolution of Humans have been asked of the Orbs.

These are the same questions that were asked of the Nordic. A dialogue is requested with the Orbs on how to combine experience and wisdom, technology with empathy, for direction and insight into the coming events.

Q: Welcome Orb and thank you for agreeing to dialogue with us.

O: The concerns outlined are many and complex. Each one has its own path and each one has its own outcome yet interplay with each other.

Q: The Orb uses multiple words for each concept but I am using the one word that best describes what is being conveyed.

O: The warming of the Earth is predictable and planned (?) many millenniums ago. The Earth is a living organism and has cycles of ebb and flow, cooling and heating and other cycles within its shell. The Earth was in a state of equilibrium before Humans. Humans have upset the equilibrium. The Earth was not meant for Humans to occupy. Humans have upset the balance of the Earth and upset its equilibrium. Humans will continue to upset the equilibrium. Humans cannot cry about this effect, they have caused it but they cannot correct it. They have hastened effects which were to take many hundreds of years to achieve. There was a balance to the Earth and this balance can no longer work. It will always be upset and not work as planned.

Q: I have many questions about the planning of these cycles. Can you answer these for me?

O: No. Not at this time.

O: Humans have their own agendas and plans and they do not consider the Earth or its cycles. Humans do not value or understand their own cycles. When Humans first came to the Earth they lived and passed at respectful periods, sometimes in small numbers and sometimes in large numbers. Now Humans do not pass as they should, as they have cycled in the past, and this has upset the equilibrium of the Earth. There are several messages that are needed to be conveyed to Humans.

O: That Humans need to respect the equilibrium of the Earth.

O: They need to learn and understand their own cycles and live and pass accordingly.

O: They must know that they cannot reverse the Earth to its old rhythms and cycles: that this must continue as it has been changed.

O: Humans must learn to live with the changes and adapt their living accordingly.

O: Humans must learn not to meddle in something that has been in effect for longer than Humans have been on the Earth.

O: Humans are greedy and use more of the Earth's resources than they need and do not consider other races.

O: Humans are closed to communication with the other races and do not know what the other races want from Humans although we have been trying to tell you.

O: Humans do not even consider other Humans and their needs.

O: Humans try to change everything and then, when things are in a mess, they cry and try to mend what has been broken. With their limited understanding, Humans think that they can mend anything but there are some things beyond mending and things which must be adapted for. Humans need to understand that living with the Earth's rhythms and cycles is the best way. The cycles of night and day have been altered, the seasons have been altered, even time has been altered by Humans. When basic cycles are changed then the circumstances also need to change and Humans have to adapt to these changes and changed cycles.

O: Humans do not seem to understand that everything revolves around the cycles and rhythms of the Earth itself: that these cycles were put in place for a reason and for a purpose. Meddling with them only causes disaster. Humans have meddled for the past two hundred Human years (which we can estimate) and this has undone millenniums of cycles and rhythms. Now Humans are wondering why the Earth is changing and why

O: Humans are being subjected to disasters and future disasters that are predicted. Humans are not able to connect the many factors that have caused these effects. Humans sort out one problem while, at the same time, they are causing new ones to happen. Humans do not seem to understand that repairing one problem is not the answer; they are just causing new problems. It is very distressing to the other races to see this.

O: The only answer (information) that we have is that Humans stop altogether trying to mend other problems while they are waiting for one problem to be solved. This way they will not confound the problems. Humans create many solutions but it is not always the most efficient solution that is used to mend a problem. Often the solution to mend a problem is used because it entails great financing and people profit, or it creates revenge on another people, or it causes prestige for the person suggesting the solution. If Humans could just use the most efficient solutions regardless of money, revenge or prestige, the problems would get mended. The questions that you have asked at the beginning of this dialogue are meaningless in the bigger view, the longer view, which extends back past Humans and will extend way past Humans in the distant future. That is all that we have to say at this time.

Q: Thanks you. That sounded more like a diatribe than a dialogue but I will pass on the information.

Questions for the Orbs.

Q: Where do the Orbs receive their information, from where and from whom?

The information for this session came from the Orbs, who collected the information from the Elementals, who collected the information from the Void.

Q: Is the Void the same as what remote viewers call the Matrix? (The Matrix in this context is defined by remote viewers as "Something within which something else originates or takes form or develops. A place or point of origin or growth.")

O: It is similar but much more extensive. It does not just include Human information but information for everything, everywhere.

Q: Where might we go directly to dialogue on these issues?

O: The information for any subject can be contained in the same way. However Humans may not be ready to hear, understand, and receive everything that is in the Void. The Void contains much information that the Human mind is unable to understand. Humans pride themselves on their understanding but they have a limited understanding. Humans are growing in understanding but have regressed much in the past several hundred years.

Q: Regarding the races from the Pleiades, from Sirius, and Andromeda, would these races talk directly to us? Are they members of the Confederation?

O: Yes, these races belong to the Confederation but do not always have information that concerns Earth and Humans. There is much interaction between many different species but it does not always concern Humans. Humans would not understand much of it, as they do not understand the other races. As Humans evolve and come to learn more about the other races then more can be understood about these other races. Yes, they can talk directly to Humans and Humans can talk directly to them, through thought, but not everything they say about Humans is complimentary.

Q: Which other races are here on Earth and interacting with Humans?

O: You have talked with many of them. We have been taking messages back and forth about this and how more Humans are now interacting through thought with the races. We cannot tell you more about other races at this time as we would have to leave and come back with this information at another time.

Q: Did the Nordics create the Grays? Are the Grays from Zeta Reticulli?

O: No, the Nordics did not create the Grays and the Grays are not from Zeta Reticulli. The Grays are their own race and are everywhere. The race from Zeta Reticulli is a different race and does not leave its place.

Q: Was there a treaty between the Grays and the government i.e. Eisenhower?

O: NR – No Response.

Q: Please go and find this information for me.

O: Yes there was a treaty which was broken many times. It did not end in recent years, there was no stated ending time but the treaty was broken by Grays and Humans many times. There were many causes. Humans used technology that they said they would not use. Grays collected Humans that they said they would not collect. The treaty was broken again and again. The treaty was put in place but was not understood by either side, or not understood fully so there were mistakes and some of the mistakes were intentional. The treaty is in place, it has not ended but it is not really working.

Q: Have alien races altered the structure of Humans at any time in history?

O: NR.

Q: Please go and find the information.

O: Many different races, over the history of Humans have altered the structure of Humans, especially the Grays as they created hybrids and seeded them back to the Earth. This was done again and again. Some of the races altered Humans and left Earth and never returned.

Q: Are the races watching and waiting for us for when we are able to join the Confederation?

O: NR.

Q: Please go and find the information.

O: The Confederation is unsure of when Humans will be ready as a race to join the Confederation. There are times when the Confederation is happy with

Humans and contemplates Humans joining but there are always Humans breaking even the most basic of Confederation rules and the Human race will not be joining the Confederation in the near future.

Q: Are the climate changes that we are seeing inevitable and what will happen next?

O: Please refer to what we have already written earlier. These cycles and changes are permanent and cannot be remedied. Humans will have to adapt to the changes.

Q: Is all of this change necessary to produce the next evolution of Humans, to take Humans to the next level?

O: Humans are not evolving to any next level. They are at the same level or have regressed to lower levels. Some individuals appear to evolve but they are repressed by Earth's societies unless they produce activities that create wealth, revenge, or prestige for others. The Earth changes will not take Humans to any next level of evolution.

Q: Orbs, thank you for your information.

Follow-Up with the Orbs

"The Hybrids are sent out all over the Universe and we do not track them. Your hybrid descendants could be somewhere out in the Universe"

—The Orb

We thank the Orbs for the following information, for their responses, their patience, and cooperation during this follow-up session. We respect and honor the Orbs. This follow-up session asks the Orbs additional questions, some generated by the previous session, and requests the Orbs to access and relay this information to the researcher.

(We should remember that the Orbs have a unique way of communicating. They are multi-meaning, which is that for every word that they convey, each word has multiple meanings. As mentioned before, interacting with the Orbs is like interacting with a Thesaurus. Therefore, the *closest meaning* to the conveyed word will be written down in italics. If there is any problem with a definition, it will be noted and questioned.)

Some of the current questions focus on a South American woman, Elizabeth Klarer, from the city of Natal, who has since died. She claimed that she had a love affair with a non-Earth race, who took her to Proxima Centauri, where she stayed for four months, before being returned to Earth. We are interested in her story and if it is true.

Additional questions are asked regarding: the planets around Proxima Centauri; the Rall; races that might live on Venus; the feeding of Hybrids by the Grays; and other races that might have bases on Mars.

Q: We are respectfully requesting an available Orb (or Orbs) to travel to the Centauri systems and to other places as necessary, to observe and access information related to the following questions:

Q: Is Elizabeth Clarer's story true: that she had a love affair with a non-Earth race and was taken to Proxima Centauri?

O: Her story was true. She was taken, both by Grays and the race that live on the middle planet of the Centauri A system, the Scholars. The transportation was provided by the Technical race from the larger planet in the A system. The Technical race provides transportation for many races which do not have transportation or the means to manufacture transportation. The Technical race was the race that transported her but the race that brought her to their planet was the Scholar race from the middle planet of the Centauri A system. They have technical knowledge but not sufficient knowledge or resources to build craft.

O: She was taken by force during a Gray encounter. Sometimes, Grays *trade* Humans with other races and sometimes they are taken by force by other races from the Grays. This is not frequent but it does happen. There is an *inquisitiveness* about Humans by the other races. The Technical race was prohibited by the Confederation from taking Humans from Earth but they can trade with other races for Humans.

O: She was not taken to Proxima Centauri but to the middle planet around the Centauri A system. There she developed a relationship with the representative of the Scholar race and developed an *interdependency* with him. That is, she could not return to Earth without his help, so she developed a *relationship* with him. Humans have a term, which we have learned, called the Stockholm Syndrome, where a victim falls in love with their captor and looks to them to provide their safety and survival. This was so with this woman and the Scholar although he treated her well. The Scholar race was interested in her for her intelligence and for her knowledge of Earth as she was well traveled.

Q: Please describe the planets around Alpha Proxima C, also known as Proxima Centauri. Are there birds, deer, fish in the sea, grass, night and day as here are on Earth?

O: The two planets around Proxima Centauri are identical in size, orbit and *constitution.* It could be said that they are *mirror-image twins* of each other. The planets each have two zones. The middle or equatorial zone is dry and barren, much like Earth's middle zone, and the outer zones and wet and *florid*. These areas are abundant with *flora and fauna:* that is life. We have not found information about this but it is possible that the woman was taken for some time to the wetter regions of these planets before transferring to the middle planet of the Centauri A system. Many races stay on these planets for short periods but there is little atmosphere that would sustain races that come from other systems.

Q: Why is this, if there is flora and fauna, would there be oxygen and other gases?

O: There is some oxygen but the planets are high in nitrogen in their atmospheres. Many races cannot live long on these planets. The flora and fauna that survive here have adapted to the atmospheres. There is the equivalent of Earth birds, deer, fish in the waters, grass, night and day but are different in that they are *nitrogen-dependent*. They also look different in terms of size and life cycles. They are smaller than their Earth equivalents.

O: The middle planet around the A sun has a similar constitution, but a higher oxygen content than Earth, although Earth's is lower than the middle planet.

Q: Please describe what the rest areas look like, that the races use on Proxima Centauri.

O: In the dry areas around the equator of the Proxima Centauri planets the rest areas are underground and set into steep rises of land. They are very, very large and *cater* to many races. In the wetter regions, the rest areas are spread out over many *miles* and are on the surface. Artificial atmospheres are generated within both of these types of rest areas. Within these atmospheres, races are free to rest and travel.

Q: What do people who are on Proxima Centauri look like?

O: There are no *indigenous* races on the Proxima Centauri planets. The people that are there are races from many other systems. They do not stay to *habitate* the planets.

Q: What does the architecture look like on Proxima Centauri?

O: Underground, in the dry regions, the architecture takes the form of *bubbles*: rounded spaces that can accommodate craft and the races. These bubble spaces can *coalesce* and form larger spaces when needed. They can be divided to create smaller spaces. They are held by a magnetic force within the matrix of the ground. In the wetter regions, the architecture is varied and can range from simple bubbles, as seen underground, to elaborate *hard* structures of the local Earth, which is a reddish brown. These are all housed within the artificial atmosphere which is held in place by the same magnetic force as the bubbles under the ground. Any race can stay at any region of the planets as there is no one race that owns the planets.

Q: What did this woman herself believe of her experiences?

O: She believed that she had been taken by a *space stranger* who was intent on making her his wife. She believed that she was his wife according to the Scholar's traditions. However, this was not so as the Scholars do not have marriage. She was there to be studied and to be returned. She was very disappointed when she was returned to Earth. She wanted to stay in the Centauri systems but this would have damaged her physically. She always hoped that she would be taken again.

Q: Was this the "love affair of her life" as she believed?

O: This was not a *love affair* in the Human sense. She believed that she was married and thus had no qualms about certain behaviors with the Scholar. However, he was more interested in her Human qualities than *perpetuating his race* with a Human.

Q: Can the Angels communicate with spirits that have passed on? Can they communicate with Elizabeth Klarer?

O: Angels can communicate with spirits of Humans that have passed on, particularly if they have recently passed from the Human form. There comes a time, after passing on, which neither Angels nor other races can communicate with these spirits: they have other things to do and it is against Confederation rules to interfere with their journeys and purposes. This woman has passed on for too long a time for the Angels to communicate with her.

Q: The Zulu are a Human people of South Africa on Earth. Do they have telepathic abilities? It is said that some individuals of that race were witnesses to Elizabeth Clarer's experiences? Can her experiences be verified by contacting these individuals?

O: The Zulu are only one Human race that has telepathic abilities. They have no more telepathic ability than any other race on Earth. The witnesses to her collection and meeting with the Technical race and the Scholar race have since passed on and are no longer able to be contacted.

Q: This woman appeared to know more about extraterrestrial physics than many Earth Humans? Was this true? How did she know so much?

O: Yes. Being with the Scholar she was shown many things that *pertain* to the mind and to the physical universe. Some she was deliberately shown and others she *gleaned* from the Scholar by watching and listening. She was able to retain many new ideas and was able to put together *disparate concepts* to create new ones that were correct.

Q: Was her journey to the Centauri systems to replenish their hereditary stock?

O: No, her journey to these systems was not to replenish their hereditary stock. They have no need for Human DNA. The Scholar and this woman could not have *bred*: they were too different in their *composition.*

Q: Regarding the Technical race on Alpha Centauri A. Do they have a high IQ? Was this the race that brought this woman from Earth to Proxima Centauri? Or was she brought to another of the Centauri system planets?

O: The Technical race does indeed have a High IQ according to Earth standards and measures but the Scholar race has a higher and broader measure. The Technical race commits their intelligence to building craft and other technical equipment. The Scholar race can do both, mental and physical *applications*, although they do not build craft.

Q: Can the Orbs contact Human spirits that have passed on?

O: The Orbs can contact Human spirits but under the same rules as the Angels.

Q: Before we contact the Rall, can the Orbs tell us why the race that currently lives underground on Mars, started to live underground?

O: There were many *successions of assaults* from above the planet. There were many types of assault including large meteors that rained down, *flashes of energy* that bathed the planet, shifts in the orbit of the planet that created weather disturbances. Mars is in the process of a *severe heat age*, the opposite of an Earth Ice Age. This was caused by the periodic tilting of the planet towards the sun. This was precipitated by a large *meteoric bombardment*. Although these catastrophes no longer exist, the Rall have become *accustomed* to living underground.

Q: Do any of the races on Venus, also live underground and did they start living underground for the same reasons as the Rall?

O: There are three races living on Venus and all live underground due to the same problems *encountered* by the Rall. There was a very unstable period of history for the races when many of these *catastrophes* occurred. Two of the races are corporeal, that is they have bodies and one is *ephemeral*.

Q: Does that mean that this race is temporary or transitory?

O: No, it just means that their life cycle is very short and they replicate very quickly compared to other races. They are also non-corporeal.

Q: What "thought gift" could we give the Rall, whose economy and customs appear to be based on gift-giving and gift-receiving?

O: The Rall appreciate beauty and the things that sustain life. As these things cannot be transmitted mind to mind, then information related to beauty and anything life sustaining are valuable.

Q: Could I tell them about the water experiments that are being done on Earth: Dr. Emoto's water experiments?

O: We do not know this but yes that would be acceptable as water is a big part of their *sustainability*.

Q: Regarding the Grays, could you contact them for the following information? We know that the Grays have created Hybrids containing Nordic and Human characteristics, as well as those from other races. Various proportions of the different races were included in these Hybrids. Where are these descendents now? Where are my Hybrid descendents (if any)?

O: The Hybrids are sent out all over the Universe and we do not track them. Your Hybrid descendants could be somewhere out in the Universe.

Q: Could I contact them telepathically?

O: That could be possible.

Q: That is something to think about.

Q: Regarding the Hybrids. What sort of nourishment do the Grays provide for the Hybrids from birth to their placement on Earth or elsewhere? Are they fed in a Mothership? What specific foods do they eat?

O: The Grays *synthesis* food for the Hybrids. They do not have access to Earth foods but know the *composition* of the foods that the Hybrids need. The Grays *tailor* the foods according to the proportions of need of each hybrid. They could not feed them Human food or that of the other races because they could not locate them when away from the Earth. Yes, the *Mother ships* are where the Hybrids are fed; the smaller ships are for collecting and returning Humans and for other tasks. The Hybrids eat a mainly liquid diet as space travel does not always provide the *physical facilities* that are present on Earth.

Q: You mean that they have few bathrooms?

O: Yes, there are other provisions.

Q: Are there several Earth magicians, such as David Blain, who are either from another race or Hybrids? Many of the successful magicians all have darker complexions, straight dark hair, are on the tall, thin side, and have a great deal of self-confidence in what they do. Are they a separate race? (Are they Anaka?)

O: No, these magicians are Human; they are not another race or another species.

Q: Do the Hybrids have a vested interest in Earth, as many of them contain Human DNA? Do the Hybrids know about their genetic roots: are they told?

O: All of the Hybrids know of their genetic or hereditary roots but not specific information about their *sponsors*.

Q: By sponsors do you mean the Humans that provided the DNA?

O: Yes. The Hybrids do not have a vested interest in Earth or any other planet except for exploration and travel.

Q: It has been suggested that the Lyrians and other races have bases on Mars. Is this true?

O: There is no information that shows that the Lyrians ever had a base on Mars although other races such as the Grays and some of the Orange races co-exist from time to time with the Rall. The Lyrians keep very much to their own world.

Q: Many thanks to the Orbs for their service to Humans and for the information that they have conveyed to us.

15: The Exobiology Project: Talking With The Lyrians

(including site visit)

"We cannot predict for Humans. They are too complex."

—The Lyrians

The previous phases of the Exobiology projects focused first on questioning several non-Human races. This brought us into contact with many diverse races including Large Grays, Nordics, Small Grays, the Hooded Reptilians, an Indigo Hybrid, Orbs, Elementals, the Oranges, The Angels (also known as the Smooths), the Record Keeper race, The Gate Keeper race, Light Beings, the Tall Oranges, and the Anaka. The interviews with the Angels, Elementals, Record Keeper, and Gatekeeper have not been included in this record as they are primarily Earth-based.

Following the questioning stage, it was decided to dialogue with some of the races as this might give us a better insight into their mindset. Therefore dialogues were conducted with the Nordics, the Angels and the Orbs. A third phase was then added, that of visiting the actual home worlds of several new races while maintaining our first two phases of questioning and dialogue. The first race to be interviewed in this new phase are the Lyrians from the Lyriad system.

Q: How do the Lyrians describe themselves? How do they travel and interact across the galaxy. How often do they travel and interact?

L: We are an unknown people. We are very private and keep to ourselves. We do not interact with many other races. There is no need. We only communicate if there is a contact such as this one. We do not reach out to other races, there is no need. We have everything that we need and do not need to go to other races for what we need.

Q: Can you describe yourselves, please.

L: We look like many other races; we are taller than many other races and have all the features of many other thinking races.

Q: Can you describe yourselves physically?

L: We are all one tone and some would call it silvery. We have no need of clothing as our skin has all the qualities of clothing. We are all one piece, that is, there are no seams or lines that mark different parts of our body. We have yellow eyes. We do not travel; we stay on our own place. There is no need to travel. We only interact if there is contact from another race. We do not reach out. We do not communicate. There is no need.

Q: In their interactions with Humans, how often does this happen and why is this interaction carried out? For observation? Are they monitors for the Confederation?

L: We do not reach out to Humans. There is contact with Humans when they reach out to us, which is very little. We do not feel that there is anything that we can learn from Humans or that we can teach them. We are a peaceful people and do not fight. We are not monitors for the Confederation or anybody else than ourselves. We do not reach out to other races but we will respond if other races contact us.

Q: Can Lyrians help Humans if the entities are asked? How can Humans ask for help? If they can help us, in what way can we ask for this help?

L: We can only help by responding to your communications and contact. There is nothing we can do to help. There is no way to ask for our help. We do not offer help.

Q: We could learn from your ability to maintain peace.

L: We do not know how to help with this.

Q: What use do the Lyrians make of Earth resources? Do they need these for survival?

L: We do not make use of Earth resources. We have no need. We have everything that we need. We are able to survive without Earth resources. We travel only when necessary.

Q: What would be a necessary reason to travel?

L: To go to a new place that might be useful to us. We travel very few times. We have everything we need. We travel sometimes out of curiosity. We have not traveled to Earth and there is nothing on Earth that we would need. We travel by means of the mind only. We have no resources to do anything else.

Q: Are Lyrians positively or negatively oriented towards Humans?

L: We are neither positively or negatively oriented to Humans. Humans are interesting and the few times that they have contacted us have been interesting but that is all. We do not know much about Humans.

Q: Would you be interested in knowing more about Humans?

L: No, we would not.

Q: Why are Grays interacting with us on a conscious level and not others?

L: We do not interact with the Grays but we do know about them. They send vehicles here from time to time but we turn them away. There is no place for them here. We are very different and do not share their needs. We have our own needs and do not want the Grays to have these resources.

Q: Are there other entities in the Universe? Why, how, and who?

L: There are many entities in the universe and we have had contact with most of them. We do not know about the lives of these entities because we do not ask and they do not say. We keep to ourselves. We are a quiet people. They are too many to tell but we have had mental contact with Humans and physical contact with other Humanoid races but we do not permit them to land or stay.

Q: I am planning a mental visit to your world to observe, would this be in order?

L: It is in order but you cannot stay.

Q: I was not planning on staying: just coming for a short period to observe.

Q: Do the Lyrians have the ability to look into the future?

L: We can look into the future for ourselves. We live a very simple life and do not have many changes in our life, so we can predict most of what will happen to us in the future. We know that some races make predictions. The lives of most races are chaotic, including what we know about Humans, that we do not know how they can predict with any sense of reality. We live an ordered life so we can predict accurately for ourselves. How can Humans and others predict their future when their present is so disorderly? It surely cannot be done.

Q: Are the Lyrians, helping, hindering or ignoring us?

L: We are not doing anything to help or hinder Humans except to interact when we are contacted. Mostly we ignore other races.

Q: To the Lyrians knowledge is the Confederation just of our Galaxy or of the Universe?

L: We know about the Confederation but have no need of it. We are sufficient to rule ourselves and we already live by many of the rules that they offer. They have contacted us and offered us their rules and protection but we do not need it. We have everything we need.

Q: Are the Lyrians, a Galactic or Universal entity?

L: We live in both so we consider ourselves of both. But we are also Lyrians and live in our own system. There are many parts of this system but we all live much the same. We have no need for anything outside the system.

Q: Regarding the Rules of the Confederation – are these also applicable to non-members, such as the need to respect and cooperate with other races?

L: Yes, we would consider that the Confederation rules apply to everybody regardless of whether they belong to the Confederation or not. We live by the rules for ourselves and do not need the Confederation.

Q: Do Lyrians have a sense of who people are? Do they have autonomy or are they on a mission for others, or for another group?

L: We have a sense of who Humans are and that they are life and mainly we do not like them. We would ask to be left alone.

Q: Can I still ask you questions and visit you?

L: Yes. We are no mission for others but feel an obligation to respond when other races contact us.

Q: What questions should Humans ask of the Exobiology entities?

L: You should be asking nothing of us but you may. Humans should ask everything of other races and entities to learn more and become better educated about others outside their system. There is much for Humans to learn.

Q: What should the Exobiology entities be asking of us or want to ask of us?

L: Exobiology entities, those living outside of the Earth could ask about many things. Many races do not have the ability to think and reason like Humans, they do not have a sense of creativity, they do not have a sense of what is humorous, they do not rest like Humans, they do not play like Humans. Humans seem immature to many other races because Humans do these things and act in these ways.

Q: Are there Exobiology entities that are detrimental to Human interests? Are there entities that we should not interact with?

L: There are many entities in many systems that would take Earth as their own and should not be contacted. They are a long way from us and a long way from Earth. We do not know their names or interact with them but we have heard about them. You would not want them to own Earth. Perhaps they have not yet heard about Earth and Humans? That is good. Do not contact them.

Q: Do the Lyrians have a concept of God – of a Universal source?

L: We do not have such a concept of god as Humans do. There are many gods to us, we do not have a concept of a single god and the concept of a god is different for us. Our sky is a god, our land is a god, our food is a god, and each of us is a god. There is no sense to be made of just one god. We do not understand the concept of one god. How could one god cover all the duties of all the gods that we have. It would be impossible.

Q: Do Lyrians need two genders to reproduce like we do? Do they manipulate DNA to reproduce and how?

L: We possess what Humans call DNA but it is very different. It is not spiraled like Human DNA, we know somewhat of Human DNA, ours is just a rope that is coiled within us. There is no need for it to spiral. We do not produce as Humans do. The closest to Human understanding is a concept of budding. From time to time, we bud a new being and when the time is right this budding becomes a new, small person that we look after. We take great care of the budding and the new, small ones. We do not need two genders, we are all one gender, and we all do budding.

Q: Is Earth toxic to Lyrians, i.e. such as ultraviolet is toxic to Grays?

L: We have never been to Earth and have never experienced the atmosphere of Earth. But we would not be harmed by ultraviolet as we have much in our own system.

Q: How do Lyrians sustain themselves, with nutrient baths etc? All entities have the need to survive. Humans need food, water, air, sunshine to exist. Do the Lyrians need these same things or something different? Do they need warmth, shelter, etc. to survive?

L: We keep our needs very simple and have a food that we collect from the ground, where it lands and flourishes. You would call it *a mould, or mat-like fungus*. We have always eaten this and always will continue to eat this. It is everywhere. There is a rain that falls, a watering that comes every day; we do not call it rain, but it is necessary for the food to grow. It brings the seeds of the food and after a day we can go and collect the food from the ground. We can store some but have no need as it replenishes every day. We do not immerse ourselves purposefully in water but we go out when the water falls and become cleansed that way. The light from the sky also cleanses us. We have shelter that is partially above ground and partially below. That is how we survive. The sky, the Earth, the food, the shelter, this is all we need.

Q: Are the Lyrians surprised by the way that our species is socially organized? How does this differ from their social organization? It is hard for us to conceive of a species that is not centrally controlled. We conceive of centralized control as a means to prevent destruction within and between people. Is this process in place in the Lyrians' world?

L: We have no central control; every person here is able to control their lives. We keep lives very simple, so that every person can keep a simple life. There is no need for another to control more than themselves. Yes, we are surprised that other races have a centralized control or that they feel that others need to be controlled. Some races, like Humans lead very complex and chaotic lives and need control. We do not need control.

Q: Is there anything, within the next 25 Earth years (rotations around our Sun) that Humans should be concerned about?

L: We could predict for ourselves what will happen in 25 rotations of our system as our life is very predictable. That is the secret to predictions. The simpler the life, the easier and more accurate the predictions. The more complex the lives, the more difficult the predictions. We cannot predict for Humans. They are too complex.

Q: Do the Lyrians manifest a sense of creativity? Do Lyrians manufacture anything? Do Lyrians have writing, music, or art?

L: We do not have writing but we have music and dance. When we have eaten and been out in the falling water, we feel good. We hum long tunes and we weave between each other outside of our shelter. We do this to feel good and to bond with others. We do not manufacture except to form our shelter from the Earth and falling waters.

Q: Do Lyrians get sick or have illnesses? Do they have any internal or external threats? Do they die? How do they deal with death?

L: Eventually all of us die. We die as well. We begin to reflect the sky and the Earth and then we are ready we go to a place away from the others and wait. We do not follow those that leave so we do not know what happens but they do not come back. We know that when the time is right, and we begin to reflect the Earth and sky, that we will go to the waiting place too.

Q: Are Lyrians surprised that Humans can reach out and communicate with them and how often does this happen? When does this happen and from where? Is this contact carried out telepathically?

L: From time to time Humans connect and communicate with us. We are happy to respond. We do not always know where they are communicating from but it is always mind-to-mind. Many races communicate with us and we respond. After, we communicate with each other and share person to person who communicated and what they told us.

Q: Native American people, such as the Hopi and other races, have described how their ancestors had a connection to races from Sirius and the Pleiades. They claim that these races were their ancestors and that they are still interacting. There is some folklore that these beings were escaping from Sirius and the Pleiades. How did they come to Earth and are they still able to communicate?

L: We have communicated with races from these systems but do not know much about them. We do not record what we learn; it is passed from one to another. So, one group may know about another group and another group knows nothing. They all communicate mind-to-mind as we do not allow other races to land and interact with us.

Q: What potential does Earth have for Lyrians?

L: There is no potential for us except to interact from time to time with a Human. It is interesting to us. We talk about what the other race has asked us and what we told the other race. But it adds complexity to our lives and so the interaction is not remembered or recorded.

Q: Are the Lyrians are interested in our technology?

L: We know about all of the races that have technology but we do not have technology. Whatever we have we gather or make with our hands. We are a simple people. We are not interested in the technology of Earth.
Q: Is there any further information about the other races outlined in the first paragraph that will soon be interviewed? Who can we talk to? Are there dangerous entities?
L: There are many interesting entities and some are dangerous but you may have met some of these already. Use your own judgment. We do not recommend talking to anybody. If they are interested in talking with you, they will. If they are dangerous, you will soon know as you talk to them. That is all we can tell you.
Q: Thank you.

Following is a dialogue opportunity for the Lyrians. The focus of the dialogue concerns some issues relating to Humans and Earth.

Dialogue With the Lyrians

L: These are things happening in your world and have no relevance to us. We maintain a very simple life so nothing changes. The temperature remains stable; there are no variations in the temperature or of the falling water. The food continues to grow and we lead a very simple life. We have no need for the complexities that beset Earth and cause such widespread fear and change. It is our thought, after discussing these things with others, that Humans who contact us want several things. They want us to change their world for them. They want to come and visit us. They want to have what we have but when they learn that we do not have anything they leave us alone. Humans are often of one mind that they look to others to solve their problems when they have the very answers to their own problems.
Q: We do live in a difficult and complex world and one that is constantly changing. These changes are not always of our choosing or making but Humans have had to and continue to adapt to these changes. Humans, however, do tend to complicate their lives and often take the complex route over a simpler one. Humans seek diversity, change and growth and would find your lifestyle very different. It is true that the younger civilizations such as North America and the Australians are change-seekers while the older civilizations, for example the nomads and some peoples of Africa, live very simple, unchanging lives. Even if Humans lived very simple lives, there would still be climate and weather changes that we would still have to cope with.

L: That is true from what we have observed in our contact with Humans. It is possible to choose a simpler life style but it is also true that Humans would not be content with our lifestyle. It is very much the same all the time: we are not ambitious, we do not seek change and the few contacts that we have with others offer us enough interest. We do not wish to become involved in Human problems. We do not have any solutions or answers.

Q: If you have contacted other races, have they had similar atmospheric problems and how have they managed them?

L: There have been other races with similar problems but no race or world is identical. It would seem that Humans have had enough time living on the Earth to adapt and not have to answer every problem. We do not have the answers. We could tell you a hundred different stories of how other races handled their problems but none would be suitable for Earth. We do not know what to tell you. All we can say is make life simpler for all Humans and your problems will become simpler too.

Q: How could we make out life simpler? We could not make our lives as simple as the Lyrians but have you any suggestions?

L: We do not know what to say to make Human lives simpler. You could perhaps eat one food, or live simpler, or stay in one place but what we know of Humans this would not work. Humans like variety, to travel, to seek out new experiences and to make new decisions. This would not work for us and our life would not work for Humans. We are happy with how we live and do not want to change. Humans always are looking for change. Perhaps less change would be less of a problem.

Q: Would it be possible to make contact again at another time to talk with the Lyrians?

L: It would. We are welcome to contact with all races and will interact mind-to-mind but we cannot have any other race visit or stay. We cannot allow that.

Q: Thank you.

Site Visit

The home site of the Lyrians was mentally visited and the following perceptions were made. The location was very flat with just a few rounded rises in the landscape. The sky was yellowish with a faint sun or moon visible as if behind a haze. It was not a distinct, bright orb but a faint circle as if it was behind clouds. The atmosphere smelled sweet and *muggy* as if of a high humidity. The ground was composed of a solid white substance. It was not sand or gravel but felt and crumbled like plaster of Paris. Scattered around were small patches of a substance that resembled cooking pancakes when they are just beginning to get to the bubbly stage. They were of a lighter Gray color against the whiteness of the landscape. I nudged one with my foot and they did not crumble but just creased up into ridges.

I asked to see a Lyrian and a figure emerged that was difficult to look at. The whole humanoid body was thinner and taller than ours and sheathed in a metallic coating that reflected the light. There was no head covering and the flesh that was exposed was a pale white. They did indeed have yellow eyes with a vertical cat-like slit. The demeanor was calm and relaxed but wary. The Lyrian stood at the entrance to one of the rounded shapes and as I walked over to the site, the Lyrian disappeared underground.

I followed down a slope, through a half rounded entrance, into a much larger underground space. I expected to see furniture but there was none. Around the walls of the space were ledges, three tiers high, and a flattened white floor of the same substance as on the surface. There was only one space. The Lyrian stood back against one wall and while welcoming me to observe his space was still wary. Due to the Lyrians height the roof was perhaps about twelve feet high and the space about eighteen feet long in an oval shape. There were no doors or windows or other features. The Lyrian height was higher than the three tiers so was perhaps about eight feet tall and much thinner than Humans.

There were no cooking facilities or storage of any kind. I noted that the Lyrian did have a mouth and a vestige of a nose. I asked the Lyrian to open his mouth and I observed hard ridges, no teeth. There were no bathrooms so I presumed that the fungal mats produced very little waste.

There were no dressing rooms or changes of clothes. The Lyrians appeared to have only the one metallic-looking covering. I asked to see a budding Lyrian but there were none available. I asked to see an elder that was beginning to reflect the Earth and sky but there were none available. I asked to see a Lyrian dance but the Lyrian was alone. I asked him to hum but I could not hear him. The one Lyrian appeared to have been elected to show me around. I do not know if he was the one that I questioned and dialoged with. There was nothing else to see so I concluded the site visit and thanked the Lyrian for his courtesy.

16: The Exobiology Project: Talking With The Duvel

(including site visit)

"There is a wide void between what Humans consider scientific, emotional, spiritual, or evidence. They are all the same thing!"

—The Duvel

Since January of 2006, the previous phases of the Exobiology projects focused first on questioning several non-Human races. This brought us into contact with many diverse races including Large Grays, Nordics, Small Grays, the Hooded Reptilians, an Indigo Hybrid, Orbs, Elementals, the Oranges, The Angels (also known as the Smooths), the Record Keeper race, The Gate Keeper race, Light Beings, the Tall Oranges, and the Anaka.

Following the questioning stage, it was decided to try and dialogue with some of the races as this might give us a better insight into their mindset. Therefore dialogues were conducted with the Nordics, the Angels and the Orbs. A third phase was then added, that of visiting the actual home worlds or locations of several new races while maintaining our first two phases of questioning and dialogue. Several new races have been chosen: the Zeta Reticulii, other races potentially from Aldebaran, Sirius, the Pleiades, the Andromeda Galaxy, the Lyrians, and now the Duvel who may have been influential in shaping Human history.

Q: How do the Duvel describe themselves? How do they travel and interact across the Galaxy? How often do they travel and interact?

D: We consider ourselves the most mobile and traveled of all the races. We are everywhere. We travel and interact with Humans as well as many other races. We are present on Earth in great numbers. Of all the races we most resemble Humans and have been here for a very long time. We are not all of one appearance. Some of us are tall and some of average height. None of us are small. We have olive complexions and many people do not know which race we are from. Some think that we are Native American, or Spanish, or other olive-skinned races. We are not Celtic-looking or very dark skinned. We live normal lives on Earth but think of ourselves as a very distinct race. However, we would never reveal to Humans that we are our own race.

Q: Do you also call yourselves the Wingmakers, as some say?

D: No, we call ourselves the Duvel. This is a very old word that has many origins and meanings for us.

Q: I have never heard the word Duvel before.

D: That is because we do not share it.

Q: You have shared it with me.

D: Perhaps it is time. There are many people contacting us and perhaps it is time to say who we are. It is not time to reveal ourselves but perhaps time to let people know that we are here.

Q: In their interactions with Humans, how often does this happen and why is this interaction carried out? For observation? Are they monitors for the Confederation?

D: We interact with Humans all the time, on every level, in every profession, at every strata of Human life. We live with Humans but do not consider ourselves Human. We do not belong to the Confederation although there are many of us living outside of the Earth.

Q: Have I ever met one of the Duvel?

D: I am sure that have, perhaps many.

Q: How many of you are there on the Earth?

D: There are perhaps 5% to 10% of the Earth's inhabitants but we are scattered all over and less in some areas and more in others.

Q: Why do you interact with Humans?

D: We have a role of being helpful whenever we can. We aid Humans whenever possible. We are available for Humans but not all Humans are there for us. Because of our olive skin we have been the victims of hate and prejudice. We are mistaken for other races. We are not tolerated in some communities of the Earth, including North America.

Q: How long has your race been interacting with Humans?

D: For many thousands of years.

Q: Were the Duvel responsible for helping Humans develop and grow as a sentient species?

D: We did and continue to do so. It was not a one-time thing that we interacted, we continue to interact.

Q: Can the Duvel help Humans if the entities are asked? How can Humans ask for help? If they can help us, in what way can we ask for this help?

D: We do help Humans if they need help but we use our judgment when Humans ask for our help. We do not help everybody and we do not help with everything. There is a judgment made. You will find many of us in the helping professions, in volunteering, and in humanitarian efforts. We often use our own judgment as to when to help Humans.

Q: What use do the Duvel make of Earth resources? Do they need these for survival?

D: We use Earth's resources, the same as Humans do. We own houses, run businesses, work for other people, drive cars, have children, the same as Humans. But we are a completely different race living alongside Humans.

Q: This surprises me.

Q: Are the Duvel positively or negatively oriented towards Humans?

D: We are very positively oriented towards Humans and would do everything we can to help Humans. We have always been positively oriented towards Humans, from the very beginning.

Q: When was the beginning?

D: We have no conscious memory of it but we have glimmerings of a time when we were there at the beginning for Humans. We have no clear recollection of it.

Q: Why are Grays interacting with us on a conscious level and not others?

D: The Grays have their own agenda and their own purpose and we do not interfere. The Grays have been around almost as long as we have but came slightly after us. We stay away from the Grays and they leave us alone.

Q: Are there other entities in the Universe? Why, how, and who?

D: There are many entities in the universe and you have been interacting with them.

Q: How do you know this?

D: Because we know.

Q: That makes me a little nervous.

D: There is no need to be, we know most of what is going on. We know for example that your colleague has a worrying pain around his middle, but it is nothing to be worried about.

Q: Do the Duvel have the ability to look into the future?

D: We do not have the ability to predict except on historical information. We use logic as well as emotion and are able to see many things that Humans do not see. Some Humans just operate on logic, others operate just on emotion and they create problems for themselves. We have a balance of logic and emotion. Humans need to become more balanced between logic and emotion and that way they could predict for themselves.

Q: If asked would the Duvel, look at our future?

D: No, that would not be necessary for Humans as they go ahead with their future direction anyway, regardless if they know the outcome.

Q: Are the Duvel helping, hindering or ignoring us?

D: We are here to help on any level that Humans may need us but we do use our own guidance to decide where and when we will help. We do not always do what Humans ask and we often do things that Humans ask us not to do. We are our own people.

Q: To the Duvel have knowledge of the Confederation: is the Confederation just of our Galaxy or of the Universe?

D: Even though we are not part of the Confederation, we know of them. There are many Confederations throughout the universe. They mostly all have the same rules which are unchanging. We keep to our own rules, which are very similar to the Confederations. We rule ourselves and do not need the Confederation to rule us.

Q: Are the Duvel a Galactic or Universal entity?

D: The Duvel are considered universal, in that we are everywhere. We use our judgment where we need to be and avoid some places where we do not need to be. There are some places where we have completely removed ourselves.

Q: Would you ever completely remove yourselves from Earth?

D: This question has arisen many times during our stay and there have been times when we have almost left but some have stayed and continued. It is possible that under adverse conditions most of us could leave but always a small number would be left behind.

Q: Regarding the Rules of the Confederation – are these also applicable to non-members, such as the need to respect and cooperate with other races?

D: All the rules of the Confederation apply to all, regardless of whether they are members of the Confederation or not. We are not members but we still go by the rules. There are some, such as Humans, who do not go by the rules of the Confederation. Part of our goal is to help Humans go by the rules. They would be happier and more productive.

Q: Do the Duvel have a sense of who people are? Do they have autonomy or are they on a mission for others, or for another group?

D: We do have a sense of who people are, we have lived with Humans for many thousands of years. We do have autonomy and are not on a mission for others. We only answer to ourselves. We do not answer to any other group.

Q: What questions should Humans ask of the Exobiology entities?

D: Humans should be asking questions such as: How can we use all aspects of our selves: not just our logic, or our emotion, or our sense of self; and how can Humans become more balanced? There is a wide void between what Humans consider scientific, emotional, spiritual, or evidence. They are all the same thing!

D: Humans have not come to that understanding yet and create great divides between these ways of being. When Humans can realize that all of these ways of knowing are the same way of knowing, then Humans will have advanced. That is what Humans should be asking. How can Humans come to this point of understanding?

Q: What should the Exobiology entities be asking of us or want to ask of us?

D: We do not need to ask anything of Humans because we already know. We have ways of knowing that Humans have not been using for many thousands of years.

Q: Is one of the ways through telepathy?

D: Yes, that is one way but there is also a sharing of feeling between people, of sharing electrical fields, of sharing light fields and sharing energetic fields. Humans do not yet know these things. Humans are just beginning to re-understand these ways of knowing.

Q: Are there Exobiology entities that are detrimental to Human interests? Are there entities that we should not interact with?

D: You have already encountered some of them and it is wise to stay away, not that they would physically harm you but their presence would prevent you from interacting with other races.

D: There are races that would never come into the presence of some of the more dangerous entities. If the dangerous entities were welcomed in, Humans would never get the opportunity to encounter some other interesting races.

Q: Do the Duvel have a concept of God – of a Universal source?

D: We do have a concept of one god but it is not the "old man in the sky" concept of Humans. We laugh when we hear and see this. For example, Human's copying of the "old man in the sky" by the installation of a Pope on Earth. He is just a Human and could never come as god. Our concept of god is shown by groups of people, the energy that they develop and use, rather than one Human who is set apart as a leader or spiritual guide.

Q: Do the Duvel need two genders to reproduce like we do? Do they manipulate DNA to reproduce and how?

D: We do have DNA and we do produce in the same way as Humans. Our DNA is very similar to Humans except for a few differences. To a cursory look, our DNA would be identical to a test as Humans. We know much more sophisticated ways of testing the DNA and other inherent markers that Humans presently know.

Q: Is Earth toxic to the Duvel i.e. such as ultraviolet is toxic to Grays?

D: Earth is no more toxic to the Duvel than it is for Humans. Like Humans we cannot tolerate excesses of ultraviolet or other toxic light or chemicals that the Earth produces. We are not like other races; we can tolerate all the things that Humans can tolerate. We do have more energy than Humans; we are more driven and accomplish more.

Q: How do the Duvel sustain themselves, with nutrient baths etc? All entities have the need to survive. Humans need food, water, air, sunshine to exist. Do the Duvel need these same things or something different? Do they need warmth, shelter, etc. to survive?

D: We eat the same food, we live in the same houses, and live the same lifestyles as Humans. We do try to eat "clean" foods or natural foods more often than Humans, and we stay conscious of what our bodies are telling us.

Q: Are the Duvel surprised by the way that our species is socially organized? How does this differ from their social organization? It is hard for us to conceive of a species that is not centrally controlled. We conceive of centralized control as a means to prevent destruction within and between people. Is this process in place in the Duvel world?

D: As a race the Duvel are not centrally organized but living with Humans we have to live and abide by Humans rules. There is a Human need for control and management that we do not have. We have developed a personal ethic which means that we do not need to control and manage ourselves as a group. Centralized organization has never been a concept of Duvel life. We manage ourselves individually.

Q: Is there anything, within the next 25 Earth years (rotations around our Sun) that Humans should be concerned about?

D: The same as the last 25 years!

Q: Do the Duvel manifest a sense of creativity? Do the Duvel manufacture anything? Do the Duvel have writing, music, or art?

D: The Duvel are extremely creative and are singers, dancers, musicians, artists, and writers but you will not find the Duvel in any of the creative professions. We integrate our talents and creativity into our daily lives. That is the way of the individual Duvel.

Q: Do the Duvel get sick or have illnesses? Do they have any internal or external threats? Do they die? How do they deal with death?

D: The Duvel rarely get sick and generally die of age like Humans. The Duvel do not have many internal or external threats. We avoid activities that Humans need to feel that they are alive such as sky diving, roller coasters, or fast cars. We already know that we are alive! We do not need any of those activities to justify our existence.

Q: Are the Duvel surprised that Humans can reach out and communicate with them and how often does this happen? When does this happen and from where? Is this contact carried out telepathically?

D: No, it is no surprise as we communicate with Humans in this way all the time. Frequently, though, it is one-sided. They communicate with us and we do not respond or we communicate with them and they do not respond. From time to time we correspond both ways. It is not usual for a two-sided communication. Very few Humans know how to communicate this way.

Q: Native American people, such as the Hopi and other races, have described how their ancestors had a connection to races from Sirius and the Pleiades. They claim that these races were their ancestors and that they are still interacting. There is some folklore that these beings were escaping from Sirius and the Pleiades. How did they come to Earth and are they still able to communicate?

D: It is true that the native people's had communication with visitors to the Earth but most of these races no longer visit or interact with Humans. The races that communicated with these early peoples were not their ancestors but they were their teachers.

Q: What potential does Earth have for the Duvel?

D: The Earth has great potential for the Duvel as this is our home too and we will do what we can to protect our home. I understand that you also have a dialogue for us and we will tell you our thoughts there.

Q: You sound as if you share thoughts with all the other Duvel or do you share between groups?

D: We share between groups but the groups also share information between themselves so, soon, all Duvel know information that one knows. We have no goal except to survive and assist Humans.

Q: Are the Duvel interested in our technology?

D: We are only interested in Human technology in that it assists Humans to grow and develop and not kill themselves as a group. Otherwise we have no interest in technology.

Q: Is there any further information about the other races outlined in the first paragraph that will soon be interviewed? Who can we talk to? Are there dangerous entities?

D: We have covered this before. You are on a good path to talking to entities that are currently, or who have in the past, communicated and interacted with Humans.

Q: Thank you. Following is a dialogue opportunity for the Duvel. The focus of the dialogue concerns some issues relating to Humans and Earth, which are outlined in the Preamble to the Dialogue (also asked of the other races).

Dialogue with the Duvel

D: We, the Duvel, are not the people to be asking about remedying the Earth's problems. It is about time Human's stood up and took responsibility for their own problems without asking other races to provide insight and assistance in their problems. Our view of the problems outlined above is as follows:

D: These are basically cyclic in nature and will proceed with or without Human intervention and will proceed how they will;

D: Humans have caused an extension of these problems and they know how they caused the problems to become more severe, so all they need do is reverse what they have been doing; and

D: Humans, over the millennia have proven to be resourceful, creative, resilient, adaptive, capable and inventive. Whatever will be thrown at them, Humans will survive. And along with them will be the Duvel and many other races. Don't act so helpless!

Q: Thank you. If the Duvel exist elsewhere in the universe, may I do a site visit?

D: Yes.

Q: I must ask this. Are you Humans masquerading as the Duvel?

D: No.

Site Visit

The site that was visited as another location of the Duval was very, very green, even the water and the sky were green. Around the trunks of what would be trees and the stems of plants were bands of shiny, stone-like studs, like marcasite. The bands reflected back the green light. There were multiple paths weaving to and fro between the greenery, with a white, shiny substrate beneath. I looked up and realized that the green sky was in fact a roof overhead. The whole surface was covered with a green algae and the water was filled with the same green algae. I could not find a door or window to see through so I bilocated outside.

Here was the extreme opposite of what was inside the covered enclosure. The outside was burned black, stone with the same white paths. There was no green, no water, no plant life, and no algae. I did not see any life outside of the enclosure. The sky was a pale blue/Gray but no clouds, no birds, and no life.

I bilocated back inside the enclosure, to look for the Duvel. I saw the Duvel, as quiet shapes standing aside behind the foliage. They stood quietly, as if allowing me to see them but not to interact with them. They were shut off from me telepathically. They had clothing but it was neither Earthlike nor alien, just close coverings. They stood and waited, then disappeared into the background. They appeared as the Duvel described themselves; tall, thin, olive-toned, intelligent-looking, dark, straight hair, narrow rather than round eyes, long thin fingers, and decidedly Human looking. They had no facial movements while I looked at them and they did not talk to each other. I thanked them and returned here.

Q: I thank and respect the Duvel for answering my questions and for allowing me to visit one of their locations.

17: The Exobiology Project: Talking With The Sirians

(including site visit)

"We think of ourselves as a very old race, we are the old masters of the universe."

—The Sirians

A third phase was then added, that of visiting the actual home worlds of several new races while maintaining our first two phases of questioning and dialogue. Several new races, which might be interviewed, are potential races from the Orion system, and the Nurobean race. Some additional questions are what do they do to survive and what do they do for pleasure? This project was going to focus on the Nurobian (or Nurobean) race but no response was perceived from this group. They are either non-living or non-communicative. Instead, the race of beings from the Sirius system was contacted for this session.

Q: How do the Sirians describe themselves? How do they travel and interact across the galaxy. How often do they travel and interact?

S: We think of ourselves as a very old race, we are the old masters of the universe. That is how we perceive ourselves. We are not old-looking, in the Earth sense, as we do not age quickly, but look quite new to the other races. We have been in the cosmos a very long time.

Q: Were you around when the early Earth Humans were beginning?

S: Yes, and we interacted with them as a father would. We gave guidance and reassurance, we taught your fathers about light and heat and energy.

Q: Did you teach them how to use fire?

S: No, we just gave them the ideas of light and heat and energy and they worked it out themselves. We did not give them any actual abilities or skills; we just gave them the ideas.

S: We travel all of the time but have not visited Earth for a long time. We have other, more interesting places to go. We may come back to visit Earth if there is enough interest among the fathers. We travel with craft that we design and build. We can travel very great distances.

Q: You do not travel Out-of-the Body like the Nordics?

S: No, we do not have that ability. We are very conventional and stay with things that work for us. We used to think that everything had to keep advancing but there comes a time when everything is as it should be and we are happy with that way things are, then we stop trying to make new things. We consider ourselves a satisfied race as we do not have to continually strive to make new things, go to different places doing different things; we only do what makes us happy.

Q: In their interactions with Humans, how often does this happen and why is this interaction carried out? For observation? Are they monitors for the Confederation?

S: We used to interact with Humans and gave them many things, as a father would do, but then we left the Humans on their own. It seems that Humans are still striving and wanting new things and have not yet settled into that steady state of happiness that we have found. We only interacted to share some of what we had learned. We have not visited Earth and Humans for a long time. We may do so in the future. We are not monitors for the Confederation. There is no need for us to do this. They get everything they need from the Orbs.

Q: Can the Sirians help Humans if the entities are asked? How can Humans ask for help? If they can help us, in what way can we ask for this help?

S: We cannot help Humans in this respect. We visited with Humans and have told them what we had learned. Humans have taken some of this learning and applied it but the learning to be happy and satisfied has not yet been learned.

Q: What use do the Sirians make of Earth resources? Do they need these for survival?

S: The Sirians have no need of Earth resources. We are able to get what we need in the way of minerals and nutrition from our own system. Earth was only a way-station and an exploration. We have a duty to give concepts and ideas wherever we travel so that progress is maintained in the different galaxies but we have no need to return. We can interact mind-to-mind but this is usually with just one Sirian mind and one other mind. We do not share what we perceive with others like other races.

Q: Are the Sirians positively or negatively oriented towards Humans?

S: We are positively oriented towards Humans as a father would be to his children. We are interested when one of the races that we have connected with contacts us later. We can then "glean" other information not spoken.

Q: Does that mean that while we are in communication you can access other information from my mind that is not related to what we are talking about?

S: Yes.

Q: Why are Grays interacting with us on a conscious level and not others?

S: The Grays have always communicated with and contacted Humans. The Grays are our children also. We taught them many of the things that they know and brought them to Earth to interact with Humans. We have done this with many races, introduced them to each other.

Q: Are there other entities in the Universe? Why, how, and who?

S: From your knowledge you have been in contact with many races but have only a partial knowledge of these races. It is like receiving a small document from a race but not knowing all about that race. We cannot tell you all the races, there are too many to tell about.

Q: Do the Sirians have the ability to look into the future?

S: We do not look into the future. We only assess what is going to happen from what we know already. It is a safer way than trying to look at what might happen. Humans are always wanting to know what will happen in the future instead of being satisfied with what they have had and what they have now.

Q: Are the Sirians helping, hindering or ignoring us?

S: We have helped Humans in the past and from this knowledge that we have Humans they will have to find their own path and future. Humans are striving and making life much more difficult for themselves than it need be. We, the Syrians have found ways to be content with what we have.

Q: Do the Sirians have knowledge of the Confederation; is the Confederation just of our galaxy or of the universe?

S: We have our own Confederation in our system and every system has its own Confederation. Sometimes these Confederations overlap in jurisdiction but they never meet and never intrude on another's jurisdiction.

Q: Are the Sirians a Galactic or Universal entity?

S: We consider ourselves in many ways: we are local, we are galactic and we are universal, as we travel to many different part of the void.

Q: Regarding the Rules of the Confederation – are these also applicable to non-members, such as the need to respect and cooperate with other races?

S: We follow all of the Confederation rules which are mostly the same throughout all of the Galaxies. We would expect even those who are not in the Confederation to respect those same rules, they make sense to everybody.

Q: Do the Sirians have a sense of who people are? Do they have autonomy or are they on a mission for others, or for another group?

S: We only have a responsibility to ourselves, to make ourselves happy, to impart our knowledge to other races, but we have no responsibility after that.

Q: What questions should Humans ask of the Exobiology entities?

S: Humans are ever questing after new knowledge, new weapons, and new technology. They should be asking about what can make them happy and contented? They should be asking other races how they can achieve happiness and be content with what they have.

Q: What should the Exobiology entities be asking of us or want to ask of us?

S: Different races have different requirements of Earth and Humans. The Grays have their own requirements, which you have found. Other races use the Earth for mineral resources. We have no requirements of Earth or Humans and have nothing to ask.

Q: Are there Exobiology entities that are detrimental to human interests? Are there entities that we should not interact with?

S: There are many races that are detrimental to Humans and one particularly to Humans who are focusing their mind on other minds in the galaxy. These are called The Spikes. They travel very fast, very swiftly through the void and can be detrimental to Humans and to other races.

Q: Have I encountered The Spikes yet?

S: No, you would know if you had.

Q: Do the Sirians have a concept of God – of a Universal source?

S: We have no concept of a Universal source of knowledge. Yes, we help other races with information but we are not God. There is no universal source that we know as God.

Q: Do the Sirians need two genders to reproduce like we do or do they manipulate DNA to reproduce and how?

S: We are not composed of DNA as Humans are. We are a different composition and do not die as Humans die, we persist. That way we do not lose any memory or abilities that have to be relearned. The human way of replenishing is wasteful as it takes many years for a new being to acquire the knowledge that the older ones have. It is better to persist and retain all knowledge and memory.

Q: Is Earth toxic to the Sirians i.e. such as ultraviolet is toxic to Grays?

S: Nowhere in the universe is toxic to us, we can shield and protect ourselves from most damaging elements on most of the planets. Those that we cannot shield ourselves we do not visit.

Q: How do the Sirians sustain themselves, with nutrient baths etc? All entities have the need to survive. Humans need food, water, air, sunshine to exist. Do the Sirians need these same things or something different? Do they need warmth, shelter, etc. to survive?

S: We do none of these things. Our ways are far too different to explain to Humans.

Q: Are the Sirians surprised by the way that our species is socially organized? How does this differ from their social organization? It is hard for us to conceive of a species that is not centrally controlled. We conceive of centralized control as a means to prevent destruction within and between people. Is this process in place in the Sirians world?

S: We are not organized as Humans are organized. We are mainly autonomous but we do abide by the rules. Mainly we rule ourselves and are happy with ourselves and with others. We do not have to have others decide for us, we can decide ourselves.

Q: Is there anything, within the next 25 Earth years (rotations around our Sun) that Humans should be concerned about?

S: NR

Q: Do the Sirians manifest a sense of creativity? Do the Sirians manufacture anything? Do the Sirians have writing, music, or art?

S: We think of ourselves as logical and content. Writing, music, art are for others to enjoy. We do not need to produce things for others to enjoy, we satisfy ourselves. We do not manufacture anything except our means of travel and these are utilitarian and plain. Humans seem to be constantly producing things for others to enjoy and a disappointed when others do not get the same level of enjoyment as the maker. We do not strive to make other Sirians happy, only ourselves, and then everybody is happy and content.

Q: Do the Sirians get sick or have illnesses? Do they have any internal or external threats? Do they die? How do they deal with death?

S: We do not have illness or threats, we do not get sick and die, we persist.

Q: Are the Sirians surprised that Humans can reach out and communicate with them and how often does this happen? When does this happen and from where? Is this contact carried out telepathically?

S: No, we are not surprised, many have reached out to us and we respond each time. We are not required to respond but consider many races our children and still need help.

Q: Native American people, such as the Hopi and other races, have described how their ancestors had a connection to races from Sirius and the Pleiades. They claim that these races were their ancestors and that they are still interacting. There is some folklore that these beings were escaping from Sirius and the Pleiades. How did they come to Earth and are they still able to communicate?

S: We did come and help many of the first people of Earth and these memories have persisted in human memory for many centuries. We came before the Hopi and other races were gathered into their own groups. We have very early people concepts and help.

Q: What potential does Earth have for the Sirians?

S: None.

Q: Are the Sirians interested in our technology?

S: We are not interested in Earth technology; we have our own in the form of our craft and need nothing else. It is discriminatory of Humans to think that all races are wanting Earth technology, which is yet very undeveloped. It is like a child holding up a toy to a parent and asking if the parent wants the toy, the same as the child wants the toy.

Q: Is there any further information about the other races outlined in the first paragraph that will soon be interviewed? Who can we talk to? Are there dangerous entities?

S: We have told you about a dangerous entity and you know others.

Q: What do you do to survive and what do you do for pleasure?

S: We do not have to do anything to survive, we just persist. Our pleasure is to persist.

Q: Thank you. Following is a dialogue opportunity for the Sirians.

Dialogue with the Sirians

S: We have nothing to dialog. We are content and happy with ourselves. Humans appear to be never happy with themselves or with others, or the world in which they live. They are constantly seeking change although they do not like change. They damage their world then expect others to come and manage the damage. We would rather stay away and let Humans manage their own world and their own problems. This is a wise thing for a parent. We hope that Humans will eventually learn from us to be happy and content.

Q: Thank you. If the Sirians exist elsewhere in the universe, may I do a site visit?

S: Yes.

Site Visit

It was very difficult to visit the Sirian home world. I could get so far, and then all that could be perceived was a thick mist. Perhaps this was a defense of sorts to prevent intrusion from other races. I tried penetrating the mist but seemed to get turned around and directed back. There did not seem to be a way to get through these defenses. I tried going around, going above and under but to no avail. The Sirians do not appear to welcome visitors to their system, even though they gave permission.

Follow-Up

We would like to thank the Sirians for all of their responses and cooperation. We would also like to say that we honor and respect the Sirian race. As a second follow-up to the primary interview, several, additional questions were proposed.

Q: Humans do not persist, they die and Human memory is not continued within that individual. If there is life of the Human spirit after death, what happens to that spirit? Does it just live as a spirit and how can it relate to a Human who is still alive?

S: We also honor and respect Humans and will now refer to Humans and Earth on a level with Sirians. Humans prefer to live in a temporary world.

Q: What does that mean?

S: Humans prefer to live in a world in which they make everything temporary, they are always looking to the next change, the next move, the next meeting with other Humans. They do not live as if the world was permanent. It has persisted for millions of years. There have been changes but not all at once and not in the same place. Humans react as if all of the changes will occur all at once and all in the same place. Humans thus create a state of impermanence for themselves and others. Rather than enjoying what they have now, Humans are constantly looking to see what is coming, including being in the spirit world.

S: Humans, to be truly happy, need to live in the present and not be so consumed with the past and the future. There is always a need to make some plans for the future but not to make it the total focus of their lives. Yes, Humans continue to persist on different levels that are non-corporeal, after the death of the physical body and all of their memories and skills persist. When the Human chooses to re-enter the Human body, there is a taboo in most societies about past memories being present. The Human condition is engineered for new information and children are taught set patterns that exclude what Humans have already learned. There can be a two-way communication between Humans who are living on this level and Humans who are living on other levels. Bonds of family and friendship facilitate such communication. .

Q: Does the Human spirit become re-established into another Human, another life-form on Earth, or a life-form in the universe?

S: The choice is for the Human to make. Humans can become anything they want, when they leave the Human body. It is comparable to being Out-of-the-Body while the Human is living in the Human body. When a Human goes Out-of-the-Body they can become anything they want: another Human, an Earth animal or another life-form outside of the Earth. Usually this is a temporary state and eventually the Human has to return to their corporeal body. In the spirit state, the Human can also become whatever they choose and, if they also choose, they can shift their energy to become that choice in a corporeal body. If the Human does not choose to become corporeal they can stay in the spirit state.

Q: Regarding the concept of God – is there a universal energy force throughout the universe? Is there some Universal Intelligence guiding the universe? What is the Sirian's connection to such a Universal Energy or Intelligence?

S: There is a state, that is difficult to describe, that is in all of us, including Sirians. It is energy, a flux, an intelligence, that permeates the universe and also permeates us. That is what we think of in the Human terms of a God. This flux allows all beings, whether Human or Sirian or other, to manufacture events and many other things that are needed. So, if a Human has a great fear of coming future disasters, they can use the flux to create a state of non-disaster. This places them in a different "strata" than the place where the disaster occurs. The disaster occurs but the individual is not there to perceive or experience it. In the place where they are at, there is no disaster. In the place where they are not at, there is still a disaster. But would this be selfish for the Human, to want to place themselves in a place where there was no disaster, while thousands of others experienced the disaster? Humans could live their lives this way, hopping from one stratum to another, all the time avoiding catastrophes, but others would still be experiencing the catastrophes. There are great "souls" that can produce refuge for many other corporeal bodies, placing them in strata where they are safe but this is only a temporary event and the souls eventually have to return to their own stratum. Humans have a fear of change and catastrophe and could use the flux to avoid future disasters but instead should learn to cope and grow from experiencing the disasters. Humans would have never migrated and grown as distinct and intelligent people if they had avoided disasters in the past. Disasters are needed for Humans to develop new skills and intelligence.

Q: Regarding the Sirians' statement that happiness is a "steady state" – how can Humans achieve true happiness? Does it have to do with emotions feelings, what other emotions? Can the Sirians describe happiness? Is it the same as what makes us happy? Is it a "blanket term"?

S: We do not have such a term as happiness as it also means that we have to experience non-happiness in order to enjoy happiness. So, we think instead of just being and not experiencing any of the labeled states that Humans have. Humans are very invested in states of emotion, that they label, and then state that they are experiencing those emotions. Humans are constantly asking each other about their emotions and states of emotion instead of observing how other Humans are exhibiting emotions. Inquiring about emotions and thus labeling them often intensifies the emotions.

S: A sad person can cope with their sadness but when asked to discuss and label their sadness, it can intensify the sadness. That is not conducive to a steady state. We experience emotion without labeling those emotions, we just experience them. We do not even talk about happy, or sad, or disappointed, or angry as these emotions pass very quickly. If discussed and labeled they would peak beyond their original energy level and take away from the underlying steady state. Most times we are in a "steady state" that has no emotion but we do experience emotion. Humans say that they can only experience happiness when there is the absence of non-happiness. They can both exist at the same time. Happiness, sadness, anger, disappointment or joy can all happen at the same time in the steady state but are at such a low level that they can be understood.

Q: What major emotions do the Sirians enjoy and what "steady state" do they foster? Is the "steady state" related to the concept of peace, benevolence to others, what else? Is there a sense of connectedness to a Universal Energy or Source? What else does this "steady state" do?

S: In the last question, this was answered. We, Sirians, who enjoy the steady state, find that we have emotional reserves to offer peace, benevolence, and assistance to others because we are not invested in our own emotions at the high level that Humans are invested in theirs. The steady state allows us to remain balanced and able to give aid to others. If we were invested in labeling and communicating all of our emotions, instead of others perceiving our emotions, we would not have the reserves to help others. Connectedness to the flux, the universal energy and intelligence is separate from the steady state.

Q: We recognize, honor and revere wisdom and the mastery of existence that the Sirians show. What other races are comparable to the Sirians? Angels? Are these comparable races terrestrial or not of Earth?

S: The only race that is comparable to Sirians are the Angels, as they too have been able to understand and develop the steady state. Angels can persist in the terrestrial stratum as well as in other places. They can pass between strata wherever they are needed.

Q: Regarding looking into the future. Many entities can foresee the future by projecting the past and the present. Are there multiple layers of time? We assume that there are entities that can truly see ahead into the future, not just as a projection of the past and present? For example, non-steady states have cycles. For example the Earth's environment, the nature of life itself, and other factors related to the environment.

S: There are strata when both Humans and non-Humans can access information about future time. There are some Earth Humans that can do this for short periods of time and there are non-Humans that travel often in these strata. We do not understand the Human need to always know what is going to happen in the future. We have the ability to pass to the strata where the future is apparent and to take appropriate measures.

S: If more Humans were to be able to do this, to pass to the other strata to perceive future time, then they would not be so obsessed with the future. We, Sirians, do not feel it is our role to act as "strata hoppers" for Humans to see the future, when they can do it for themselves. The Orbs, too, can travel in strata that can access events in future time but Humans do not yet have the right to send Orbs to these strata. The Orbs feel the same way that Humans need to understand this ability for themselves and not keep asking other races to do it for them.

Q: Which entities can we contact who can tell us what lies ahead in the future? Will it be a continuation of what we are experiencing now or will it be different? For example, will severe weather patterns be a continuation of Earth cycles or will these cycles become accelerated, at an unprecedented speed, through Human intervention?

S: This is continuation of the same question. Yes, we, Sirians, and the Orbs and some other races can travel to strata that can access events in future time. But Humans can do this too and it is considered lazy, by the other races, when Humans ask for other races to do this for them. There are many ways to project what will happen in the future: look at the past for cycles and then try and reverse those cycles; use the flux to travel to a stratum where the cycles will not impact Humans; or learn to travel to the strata where future time can be observed. All can be equally effective.

Q: Humans are currently concerned about the adaptation of Human life on Earth in the short term only. How can they plan for and adapt to long-term changes?

S: Humans are going through "monumental" changes and have no concept what they are going through. There is a division taking place: at the moment it appears as if there are two races of Humans: those who are concerned with moral good, with nurturing, with growth, with peace, and those who are concerned with anger, with fighting, with breaking down society. This is not only apparent among Human leadership but on all levels of Human society. Within a few hundred Earth years there will be an even greater division between the two levels of society and the more base of the levels will gradually retreat.

Q: Sometime in the near or distant future a cosmic supernova could decimate life on Earth or even destroy it completely. It is possible that this could destroy the Human race? Is this a possibility? Did such an event occur in our solar system in our past? If so, did this affect life on other planets such as Mars and Venus? What happened to the races living there? How did such an event affect Earth and was Atlantis or parts of India affected by such an event?

S: We have knowledge of this happening in almost every system but the races persist. They do not always persist in the same way but they persist. This type of catastrophe is something that Humans cannot avoid if they stay corporeal. Humans can travel to a stratum where the event may not occur and they can keep hopping from stratum to stratum but will become careless and will eventually have to experience the event. Humans have the mistaken fear that Human life is solely corporeal: that corporeal life must be preserved at all costs. This is a very narrow view of life as many races exist non-corporeally and enjoy far greater freedoms than Humans in their corporeal state. It does not matter that many Humans will cease to be corporeal, if such an event occurs, as they can choose to become corporeal again when the Earth recovers or to go elsewhere.

Q: We are interested in the Sirians and thank you again for assisting us. What other entities would be helpful? So far, many of the entities that we have contacted have not been able to project themselves into the future, other than the Nordics and the Record Keepers. Are there any other races that we could contact? Our goal is to ensure that Humans persist on Earth in the long run.

S: It is our goal, too, that Humans persist but we do not experience this goal in the same way as Humans. Humans interpret persisting as remaining in the corporeal state on a corporeal world. We have a greater understanding that existence does not have to depend on a corporeal state. Humans can persist with or without a corporeal state. Humans exhibit a great need to understand what is in the future but we know that Humans can find this out for themselves, without the assistance of the other races. Humans need to learn how to do this for themselves and not keep asking the other races for help with this.

Q: Are there spirit entities on Earth and how do they differ from non-Earth spirit entities? Are some non-corporeal and just exist as an intelligence?

S: The Earth is "teeming" with life, not just corporeal but non-corporeal and some are just "wisps".

Q: What are wisps?

S: They are traces of life that exist in many different strata at once while retaining communication between all of the parts. Humans can only perceive within very narrow energy levels and cannot perceive all of the life on Earth. Humans mistakenly believe that they and other corporeal life forms dominate Earth. This is not so, there is a great sharing occurring among many races.

Q: Orbs seem to enjoy or create happiness for themselves by being in the presence of different energies. Does this happen because of curiosity, on the part of the Orbs, or is this just an experience for them, or just information to them?

S: Orbs, too, can achieve a steady state but, due to the information that they carry, they often deviate from the steady state. For example, an Orb may be carrying information that contains anger and vengeance, thus for that period of time, that is what they perceive. Orbs, like most Humans, prefer to be among positive energy but it is the Orb's duty to relay information that is not of their true nature.

Q: Why are there so many Orbs on and around the Earth? If this is the case, are there as many Orbs in all the galaxies and all the planetary systems, as well? Or are they sent here as information gatherers by other life forms, which would account for there being so many?

S: Orbs are everywhere; they are "ubiquitous" and are observed throughout the void. They can travel anywhere but prefer to cluster near where they were last needed. They go where they are needed but stay, usually, where they last relayed information. Partly, this is in case there is return information to relay or partly just to return to the steady state.

Q: All the entities talk about Humans as a race but we are not a cohesive race as we are all separate races with separate consciousness. Are there any races that could help specific individuals to better cope with their lives?

S: As mentioned Humans are dividing into two races, that will persist for several more hundred years. The many races will then become one for a long period of time.

Q: Could an individual establish a helpful relationship with another race that would benefit other Humans and other races? Humans are separate entities. For example, could an individual Orb be helpful to an individual Human entity and in what ways? Is such knowledge helpful or hindering to us? What information should we be seeking to help our own races and other races?

S: Humans have not yet understood on a large scale, although individual Humans have understood this, that Humans can change their status. Humans can alter events and Humans can change their state of being. Humans do not need other races to be able to do this. Humans have a far greater potential than Humans understand. It is of great help for Humans to befriend and assist other races, as other races will help when needed. However, we will not help Humans if they can help themselves. Some help would not hinder Humans but much help would hinder Humans. We will continue to communicate and help when needed.

Q: Thank you.

18: The Exobiology Project: Talking To The Aldebarans

"Other entities and races should be asking Humans why they choose to ignore the Confederation rules and do not wish to be part of the Confederation."

—The Aldebarans

Part 1

Q: What do the race or races from the Aldebaran system call themselves. How do these races describe themselves?

AB: We have a name for ourselves but you can call us the Aldebarans as we are from that system. Our name is the Fish and we have our own vocabulary, the Fish is the closest we can come to Human language. We are not one race but many races scattered across this part of the system which includes planets that you know as Saturn and systems that you know as the Pleiades. We are ancient and have great knowledge.

Q: Does the Aldebaran race share information; for example, is the entire Aldebaran race aware that we are communicating?

AB: Yes.

Q: Do they travel and interact across the galaxy. How often do they travel and interact?

AB: We are able to visit all aspects of the Universe and can choose to take the shape of the race that is present. We are a race that is able to change shape to travel, like the Nordics which you have interviewed. We do not need craft although we will travel with other races if that is required. We travel often and are traveling in the Universe as we speak.

Q: Does that mean that you, individually, are traveling as we speak, or the Aldebaran race?

AB: Both.

Q: Are there times when you are based on your home world and do not travel?

AB: Yes.

Q: When is this?

AB: When we rest and when we interact with others.

Q: In their interactions with humans, how often does this happen and why is this interaction carried out? For observation? Are they monitors for the Confederation?

AB: We do not interact much with Humans as we do not have any directives to interact with Humans. We interact only when Humans contact us, as you are now doing. There are other groups in this system that travel to Earth and interact with Humans, such as the Angels from the Pleiades.

Q: I never associated the Angels to be from the Pleiades.

AB: There are many types of Angels and some are located in the Pleiades system. We are not monitors for the Confederation although we are members of the Confederation.

Q: Can the Aldebarans help humans if the entities are asked? How can humans ask for help? If they can help us, in what way can we ask for this help?

AB: We can help in a non-local way by offering advice, if we are aware of the information. Humans can ask for help by asking us questions but we are unable to help in a practical way. There are many other races, including the Angels, who can help in this way. Help can be asked for in this way from Human to Aldebaran.

Q: We have several sets of questions to ask you and thank you for your patience with us.

Q: What use do the Aldebarans make of Earth resources? Do they need these for survival?

AB: The Aldebarans do not make use of Earth resources and do not need these for survival. We get everything we need from our own system.

Q: Are the Aldebarans positively or negatively oriented towards Humans?

AB: The Aldebaran race is neutral towards Humans. Humans have only just reached our system with the flying probe around Saturn. There is nothing to fear or feel about Humans at this point. If Humans were to become aggressive towards us we would need to reassess how we feel about Humans in our system.

Q: Why are Grays interacting with us on a conscious level and not others?

AB: Grays are not all one race; they are a combination of Gray, Human and many other races. They look alike on the exterior but in their composition they have some aspects of many different races. That is how they can understand and communicate with Humans on a conscious level.

Q: We had not heard this before, that the Grays combined many different races within them. Are you sure that you are not talking about the Hybrids?

AB: We are sure. Grays were the first Hybrids, before they refined the process to include individual differences of all of the combined races. The Grays were also unable, at some point, to show exterior differences related to emotional states and movement. For many centuries they showed just one type. Now there are many types and some Grays are often mistaken for Humans by Humans on board the Gray craft.

Q: Are there other entities in the Universe? Why, how, and who?

AB: There are too many entities and races to go into. You are meeting most of the main ones, the ones who are mostly interacting with Humans. As you venture out of your nearest systems you will meet more. Humans are not yet ready for the Universes that exist outside their own Universe. The Human mind is not yet ready for the complexity.

Q: Do the Aldebarans have the ability to look into the future?

AB: We have a limited ability to look into our own future, not that of other races. Sometimes we will heed a warning of an upcoming problem and can warn a race of what is coming but that is not frequent.

Q: Are the Aldebarans helping, hindering or ignoring us?

AB: We are doing neither; we are just interested in Humans. Mostly we ignore Humans unless they come into our space, either as a traveling probe around Saturn, or as a mind communication such as yours.

Q: Do the Aldebarans have knowledge of the Confederation; is the Confederation just of our Galaxy or of the Universe?

AB: There are several Confederations in each system and one Confederation over the smaller Confederations. We assume it is the same in all systems. The Confederation is a group of races that decide on the rules and the norms and adjust accordingly.

Q: Are the Aldebarans a Galactic or Universal entity?

AB: We are a Universal race that can travel wherever we choose. We are able to travel wherever we like and interact however we choose. This has always been and will continue to be. There are too many of us for it to be any different.

Q: Regarding the Rules of the Confederation – are these also applicable to non-members, such as the need to respect and cooperate with other races?

AB: All of the rules of the Confederations apply to everybody and every race in the Universe. Some races choose not to follow the rules and are therefore not included as members of the Confederation. They are then unable to be included in the decisions that are made for the Universe by the Confederations. They are lesser races because they have to abide by rules that others make. If these races were members of the Confederation they would have a share in the making of the rules.

Q: Do the Aldebarans have a sense of who people are? Do they have autonomy or are they on a mission for others, or for another group?

AB: The Aldebarans have a sense of who all people are. We are autonomous and do not answer to other races, except the Confederation. We are not on a mission for others, or for another group.

Q: What questions should humans ask of the Exobiology entities?

AB: The questions that Humans should be asking of the entities are: how can Humans learn to abide by the rules of the Confederation and become part of the Confederation? Also, Humans could be asking how Humans can learn to quickly abide by these rules of the Confederations, as they surely do not at the present. This is hindering their joining the Confederation and becoming part of the decision and rule making.

Q: What should the Exobiology entities be asking of us or want to ask of us?

AB: We do not need to ask anything of the Human race as we can visit at any time and learn what we want to learn. Other entities and races should be asking Humans why they choose to ignore the Confederation rules and do not wish to be part of the Confederation.

Q: Are there Exobiology entities that are detrimental to human interests? Are there entities that we should not interact with?

AB: If you haven't already met them, you will. You will learn about them as you meet them. That is all we can say, Humans have to learn about them themselves.

Q: Do the Aldebarans have a concept of God – of a Universal source?

AB: The Aldebaran God is not the same as the Human God. We see all the collective energies and spirit of all the races as the concept of God. The Human concept is that God is omnipresent and omni-wise: so this includes all the knowledge possessed by all the races and the fact that the races are everywhere. So, this concept of God is accounted for by all the races in the Universe. The Aldebarans do not have a sense of a God that is detached from the races.

Q: Do the Aldebarans need two genders to reproduce like we do? Do they manipulate DNA to reproduce and how?

AB: We do not have DNA, it is very different and we cannot explain. It has to do with energies and magnetic fields. Some days we just split and there are two or more of us with our abilities, skills, and memories. It is more than cloning; Human cloning only clones the physical body, each clone then has to develop its own skills and memories. We only have one gender, we do not need two.

Q: Is Earth toxic to the Aldebarans i.e. such as ultraviolet is toxic to Grays?

AB: Earth is not toxic to us: we can adapt safely to any environment.

Q: How do the Aldebarans sustain themselves, with nutrient baths etc? All entities have the need to survive. Humans need from food, water, air, sunshine to exist. Do the Aldebarans need these same things or something different? Do they need warmth, shelter, etc. to survive?

AB: Yes, we have the need to survive but we do not survive the same way as Humans. We do not need shelter; we can just move our location, if we need to. We get food our environment. Our atmosphere contains everything that we need; also we can make some food ourselves from the solar light. If we need to change our location to find an optimal supply of these things we just move ourselves.

Q: Are the Aldebarans surprised by the way that our species is socially organized? How does this differ from their social organization? It is hard for us to conceive of a species that is not centrally controlled. We conceive of centralized control as a means to prevent destruction within and between people. Is this process in place in the Aldebarans world?

AB: We, the Aldebarans, do not have a centralized social organization. But the Confederations could be considered centralized and organized. As we abide by the rules and laws of the Confederations, you could say that, in that way, we are organized. So, we are not surprised that other races have this sort of organization.

Q: Is there anything, within the next 25 Earth years (rotations around our Sun) that humans should be concerned about?

AB: There is nothing that we can see that Humans should be concerned about. Humans are always getting worried about something. We do not see any signs; such as comets traveling too close to Earth, or suns ready to blow out, that should cause Humans to be concerned.

Q: Do the Aldebarans manifest a sense of creativity? Do the Aldebarans manufacture anything? Do the Aldebarans have writing, music, or art?

AB: We do not have the same sense of creativity that Humans possess. We consider that we are the ultimate in creative races as we can change our appearance to anything within the Universe. We do not need to create anything outside ourselves, we can create ourselves to be anything that we wish or need. We do not have writing, music or art as we are all of those things and can communicate without those things.

Q: Do the Aldebarans get sick or have illnesses? Do they have any internal or external threats? Do they die? How do they deal with death?

AB: We do not die in the Human sense where one entity ceases to be. We divide and in doing so continue as separate entities. There is no concept of death among the Aldebarans, so we do not have to deal with death.

Q: Are the Aldebarans surprised that humans can reach out and communicate with them and how often does this happen? When does this happen and from where? Is this contact carried out telepathically?

AB: We are not surprised as many races can do this already. Humans have been able to communicate this way forever but seemed to have lost the ability. It is now becoming apparent that many Humans are rediscovering this form of communication. The Human mind has always had the ability to communicate in this way, so we are not surprised. Most of the races in the Universe communicate this way. It is only on Earth that this ability is denigrated, ridiculed and suppressed.

Q: Native American people, such as the Hopi and other races, have described how their ancestors had a connection to races from Sirius and the Pleiades.

They claim that these races were their ancestors and that they are still interacting. There is some folklore that these beings were escaping from Sirius and the Pleiades. How did they come to Earth and are they still able to communicate?

AB: Firstly, many of the races from this system have visited Earth in the past and imparted knowledge. You would have to talk to the individual races to find out what they left behind. Secondly, races from this system are still visiting Earth, in many guises, and giving knowledge. As more Humans remember how to communicate directly with the races in each system, then more knowledge will be given. It is hard to be more specific because the breadth of the knowledge already given is so great and the races so many.

Q: What potential does Earth have for the Aldebarans?

AB: Earth has no potential use for the Aldebaran. We can travel where we please and receive everything we need from our system. The only benefit would be if Humans joined the Confederation. Then we could communicate as equals.

Q: Are the Aldebarans interested in our technology?

AB: Technology is only interesting to those who have solid bodies, such as Humans. We can choose to have solid bodies that this is transitory. As we do not have solid bodies most of the time we do not need technology.

Q: If we were to call an Aldebaran to materialize into a solid body, would we be able to see and communicate with that entity? How would we know that this was a race from the Aldebaran system?

AB: We would only come if there was a specific reason to come to Earth and materialize for a Human. You would not know it was one of us as we would look entirely like a Human and would interact in the same way as a Human. It is possible that you have interacted with our race, in the past, and did not know it was us. That is all we can say.

Q: Thank you. There are three other sessions to follow. We thank and respect the Aldebarans for their patient and help.

Part 2

We would first like thank the Aldebarans for this additional interview, for their responses and cooperation. We respect and honor the Aldebarans for their help in answering these questions and aiding our understanding of our cosmic neighbors.

Q: The Sirians claimed that they persist in a steady state and that they are a happy race. We ask the Aldebarans the same questions as we asked the Syrians. What can make us happy? What can make us satisfied and content?

As a race we are not satisfied, or content. What can the Aldebarans tell us about this?

AB: We have observed that the majority of Humans are happy. They are not happy all of the time but they appear to be happy overall. We are not just talking about the group that calls itself North America but the whole of the World. The North Americans have the idea that nothing else exists outside of their part of the world except people to fight. We have noticed this on other worlds and even in our own system. In the rest of the world, Humans seem quite happy with their lives and do not seem to be always striving for happiness. Humans forget all that they have and want what they cannot have, especially North Americans. They are like children or adolescents. When they cannot get what they want, immediately, they fight and become very negative. Humans have lived in simpler times and have been happy, they now live in more complex times and nothing much has changed regarding their basic needs. It has been our understanding that those who have the least are the happiest on the Earth. Happiness is a fleeting emotion and it should not be happiness that is discussed here. What should be discussed is satisfaction with life. What is it in life that makes a Human satisfied? Happiness follows satisfaction.

Q: The Sirians claim to have given early Humans concepts and ideas that promoted civilization on Earth. What concepts and ideas would the Aldebarans give Humans if they were to visit today?

AB: The Aldebarans have given plenty of concepts to Humans in the past and continue to give them where necessary.

Q: Can you say some of these things that have been given to Humans?

AB: The concept of justice is one of the concepts that we have given Humans. There was a time when Humans took and fought and there was no justice. Then there came a time of justice as the idea took hold and spread to other Humans. It was not well received as those who acted outside of justice could not do what they wanted. Then there came a time of overuse of justice and everything became a rule or a law and many died for small injustices. Now there is the time of unequal justice, when justice is used only for those who want it, rather than for those who need it. Eventually, the concept of justice will equal out and become what it was meant to be.

AB: If we were to give Humans a concept now, it would be something that they did not already have. This would be something that some were ready for but not everybody. The concept would take hold slowly and would grow, would have the same history as the concept of justice and would eventually have its place in society. What we would give Humans now would be the concept that systems like ours, the Aldebaran system is not as far away as Humans think.

AB: Humans have a wrong idea about the speed of light and it is not what they think it is. Humans state that it would take so many light years to reach certain planets and systems. In fact, this is erroneous. Light bends and twists, increases and decreases in speed, depending on the part of the Universe that it is in. There is no need for "wormholes" and "bending time", just an understanding of light.

Q: How can we persist and retain knowledge and memory given our DNA composition?

AB: The persistence and retention of knowledge and memory is not dependent on DNA as Humans teach. Knowledge and memory transcend DNA and persist beyond the decay of DNA. DNA is solely utilized by Humans to transfer physical and mental characteristics to their offspring. These offspring come into the DNA body already equipped with knowledge and memory that has transcended their previous DNA body. Humans have the idea that once the Human body dies that all knowledge and memory die, but it does not.

Q: How is it possible for us to settle into a steady state of happiness?

AB: As said before, find what brings satisfaction and then happiness will follow. If you continue to do those things that bring satisfaction, then happiness will flow concurrently in a steady state.

Q: What is interesting about the Earth that is different from other places in the Universe?

AB: Earth is interesting to the other races because of the diversity of life, not just Humans, but plants and animals. Most of the other planets and systems do not have the variety and diversity of life that Earth has. Humans put examples of this diversity in zoos, all we have to do is come to Earth and wander around and we can see this richness of life. Humans are very diverse, too, in culture and development. Earth is like a living school for many races that come to Earth to learn. The Aldebaran are interested in Earth because of the oceans and the life in the oceans, as we do not have such oceans in our immediate system. It is a wonder and an experience to visit the Earth.

Q: How do we avoid contact with other races in the Universe that could do us harm?

AB: You cannot avoid them if you continue to explore the Universe. All you can do is to learn to deal with them and any negative effects that they may have.

Q: How can the Aldebarans and Humans better communicate? How can Humans better communicate with other races?

AB: Humans can communicate with us in the way that we are now doing. This will eventually be learned by more people and it will not seem so strange.

Humans can also learn to communicate, in this way, with many other races throughout the Universe. However, Humans do not have a good record of communication among themselves and need to understand their own communication before setting out to communicate with other races.

Q: Do the Aldebarans have a home world or are they scattered around the Universe? Could Humans visit the Aldebarans' home world?

AB: The Aldebaran are not just one race, we are a collection of races that live in our home system. There is no home world as we rest and replenish wherever we want to. Humans could not visit the Aldebarans' system at this time because they have not understood light travel. Humans have sent a traveling probe to Saturn but this is using ancient physics, which we left behind a long time ago. When Humans begin to have some idea of light travel, then we will invite Humans to visit us.

Q: Did the Aldebarans have a role in the evolution of early Humans? Have Aldebarans helped Humans evolve to a state of heightened knowledge?

AB: Yes, the Aldebaran have helped Humans with many concepts, such as justice and sharing. Early Humans did not know the concept of sharing. They found or took what they could and kept it to themselves and their family group. We also taught the concepts of altruism and cooperation to Humans. Humans are still trying to understand these concepts, much to our dismay.

Q: Have the Aldebarans heard of the Nurobean race or the other races that were mentioned in the recent emails that were sent to a colleague? Are the contents of these emails true or false? Who are the authors of these emails?

AB: We have not heard of such a race or the others in the article. The emails, which we monitor, are partly true but are muddled with falsehoods. The authors have an interest in getting some information, without being identified, and so muddle the true information with false.

Q: What other places in the Universe do the Aldebarans visit and what do they do there?

AB: We visit almost every place in the Universe. Mostly we travel for the joy of it, we help where needed, we give knowledge where needed, but mostly we just are. It is hard for Humans to understand a race that does not work, that does not have goals and aspirations but that is what we are.

Q: Humans do not persist, they die and Human memory is not continued within that individual. If there is life of the Human spirit after death, what happens to that spirit? Does it just live as a spirit and how can it relate to a Human who is still alive?

AB: We have observed that Humans believe that Human memory and experience die with the physical body. This is not so. After the death of the body, the spirit flies free and for a time floats free in the Universe until it is called. It does not have a body but has all of the manifestations of life. The spirit does not eat, does not drink, and does not sleep, or do any of the other bodily things that humans need to survive. There is no need and no desire.

AB: Sometimes, the system goes wrong and a soul remains trapped close to where its physical body last existed. We have observed that Humans who have an unusual attachment to things of the body and the Earth are the ones that get trapped most easily. It is these spirits that have the most contact with the living. When it is called, the spirit has a choice of many different destinations or missions. It is a huge Universe and spirits can go wherever they wish. Most Human spirits choose to return to the Earth.

Q: Does the Human spirit become re-established into another Human, another life-form on Earth, or a life-form in the universe?

AB: It is our experience, as mentioned, that most Human spirits return to Earth but they have a choice to go anywhere they choose.

Q: What major emotions do the Aldebarans enjoy and what "steady state" do they foster? Is the "steady state" related to the concept of peace, benevolence to others, what else? What else does this "steady state" do?

AB: We are mostly satisfied with what we can do and where we can go, so we have happiness too. This is the steady state for the Aldebaran. We follow the rules of the Confederation but apart from those we are free to go wherever we want and to do whatever we want. This steady state keeps us together as a race instead of tearing us apart with different needs and wants.

Q: Why could the Angels not help more with my colleague's medical problem? Was there something else that he or they needed to do?

AB: There was nothing else that the Angels could do. He knows how this happens and he forgets. Then he is upset when he is not able to move. He gets very angry and denies that he has not done the right thing. He must also remember that the Human body is not a perfect machine and does have its problems.

Q: 200,000 years ago, there were few Humans on the Earth. If each of these has a soul, where did all the extra souls come from to be included in all the millions of Humans that are alive today?

AB: The extra souls come from what we call God: the energy that is contained in all of the races and beings in the Universe. It is not just Human souls or spirits that come back to Earth: they come from all over. There is no lack of souls to come to the Earth.

Q: Are there wars that are being conducted in space, what we would call Star Wars? Are the races that are fighting good or evil?

AB: There are always wars, especially between the races that are not members of the Confederation. These, however, do not often infringe on Earth or its system. We observe them but do not intrude. When they are ready to live by the rules, they will not fight. We do not have such concepts as good and evil, just those who live by the rules and those who do not live by the rules.

Q: Why do the races in the Universe allow Supernova explosions?

AB: The races have no control over or "allow" Supernova explosions, just as Humans do not control or "allow" earthquake or volcanic explosions. They just happen; we get out of the way and deal with the aftermath.

Q: Is the Earth a living entity? We call the Earth Gaia and personalize our planet. Does Gaia have intelligence?

AB: The only living part of the Earth is the covering that contains life. This has an existence of its own: it has cycles, and intelligence. The inner cores of the Earth are the engines of the Earth and without these all life on the surface would cease. It is good for Humans to think of the Earth as a living thing.

Q: Thank you. Two more sets of questions will be asked soon.

Part 3

We would first like to thank the Aldebarans for this additional interview, for their responses and cooperation. We respect and honor the Aldebarans for their compassion and help.

Additional Questions for the Aldebarans.

Q: What other races are comparable to the Aldebarans? Are these comparable races terrestrial or not of Earth?

AB: The part of the Universe that encompasses the Aldebaran system has many races living here. There are at least one Earth dozen. We have all been here a very long time and live as neighbors. We are peaceful together. We do not fight unless there is an intrusion by a race from another system. We allow other races to fly through our system, if we know them already. One of these races has spread throughout the Pleiades system and you will eventually meet them. They have visited Earth many times and know Humans quite well. They are very similar to Humans in many aspects regarding intelligence and sensibility.

Q: Regarding looking into the future. Many entities can foresee the future by projecting the past and the present. Are there multiple layers of time? We assume that there are entities that can truly see ahead into the future, not just as a projection of the past and present? For example, non-steady states have cycles such as the Earth's environment, the nature of life itself, and other factors related to the environment.

AB: Yes, there are multiple layers of time but these layers can be viewed as circular, rather than vertical or horizontal layers. They wrap around each other and overlap in areas, so that some time can become intermingled with other time. We use the layers to travel and to visit other locations at different times. We cannot see into the future as the layers are constantly moving and updating, so a definitive future is never apparent. The future twists and turns and is rapidly being caught-up with by the past, and intertwining with other times, so it is very difficult to see a future event for us. Perhaps we are too close with the lines. Yes, the future can be predicted from the past and present and the future can be forced to occur, by traveling the time line.

Q: How does a person, Human or Aldebaran, travel the time line?

AB: We can physically attach to a particular time line but Humans have to travel with the mind only. We see the Earth as static, in terms of nature cycles and the Earth's environment. You must remember that the Aldebaran view time in a different way and see a "bigger picture" than humans. To us, the Earth seems static and does not change much.

Q: Which entities can we contact who can tell us what lies ahead in the future? Will it be a continuation of what we are experiencing now or will it be different? For example, will severe weather patterns be a continuation of Earth cycles or will these cycles become accelerated, at an unprecedented speed, through Human intervention?

AB: We are not the ones to contact for this information. The Record Keepers can project from past events. One thing to remember is that every catastrophe or major events sends ripples in time both ahead of itself and behind it. Humans already know this. So, look for the ripples that will indicate something big is about to happen. There are many sensitive Humans who are able to detect these ripples. They are a better resource than asking some other race what is to happen.

Q: Humans are currently concerned about the adaptation of Human life on Earth in the short term only. How can Humans plan for and adapt to long-term changes?

AB: Humans don't need to do anything beyond what they are already doing. It seems to Humans that life progresses in chunks of time and action. This is not the case. Progress is made one step at a time and these small steps make up the chunk. Humans are constantly adapting, as are all the animals and plants on Earth. There has never been a time, and never will be a time, when Humans and other Earth life are not adapting. Adaptation cannot be planned for, it just happens.

Q: Sometime in the near or distant future a cosmic supernova could decimate life on Earth or even destroy it completely. It is possible that this could destroy the Human race? Is this a possibility? Did such an event occur in our solar system in our past? If so, did this affect life on other planets such as Mars and Venus? What happened to the races living there? How did such an event affect Earth and was Atlantis or parts of India affected by such an event?

AB: Events such as Supernova cannot be predicted, they just happen. We have no knowledge of any supernova that happened to destroy other planets or systems or to the races living there. We do not keep such knowledge.

Q: Are there spirit entities on Earth and how do they differ from non-Earth spirit entities? Are some non-corporeal and just exist as an intelligence?

AB: The variety is enormous. There are both corporeal and non-corporeal races inhabiting the Earth. Humans think that they own the Earth but they are just co-tenants of the Earth. They are neighbors, even if they do not see each other. The only difference is that most corporeal entities are tied to Earth's atmosphere, non-corporeal have the Universe in which to travel. There are very few that exist just as intelligence and these are found very rarely on Earth.

Q: Orbs seem to enjoy or create happiness for themselves by being in the presence of different energies. Does this happen because of curiosity, on the part of the Orbs, or is this just an experience for them, or just information to them?

AB: The whole purpose of the Orbs is to carry information and to collect and deliver information. That is what makes them happy, when they are carrying out their role. Nothing more.

Q: Why are there so many Orbs on and around the Earth? If this is the case, are there as many Orbs in all the galaxies and all the planetary systems, as well? Or are they sent here as information gatherers by other life forms, which would account for there being so many?

AB: They are doing their job. They are everywhere in the Universe. Some are seen, most are not seen. Many races utilize the Orbs to send and receive information.

Q: All the entities talk about Humans as a race but we are not a cohesive race as we are all separate races with separate consciousness. Are there any races that could help specific individuals to better cope with their lives?

AB: We know this and do not understand why Humans have not become more cohesive. Humans know quite well what it takes to become a cohesive race but resist doing this. There is nothing any other race can do to help Humans until Humans become cohesive themselves.

Q: Could an individual establish a helpful relationship with another race that would benefit other Humans and other races? Humans are separate entities. Is such knowledge helpful or hindering to us? What information should we be seeking to help our own race and other races?

AB: This is a first step, for Humans to be contacting and interacting with other races. This is very helpful. Many Humans, from many different parts of the Earth, reach out this way to the different races. Such knowledge that the other races can offer could only be helpful, especially from those races that are part of the Confederation. Asking the Confederation races for assistance is very helpful to understanding the rules that the Confederations set.

Q: What do the Aldebarans think of our projects? Are we going about these projects in the right or the wrong way? When we are talking to the Aldebarans are we talking to all other Aldebarans? When we talk to the Aldebarans do other races also hear the discussion? What other Humans have communicated with the Aldebarans, other than those asking for help?

AB: We think this is a great project but needs more Humans talking to the races. There are so many races and very few Humans who are reaching out like this. More Humans need to be trained to do this. Some can do it naturally but others need to be trained. We are thinking of a school. This must be International.

Q: I have also had this idea.

AB: These are our ideas, too. We have similar schools for contacting other races.

Q: Do Humans have a personal Angel or do we draw from a group when we ask for help? To what extent can Aldebarans help Humans and are there any limits?

AB: We know of the Angels but do not interact with them in a major way. We know that they help Humans and will help other races if asked. We have not needed to ask. We can only help Humans in a very limited way, perhaps not at all.

Q: Regarding a medical condition that may suffer from in modern society: occasional vertigo; what are the causes and what else can be done to eliminate this annoying condition?

AB: The condition is caused by frequencies that occur outside of the body. Some people are very sensitive to these frequencies. The frequencies are generated by Human technologies.

Q: Such as cell phones?

AB: Humans are constantly creating frequencies in the atmosphere and some people are sensitive to these. One frequency alone may not cause a problem but many overlapping frequencies can affect Humans.

Q: I thought that it was certain foods or substances, such as artificial sweeteners, that was causing the problem.

AB: They can aggravate the problem. Humans can adjust their frequencies so that they are not so sensitive.

Q: The responses by the Sirian's sounded very Buddhist? Are there similarities between the Sirians and the Aldebarans?

AB: We know of the Sirians but do not have much interaction. They do not have much to say to us and we do not have much to say to them.

Q: We would still like to understand the Aldebarans' concept of God. Do the Aldebarans interact with God, What is the nature of God? Is it different and how is it different from the Earthly concept of God? Some of the other races have no concept of God, why is that?

AB: As we mentioned before, our concept of God encompasses all the energies of the races and beings in the Universe. It is a very simple matter to understand and cannot be questioned as it is questioned above. We have already told you how your concept of God is different from ours. There are many differences: your God is confined to one figure; ours is spread out over the Universe. Your God only seems to service Humans: ours services everybody and everything in the Universe. Your God is judgmental and cruel; ours is benevolent, intelligent and compassionate. The only races that do not accept our definition of God are those that do not follow the Confederation rules.

Q: We would like to elaborate on the recent email that held some true information and some false information. We would like to know who was behind this email and why it was sent. Is there any other information that might be relevant?

AB: The Humans behind this email are a group of individuals who are also looking for information about the other races. But they are limited by scientific and idealistic confines that hinder their sense of openness. They feel that they have to only partially disclose what they know or there will be consequences from the authorities. They realize that what they publish will cause confusion but also know that there are those that will take some of the information, add it to what is known already, and increase what is known about the races. They are deliberately misleading but with a purpose.

Q: The Aldebarans said that Human spirits float free in the Universe until "they are called." Who or what calls them?

AB: We do not know what calls them back to Human or other form. It is an intangible thing. We just know that spirits suddenly have an urge to move to another part of the Universe where they become reincorporated; that is, they become corporate again. We do not go through this process so we do not know what this call is; we just know that it happens.

Q: There is a system called Alpha Centauri in Human terms and within that system is a star that we call Proxima Centauri. Within this star system is a planet that has been referred to as Menton. Can you please describe the race that inhabits this region? Are they Human-like? What interactions do the Aldebaran have with these people? Where did the people on Menton come from?

AB: First, we have not heard of Menton, either from other Humans or from other races. There are many, many stars within the Alpha Centauri system and we know of Proxima Centauri. We have interaction with all of the races in this system. They do not appear Human or act Human. They can be referred to as the Craft or Kraft, in Human terms.

Q: I will refer to them as Kraft, so as not to confuse the term ship or craft.

AB: They do have an intelligence that can be interacted with. They are closest to the Nordic, who can assume Human shape. The Kraft cannot assume the shape of other races. Please do not assume that because other races can interact mentally, that they all have Human shape. That is not the case and should be remembered.

Q: In the 1900s of Earth history there was an anomalous explosion in the Tunguska region of Russia. What happened here? What role did the ET races play in this incident?

AB: From our records and from interacting with other Humans, we find that this explosion was the result of a craft from a very far system, which caused the damage. There are particles of its energy system still present in the water and the soil of the region. Scientists are aware of these particles and they are not from a meteor or from an Earth accident. This craft became wildly unstable and efforts to stop it failed. It was diverted to a mountain region of Earth where it would do least damage. Many races were involved in trying to stop the craft and to divert it. Many races stayed around to monitor the crash and the damage and there are records of this in Earth history that few people know. Humans would prefer the damage to be natural than to be caused by something else, from outside the Earth.

Q: If there are races on Saturn, did they originally come from Venus and why did they travel there?

AB: That is not so, each system has its own races that have been there for a very long time, longer than Humans can conceive. It is pointless to speculate that some races came from other places. Even, if races travel, there are still people from their race in the location where they stay.

Q: There is a region on Earth that is called the Bermuda Triangle, where numerous boats and planes have disappeared. Non-Human craft have also been seen in the region? Is there any connection between these non-Human craft and the disappearance of the boats and planes?

AB: Humans would be surprised to know of the many races that live under the waters of Earth, as well as under the land. Many races fly their craft in and out of the waters of Earth and have had to put in place energies to enter and exit the waters. Sometimes Earth air and water craft enter these energy regions and enter into the areas where the other craft are operating. The other races do not want these Earth craft in their spaces so place them back outside, usually on the bottom of the water but away from the non-Human entrances and exits. The other races assume that Humans will eventually find their air and water craft and will understand what happened. However, the other races do not want Humans to know about the other race's locations. Because the other races operate in these areas, it is to be expected that they will be seen from time to time.

Q: Thank you for your answers and cooperation. There is one more session to follow when the remainder of the questions we have will be asked.

Part 4

This remaining fourth section – communicating with the races from the Aldebaran system - proposes some additional questions that focus on some new topics. We would like to thank the Aldebarans for this additional interview, for their responses and cooperation. We respect and honor the Aldebarans for their assistance.

Q: Humans have difficulty in communicating with those who have passed from the corporeal world to the spirit world. How can Humans best communicate with those who are now spirits?

AB: Other races have told you this and we say this too, that there are many Humans in the spirit form and they are now out in the Universe getting ready for their return. When they are out in Universe, there is no communication with them. There are spirits that are trapped on the Earth for various reasons, such as being trapped by excess emotion to one place or person. These spirits can have communication but all that the Humans will learn is why the spirit is suffering or has suffered. It is not good for either the Human or the spirit. It is not good for the spirit because it reinforces their misery. It does not do the Human any good because they have impression that the spirit world is filled with misery. This is not the case. Most of the spirits out in the Universe are joyful and free.

Q: How could people best communicate with people who are now in the spirit world? What are they doing now in the spirit world?

AB: If they are now out in the Universe in spirit form you cannot communicate with them. If they are trapped on Earth, and you communicate with them, their misery may become your misery and neither will be happy. So, it is better not to communicate with them.

Q: One of the races that have been contacted is the Companions. They talked about how the hybrids (that the Grays are developing) are part of a "sacred act" Can the Aldebarans talk more about this and why hybrid births are thought of as "sacred?" Is it to do with the creation of life itself or the manipulation of life or the role of the hybrids?

AB: All creation of life is sacred. This is one of the Confederation rules. Wherever life is formed and by whatever means it is sacred. Even though the Grays do not belong to the Confederation, the life that they create is considered sacred. The Companions also consider life sacred and revere it.

Q: The Sirians talk about there being alternative strata, which we can visit, explore, and perhaps, utilize? Can the Aldebarans tell us more about the strata?

AB: We have discussed that in an earlier session, when we talked about the strata being circular, rather than horizontal or vertical. We also talked about how some of the strata can overlap and interconnect for communication and travel. We have nothing more to add to this.

Q: The Grays continue to interact with Humans. Are the Grays also hybridizing other races, and why? Please note that we are not denigrating the Grays but are interested in all races and how they function. Are the Grays hybridizing the Aldebarans, if not, why not?

AB: The Grays do not hybridize the Aldebaran. We are not a species that has DNA. The only races that the Grays can hybridize have DNA. We know that you are not denigrating the Grays and that you are only trying to understand them.

Q: Have the Aldebarans played a role in the Confederation? Are they the Confederation? Do they play a small role or a larger role in the Confederation? Were the Aldebarans involved in the creation of the Galactic Confederations?

AB: The Aldebarans have been around since before the Confederation and were there in the early stages of the Confederation. We were not involved in the creation of the Confederations, just there. The Confederations grew from simple groups to Universal wide groups. We are not the Confederation.

Q: Do Aldebarans have any influence in the role of peacekeeping in the Universe?

AB: We do not have a Universal role in peacekeeping. The only role that we play is as part of our Confederation where we promote the rules of the Confederation. If the races abide by the rules of the Confederation there will be peace. Humans do not abide by the rules of the Confederation, so there is no peace.

Q: We would like to give the Aldebarans an opportunity to add anything else that they feel is important for Humans to know. We have been asking a lot of questions but this is an opportunity for the Aldebarans to tell us what they want us to know.

AB: We would like to talk about color: which we have not been asked about. We mentioned that not all races have a physical form. Our form is in the appearance of color: many different colors. By Human standards we would be very beautiful. If a Human could imagine a metallic rainbow but without substance; that would be us. Our world is a colorful world. We do not perceive color, as Humans do, with eyes but as frequencies. Our entire world is in color and we enjoy our world and its colors. Earth has some colors but nothing as vivid and beautiful as ours.

Q: Why is it that some people can physically perceive Aldebarans? Under what circumstances do Aldebarans come to Earth in physical form?

AB: Very occasionally we can travel to Earth and you would not perceive us. Humans would perceive a flash of colored light, as if a bird flew past a rainbow. That would be us. But it is very rare for us to visit Earth.

Q: Are other races, apart from the Grays hybridizing Humans and other races?

AB: The Grays are the main race that is hybridizing other DNA races. We do not know of other races that are hybridizing Humans or other DNA races.

Q: Did the Grays destroy their own world with atomic weapons or something similar?

AB: We do not have any information about the Grays or their world. We only know of them through interacting with them on our travels.

Q: There is some evidence that some races can neutralize Human atomic weapons, are the Grays doing this or some other race?

AB: This question needs some understanding of matter. Everything is matter, energy and information. Atomic weapons are only various grades of matter, energy and information and no harder to control than a Human can snuff out a candle. It is easy for us and other races to manipulate these things. Different races neutralize different energies for different reasons, such as needing the energy for their own purposes.

Q: If some of the extraterrestrial races are so advanced why would they need Human DNA to hybridize other species? Would they not be able to synthesize DNA or manufacture what they wanted in some other advanced way?

AB: The Grays are able to synthesize DNA but there is a limit to the amount of times that the DNA can be replicated. It is the same with Human DNA; it can only be replicated so many times before it is unusable. So, the Grays have to continually collect Humans and collect their DNA. Also, the production of sperm and egg are more difficult to synthesize and these must be collected frequently from Humans.

Q: Do the Aldebaran races have a concept of time?

AB: We do not have a concept of time as it is utilized on Earth. We have discussed this before. Earth time is seen to be linear and created by the circling of the Earth. That is the Human concept of time. Other races have no concept of time, as Humans know it. There have to be time posts, markings in space or in the material of the Universe, between which time is measured, and there are not. There would need to be uniformity of time, between the races, and there is not. The Universe would have to remain static and unchanging for time to exist, and it does not. So, we have no concept of a linear, non-static time.

Q: Regarding Earth and its many changes, how does the Earth rebalance itself: with heating, cooling etc?

AB: The Earth can be seen as an orthostatic planet. Its movements around the sun and between the other planets contribute to its temperature, shape, tilt and everything else the Humans measure on the Earth. We would never bother with constantly measuring the Earth; we would just get on with the matter of living.

Q: There is a mythical island state or country called Atlantis by Humans? Did such a place exist? What happened to it?

AB: We do not know about this island state or what happened to it. We also know of the myths but do not have any other information or what happened to it.

Q: Regarding the Martians, who refer to themselves the Rall, are they still surviving?

AB: Yes, the Rall, are still surviving, as you will see when you talk to them. However, don't expect them to be as gracious and communicative as us.

Q: Are they surviving underground on Mars and how? What happened to their planet?

AB: Yes, they have an underground existence. Nothing happened to their planet, they are still there. You will need to ask them more questions, as they will be able to give you the answers.

Q: Did the Rall destroy their atmosphere? If so, how was it destroyed?

AB: Ask the Rall, not us.

Q: We will be talking with the Rall in our next sessions, is there anything specific that we need to know before communicating with them?

AB: Just that they are quieter, sometimes ruder, sometimes less communicative than us. We are always available for communication. The Rall are not always available. Be patient with them as they are still learning how to interact with the other races.

Q: Thank you, Aldebarans, for your patience with us, for your answers and your cooperation.

19: The Exobiology Project: Talking With The Rall

"Life is everywhere in the Universe. It would be unusual not to find it, rather than be surprised to find it. Keep looking everywhere."

—The Rall

We would first like thank the Rall for this interview, for their responses and cooperation. We respect and honor the Rall. During 2006, the Exobiology projects have focused on interviewing many non-Human races. This current session is with the Rall, the race that lives on Mars.

There is an intuitive understanding that the Rall like to receive gifts. As we cannot offer a physical gift; we offer a blessing in the form of positive thoughts and intent to the Rall.

Also, we understand that the Rall respect water and information so we would like to offer the following as gifts to the Rall: photos of the water crystal experiments by Dr. Masaru Emoto notably water responding to Mozart's Symphony; and Love and Gratitude. We also include here some pictures of some of Earth's waterfalls to show the Rall their beauty and wonder! We also thought that the Rall would appreciate some poetry about water: a poem about rain by a famous Earth poet, Henry Wadsworth Longfellow, "Rain in Summer".

Q: What do the race or races currently living on Mars call themselves, are they the Rall? How does this race describe themselves?

R: Please read the questions to us slowly, leave, and then come back for our answers...

R: We are the Rall and accept your gifts of words and pictures. Water is precious to us and we value this information. We are a race that is very like many other races but we have had to undertake an unusual lifestyle. We live beneath our planet and do not travel. We call ourselves the Rall. We are many. We have limited resources although we are many. We have emotions, thoughts, feelings as many other races. We do not belong to the Confederation although we know of the rules. We do not follow all of the rules. Our history and lifestyle dictate that we do not follow some of the rules. We do not believe in the rule of balance. We do not believe in keeping a balance in war such as other races do. We do reciprocate with gifts when gifted.

Q: Do the Rall ever travel to Earth?

R: The Rall do not travel to Earth, we do not have a need although we did in the past. We did not contribute to Humans. We are separate and we are the Rall. We do not manufacture craft but we are visited by other races with craft.

Q: Are there any Rall living on Earth at this time? If so, do the Rall interact with Humans?

R: There are no Rall living on the Earth with Humans at this time.

Q: Are the Rall, Human-like? Or are they energetic and non-corporeal?

R: The Rall are somewhere between these two. We are not like Humans as we are much more delicate in appearance and might appear non-corporeal. We are not bulky like Humans. We have no need to carry anything in or on our bodies that is excessive. We have become developed down to the bare needs of existence. Our lack of resources has caused us to be thin and delicate compared to Humans but we are very strong.

Q: It is understood that the Rall live underground. If so, how long have the Rall lived underground and why?

R: The Rall have lived underground for a very long time, past many generations of Rall and their remembrance. We are an oral society, not having the written word like Humans and having no need of it. The written word controls individuals and we have no need of it. Before the written word on Earth, Humans were able to make their own decisions with their lives and so it is still with the Rall. In the past, when we visited Earth, we found that the written word controlled, directed and managed Humans. We did not want it so did not develop it.

R: We remember very well and can convey what we want to our children, and their children. In this memory we have a distant remembrance of large rocks that fell from the sky and a jolting of the land and the following heat and dryness that came quickly. It was not a sudden warming but arrived each successive day a little more strongly. There was nothing like it in memory at that time and so we did not know what to do except to escape it. We went to caves and holes and from there learned to live under the surface. One day, we will return to live on the surface but now we have our communities and our living under the ground and it seems natural to us.

Q: Given the Rall experience with, possibly, living longer than Humans, what advice can the Rall give Humans?

R: Some of the advice that the Rall can give to Humans is to respect and enjoy the water that you have, it can disappear so quickly. We do have water but it is very little and we manage it carefully. At one time our planet was as rich in water as the Earth, and as green and as blue and as beautiful. The other advice is not to let the written word control and manage your lives. Let your own guidance and judgment guide you rather than the written word.

The spoken word has more authority and wisdom that the written word. Listen to what people say rather than what they write.

Q: Are the Rall concerned about our landing space probes on Mars and the eventual landing of a manned mission?

R: At first we did not know what to do with the craft that came to our planet. We have protective mechanics that roam our planet and these first saw the visiting craft. We did not identify them as belonging to any race that we knew. Some thought that the craft were gifts sent ahead of visiting Humans and so we collected them and waited for the Humans. But no Humans came. More craft came and again we waited for the Humans who had sent these craft ahead of themselves as gifts. No Humans came. Now we understand that these are not gifts but extensions of the Humans themselves who will come when they are ready and able. When will the Humans come?

Q: I do not know.

Q: Were some of Earth's space probes, which landed on Mars, disabled or taken by the Rall?

R: Yes, most of the first craft were taken and dismantled by the Rall, eager to understand the gifts. When they could not be identified as coming from any race that we know, we deduced that they were from Humans because of the written word on them. They did not broadcast the spoken word like some craft. We have a collection of these craft and their parts which we will return to Humans when they come to visit.

Q: Why do the Rall continue to let some of the probes, included the most recent, roam freely without disturbance?

R: Now that we understand that the craft are not gifts but extensions of the Humans we leave them alone, we just watch because we do not want to harm or upset them.

Q: Can the Rall tell us why Humans have not been back to the Moon and why so many of the Moon probes failed?

R: There are many races who call the Moon theirs including Humans. It is indeed owned by many races and not by one race. The Moon does not belong to Humans alone. Craft and probes from Earth have been a nuisance in the past. Most of the races have a schedule and know when each one has the time and space to bring by their craft or probes. Earth's probes did not match the timetable and interfered with the craft from the other races. The Moon is a good resource for landing and waiting but Humans need to understand the scheduling and only come when it is right. It is our understanding that some of the races told Humans about this scheduling but it was ignored. So, some of the Humans probes were destroyed because they ignored the schedule.

Q: Did the Rall ever live above the ground? Why have the Rall moved underground?

R: We have told you this already. Conditions on the surface became so dangerous to the Rall that we retreated. This was not a sudden event but gradual and our moving underground was gradual. But once underground this is where we have stayed.

Q: Was there a race on Venus? Are they still there? If not, where did they travel to, another star system?

R: There is still a race, in fact several races still remaining on Venus and living much the same way that we do. They are different than us in that they can travel and do venture onto the surface of their planet. We are in spoken word contact with them as well as mind word contact, as we are doing now. We do not know of a race that traveled away from Venus.

Q: Are the Rall able to travel away from Mars at all?

R: Not now, although we did so in the past. We are content to live our lives below the surface and have become accustomed to this. On our last visits Humans had become very managed by the written word and had almost forgotten the spoken word and their own judgments.

Q: One Human has claimed that a great catastrophe damaged the Martian atmosphere and that Martians escaped in a craft and came to Earth to hide under Mt. Baldy in New Mexico. How valid are these claims?

R: There were several catastrophes that damaged our atmosphere but we did not leave the planet or go to live underground on Earth. This Human has some of the knowledge but not all of the knowledge.

Q: Humans have been shown photos in the media of very large worm shapes that appeared to move in and out of the Martian surface? What are these? Are they biological?

R: These belong to the Rall and are a form of transportation, nothing more. They are part biological and part mechanical. In this way the Rall can reach the surface without becoming endangered. It is a common way to travel.

Q: Regarding the rock that was found by our scientists and evaluated as having come from Mars, were the shapes found within the rock actual bacteria or something else?

R: It is possible, as many organisms exist that are both beneficial and harmful to the Rall. It is also possible that rocks left our planet and landed on Earth during the catastrophes but we do not know. If Earth Humans say that these are Martian organisms we might believe then: if they write that they are Earth organisms we might not believe them. We would use our own judgment. In our judgment they are real.

Q: Did the Martian atmosphere contain more oxygen and what happened to it?

R: Two things happened to the oxygen that was on the surface of our planet. The first was that when the waters stopped flowing; the air stopped circulating in patterns that distributed the water. Thus much of the atmosphere settled to the ground or drifted off planet. Some of the atmosphere that settled to the ground was then engineered into vast reservoirs underground for our use. However, we learned how to manufacture most of the air we breathe, the water that we drink, and the food that we eat. But our resources are low and we have to manage what we have.

Q: Did the Martian landscape contain more water in the past and what happened to it?

R: The same happened to the water, as happened to the atmosphere. Some was lost and some we were able to save.

Q: Do the Rall contribute to any wars?

R: No, the Rall do not contribute to any wars. We are one race and are harmonious in our dealings with each other. We understand that Humans war over resources but the Rall cooperate when resources are low.

Q: Do any disasters befall the Rall? When and what were they?

R: We have already covered that in our other answers. We still encounter disasters, when rocks fall underground or a well dries, or sickness comes but these are always happening and we deal with them.

Q: If Mars once had an atmosphere, what happened to it?

R: We have already answered this question before.

Q: How old is your race?

R: We do not know how old our race is. We think it is as old as our planet. Our memory stretches back for five to six generations of Rall and then becomes unreliable except for the major happenings. It is not important what happened more than six generations ago, what is important is what is happening now.

Q: Did the Rall evolve earlier or later than Humans?

R: We think that the Rall and Humans evolved about the same time and perhaps came from the same place or from another parent race. We do not know; information from that far back is unreliable.

Q: Which of the races that we have interviewed so far have been the most helpful to Humans? Which of these races has been helpful to the Rall?

R: We do not know what other races you have interviewed. We only know which races have been helpful to the Rall and there have been a few.

Q: Can you tell me which ones?

R: We do not have the same names as Humans use but they are ones that have technical craft and can come and go from our planet. They come for minerals. We have not yet met the Humans, although some say they have. We are not sure of this.

Q: How did the Rall continue to evolve on an arid planet?

R: There was no major decision to go underground but it did help us evolve. It may be arid on the surface but we have water underground. It is sufficient to help us live. There may be a day when we can live above the ground once again.

Q: There is some speculation that some races monitor Human's telecommunications including the Internet. Could some races actually communicate using the Internet or other resources?

R: This would not be the Rall as we only monitor ourselves. It must be some other race. We are sure that this could happen as some of the races have high technology.

Q: There is a group of scientists, loosely associated with NASA, which wants to make contact? What would you advise them to do to facilitate this contact?

R: We would advise them to disregard the written word and to rely on spoken word and mind-word.

Q: Our scientists rely much on written word for proof.

R: We do not need such proof, we know that we exist and we know that you exist, that is all the proof there is. We do not need written proof that we exist.

Q: What do the Rall think of the SETI initiative to identify signals from other races? Has SETI succeeded? If not what else can Humans do to initiate or receive contact from the other races?

R: We do not know about this but the other races do emit signals, including Humans, some of which we can interpret with our limited technology. Human signals are too bound up with the written word to be of use or helpful to the Rall.

Q: Our space agency NASA has reached as far as Saturn with an unmanned probe. Where else should Humans look for life and contact?

R: Everywhere. Life is everywhere in the Universe. It would be unusual not to find it, rather than be surprised to find it. Keep looking everywhere.

Q: We share the same Sun and the same cycles that this sun generates. Regarding the Sun's cycles, is there something that we should know about its cycles that might cause problems to Earth in the future? There is the possibility that around the year 2012 the Sun may cause some major changes for Earth. Can you give us any information about this?

R: Our memory only covers five to six Rall generations and does not have detailed information about the Sun's long-term cycles. Our judgment says that if you anticipate and perceive changes in the Sun's behavior, that heralds a disaster, then you should do something to protect yourselves. We are already protected under the ground. Will you tell us if you perceive anything that might affect us?

Q: Yes, we will.
R: Thank you.
Q: Thank you for reciprocating our gifts with your gift of a mind-word response.

20: Talking With The Anunnaki

In October, 2013, a new venture began dialogues with another ET race. These three sets of questions from NF, SJ, and NG (with clarification questions asked by ATS) are requested of a non-Human race called the Anunnaki. It is to be remembered that these interviews involve non-Human intelligence and much of it will not, necessarily, be understandable to our human logic or understanding. We cannot expect their logic to be the same as ours. It is akin to interviewing an indigenous race that has had restricted face-time with other humans. This is an atypical project that is carried out with diplomacy and respect.

Q: (NF) Greetings: are we correct in saluting you as our creators and parent species?
Anunnaki: Yes, you are correct.
Q: Are you part of the Federation?
Anunnaki: Welcome. We have always been part of the Federation even before it was the Federation. It was not always the Federation.
Q: What was it before it was the Federation?
Anunnaki: It was nothing, it was void, it was a collection of us. We became the Federation and we are the Federation.
Q: Some of the other races said that there are many different Federations (Confederations) in many different Galaxies? Is that so? Are you of the Federation of this Galaxy or other Galaxies?
Anunnaki: We are of all Federations and we are this Galaxy's Federation.
ATS: For clarification – other races can also be part of the Federation?
Anunnaki: Correct. We are the Federation and also part of the Federations.
Q: Are you accepted as a species in stellar society?
Anunnaki: A species implies something corporeal and living. We are living but non-corporeal but we can become corporeal for a task. So we are a species and not a species. Other races accept us when we are corporeal and when we are non-corporeal.
Stellar society implies something around a sun and society as having set norms and standards. We are of many suns and many societies and are accepted in all. This was not always so.
ATS: Can you tell me why this was so?

Anunnaki: We are not always in favor with the other species.
ATS: Why is this?
Anunnaki: NR
ATS: Why didn't the other races mention you in the Exobiology Interviews?
Anunnaki: The right questions were not asked of the other races.
ATS: Thank you. Please accept these questions as being asked with diplomacy in a search for understanding. Also, I am asking the questions on behalf of three other Humans. We only want to understand.
Q: Did you have difficulty getting accepted into stellar society because you created us as a species or, more specifically, as a slave species?
Anunnaki: We were not the only ones using this process. Humans misunderstand. Slaves have nothing in return. We gave much to Humans. Humans are our children. We worked together. We had no difficulty in being accepted by other races. There is a Human term: paternalism. In some societies it is a negative term, in ours it is a positive term. We did not birth Humans but created them. Humans use things they create and design. They have attachments to these things and look after them even if they are not perfect. We have noticed that Humans prefer imperfect things and value them. Humans are imperfect but strive for perfection. Humans are created as they are.
Q: Have you evolved or changed in some way that has allowed you to be accepted into stellar society?
Anunnaki: We are both part of and apart from stellar society. This is different than being accepted. We are accepted but not always part. All things evolve and change. We have evolved and changed, too but not according to Earth standards.
Think of a rock: it evolves and changes but stays much the same for thousands of years. It is the same with us; we evolve and change but stay much the same. Whether we evolve or change does not affect how we are seen by other races or stellar societies.
Q: How many alien species do you know and interact with?
Anunnaki: How many grains of sand on the beach: how many stars in the sky?
Q: Do you have a colony on Earth?
Anunnaki: Yes, always. We come and go. We do not always have many but there are always some. A colony implies a group: sometimes we are just one or two, not a colony. Sometimes we are more but never a colony. All groups are constantly changing.
Q: Are any of you resident here on planet Earth now?
Anunnaki: Of course, there are always Anunnaki on Earth. A colony implies a group that is new to an area and starting a new life in a new place. We

are not a colony. We have been here longer than Humans. Humans are the colonists. We are represented in every place on Earth. Resident implies being in one place for a long time. Sometimes we are on Earth for a shorter time: sometimes for a longer time but we stay for some time.

Q: Are you directing events in the world through selected government or other organizations and/or individuals?

Anunnaki: We know that we are influential to Human affairs. We do not direct, only guide as we see necessary. We do not select. Wherever we are, we assist and direct as we can. We do not choose.

Q: What is your position relative to humanity in general?

Anunnaki: There is a Human understanding of wise people and personify this as fictitious people with powers beyond being Human. That is how we are. We have powers beyond being Human. We are not above or apart from Humans: we are different.

Q: What humanoid species did you use to impinge your genes on to create our species?

Anunnaki: At the beginning there was an early humanoid race on Earth that we assisted. There is no "missing link" as Humans think. It was a gradual process. It would have been devastating to evolve Humans too fast and too soon. It did not happen all at once. We did not just use our genes but from many other non-Human races. Our genes alone would have devastated early Humans.

Q: What percentage of the human gene code is from you originally?

Anunnaki: Humans are an amalgam of many different non-Human races. Over time, the percentage of gene material from us has varied. There is very little now but enough to enable Humans to evolve. We cannot say that every Human has this much of our gene material in this percentage. There are some Humans with more and some with less.

Q: Are you involved in any kind of abductions, genetic sampling, crossbreeding with humans?

Anunnaki: We do not abduct Humans: Grays and others abduct Humans. To abduct implies to take without permission and to not treat with respect. The Anunnaki will ask before taking a Human and the Human has a choice. We treat Humans with respect unless there is a condition where we do not.

ATS: What does that mean: under what condition would the Anunnaki take Humans and not treat them with respect?

Anunnaki: NR

Q: Can you honestly guarantee and demonstrate to those humans who fear that you are returning to take over the planet Earth and dominate our species that your intentions and agenda are benevolent and positive and that contact and interaction will facilitate our independence and evolution?

Anunnaki: History speaks for itself: we have been visiting and living with Humans for multiples of thousands of years. If we were planning on taking over the world we would have done so. We glory and also despair in the evolution of Humans. We cannot guarantee anything. How can we demonstrate this? Humans have always feared us and will always fear us. Contact with us will always facilitate evolution in Humans.

Q: Would you name human individuals whom you have enlisted to assist you?

Anunnaki: NR

Q: What must we as a species do to create the conditions under which you will be satisfied that you can make safe and comfortable contact again?

Anunnaki: We make contact with Humans every day in every location. If we came in our original form Humans would again fear us and be threatened. We will never come again in our original form.

ATS: I had a dream the other night of the Anunnaki: ten or more feet tall, very large, like Viking Warriors. The dream creatures had helmets with horns but there was an understanding that these were not horns but technology. People were afraid and running from these creatures. I did not run but was prevented from seeing them by another species. Was this a true depiction of the original form of the Anunnaki?

Anunnaki: Yes, close to the original form.

Q: How essential is it that we reunite, reconcile, and resolve the relationship between our species before we begin to contact and interact with other advanced species?

Anunnaki: That is not necessary. All species, even what you call advanced species, are not resolved. Humans already have the capability to contact and interact with advanced species. Humans are as they are. Some will evolve, some will not. The evolved ones can contact and interact with other species. It is not essential to reunite, reconcile and resolve but some will.

Q: We wish to ask you about translations and interpretations by the scholar Zecharia Sitchin of the Sumerian records of your history on planet Earth. Are those writings very accurate and trustworthy?

Anunnaki: Just as modern Humans have historical writings that tell of earlier times, so the Sumerians had the same. Not all was correct but enough for Humans to learn about us. Humans have a word-of-mouth history and a written-history and both are not the same. There is some truth in both but many fallacies. Humans should not take the Sumerian writing as all of the truth about us. You can ask us what you need to know.

Q: Did you guide Zecharia in that process?

Anunnaki: We did not.

Q: Why not and what interpretation should be accepted as the truth?

Anunnaki: We did not learn about this until it was finished. It was read with compassion but also mirth by some of us. Not all was correct. Some was a misinterpretation of the truth as perceived by the Human mind. Some of the mistakes were the original Sumerian writers and some from the interpretation.

Q: As Sitchin has claimed, is Quetzalcoatl the Mayan name for Ningishida?

Anunnaki: Much has been changed through history. There was an original being called Ningishida. The name has changed over the centuries and there were multiple Quetzalcoatl. The original Ningishida was mostly Anunnaki: the multiple Quetzalcoatl had reducing proportions of Anunnaki. Because two entities are called by a similar-meaning name does not make them the same person.

Q: In teaching the Mayans that the calendar date of December, 2012 was going to be significant, did Ningishida intend it to mark the beginning of a new period in which you would reestablish full contact with us, the human species?

Anunnaki: No, there will never be full contact in our original form with Humans. We will continue our current contact and integration. There is no need for full contact. The Mayans had a true understanding but this has changed over the centuries. What was correct for the Mayans is not true for modern Humans.

Q: The person who formulated these questions for us --- who does not feel he has to be named --- says he has been cooperating with you since being enlisted by you at the age of ***** in ***** to help you "get introduced into the planet". Is he correct in saying that he wrote these questions directly under your guidance in a kind of automatic writing? Is that the truth?

Anunnaki: That is true. However, we are already introduced to the planet. What we requested then and what we are requesting now is that Humans recognize those who are here now and have contact with those of us who are not here now.

ATS: Am I communicating with an Anunnaki who is here on Earth now or one who is not currently here on Earth.

Anunnaki: You are communicating with a group of Anunnaki who are not currently on the Earth.

ATS: Thank you.

Q: Is this interview seen by you as a part of that process and has my part as interviewer and this interview process, in itself, been gradually brought about through your direct influence for that purpose of full species contact?

Anunnaki: It is so. Your role as interviewer is part of an ongoing and extended process. There will never be full species contact. Only some Anunnaki will interact with some Humans. This is how it has been and how it shall continue.

Q: (If not) then how should we understand what is happening here?

Anunnaki: This is the process by which we can interact at present. There are other ways to interact and these will be discovered.

Q: How do you intend the process of full contact between our species to unfold? Under what required conditions? According to what timeline? How best may we cooperate?

Anunnaki: We cannot speak for all of the Anunnaki. While we have unlimited communication on some things there are regional and personal communications on others. So, while we can speak for off-Earth groups, we cannot speak for the on-Earth groups. There has always been contact between the on-Earth groups and Humans; only Humans have not recognized it as such. Off-Earth groups have had limited contact with Humans. Contacts such as the current communication are rare. They are welcome and tolerated.

Further contact is up to Humans. If further contact, or contact in a more tangible form, are requested this could be discussed and formulated. The Anunnaki have never had a plan in place for full contact with all Humans. Limited contact with limited Humans can be formulated. There is no time-line.

Q: Is there a human group that you would prefer to represent the human species in the process of re-acquaintance or no group would be better?

Anunnaki: Individual contact is preferable for off-Earth contact: group contact with on-Earth Anunnaki has always been available.

Q: Is there a particular location where meetings could best take place such as the ancient sites in the former Mesopotamia?

Anunnaki: There are no preferred locations: Anunnaki are already present in on-Earth form in multiple locations. Physical meetings with off-Earth Anunnaki may not be possible. This would have to be discussed and formulated.

Q: Do you have special physical requirements to accommodate to current conditions on Earth that we may provide?

Anunnaki: On-Earth Anunnaki would need no special physical requirements: off-Earth Anunnaki would need some accommodations for meeting. This would have to be discussed and formulated.

Q: Are there advanced technologies that you would like to give us?

Anunnaki: NR

Q: Would you teach us how to remove obstacles and limitations such as short life spans that you imposed on us at the beginning?

Anunnaki: Humans already know how to extend their short life spans but mostly ignore this knowledge. We did not impose the short life spans; this was a consequence of the pattern of development of Humans. Humans cannot live as long as Anunnaki. Humans are already extending their life span. Having a longer life span is not always a positive thing.

Q: Is the information about monatomic gold as claimed and published by David Hudson and Sir Laurence Gardner true and accurate? Do you still ingest it?

Anunnaki: We ingest many minerals provided for us by other races. Monatomic gold and other mineral nutrients are essential to us. While we often operate in a non-physical body, electrolytic solutions are needed for our function.

Q: What is the position of Nibiru in its orbit now and when should it reach perigee? Will the next Passing be a milder or cataclysmic on for Earth?

Anunnaki: We do not call this Nibiru, we know of it, having seen its rotation many times. It is approaching perigee. It will bring change to the Earth but not cataclysm. Humans do not like change: Nibiru will bring change. Humans need to adapt to the changes. It will not reach perigee for several Earth years. It will be far enough away from Earth for its effects to be felt geologically but not devastation.

Q: Is your home planet Nibiru degrading in habitability or is it stable in that mode? Will you need gold from the Earth to maintain conditions of your planet?

Anunnaki: Nibiru is not our home planet. We are from many different regions. Nibiru has one part of our group inhabiting it. Nibiru should be greeted with excitement and a sense of discovery. We would be grateful for the gifts of gold, if offered. But we already obtain gold and other minerals from many other races and, indirectly, from Earth.

Q: Could you and would you be able to give us technologies that would solve the major crises and conflicts among humans currently?

Anunnaki: The current major crises and conflicts among humans do not need technology to resolve them. The conflicts and crises have arisen because of technology. The Anunnaki have technology that could solve the conflicts but these are extreme and would not be liked by most Humans.

Q: Do you do interstellar travel? Intergalactic travel?

Anunnaki: Off-Earth Anunnaki travel both by our own technology and with other races. It is both interstellar and intergalactic. We have done this for as long as we have existed.

Q: What technology do you employ for space/time travel?

Anunnaki: Travel depends on who we travel with and where we travel to. The technology is beyond current Human understanding.

ATS: Can you please try and explain. It might be beyond my understanding but there are Humans that might understand it.

Anunnaki: We will try and put this into an allegorical form for understanding. Imagine an Earth mollusk creeping on the ground. If the mollusk's time perception is speeded up, so will the mollusk. The mollusk's rate of speed will be proportional to its increased time perception. That is the closest we can come to an explanation.

ATS: We have only touched the surface here. May we communicate again soon?

Anunnaki: Yes, we are open to communication.

Anunnaki Questions (CBSJ)

Q: Do the Laws of the Federation restrict you from contact with and support of Earth and its citizens? Does the Spiritual Hierarchy expect this from you because of our previous ancient relationships?

Anunnaki: The Laws of the Federation do not restrict us from contact, support or communication with Earth and its citizens. The Laws restrict us from certain actions such as interfering with another race that is interacting with Earth. Humans are not the only citizens of Earth: they are co-inhabitants. There is an ancient relationship between the Anunnaki and Humans but Federation Laws supersede these.

Q: Do you believe that a global dialogue about the ancient history of ET/Earth contact and the impact of future contact is necessary? If yes, are you willing to play a significant role in supporting that dialogue?

Anunnaki: There is a great benefit of uncovering and discovering through dialog the history of Humans and non-Human races. Future contact and communication is considered to be important yet restricted. The Anunnaki role would be important but, again, restricted.

Q: Did you have any significant contact with the ancient cultures of what is now China?

Anunnaki: We have had contact with each civilization that has arisen throughout Earth's history. There has been a radius of contact from the beginning radiating, out from the lands of Human origin with significant contact, to the outer limits of the radius with minimal contact. All parts of Earth have had contact.

Q: Are you willing to communicate through this channel to answer questions from Heads of State and other senior government officials? The questions would include global politics and economy, and technologies that would serve humanity in such areas as energy, food production, environment, global warming, health, and life extension.

Anunnaki: All questions and communications would be welcome with the provision that the information does not conflict with other races currently visiting/sharing Earth's resources. The Anunnaki have an interest in facilitating Human development.

Q: Are you willing to assist colleges and universities in researching and writing White Papers on the opportunities and challenges following formal disclosure? If so, would that assistance be through this channel, other channels, in person, or all of these?

Anunnaki: The Anunnaki are eager to assist this channel and others as needed in the future. The same provisions remain as were outlined in the previous answer.

Q: What do you think about the Outer Space Security and Development Treaty?

Anunnaki: This Treaty is a step forward for safeguarding all who enter within the Earth's and Humans' zones. The races that share Earth resources already have in place protections and Humans need to realize that hostility from Humans may be met with hostility, thus making the Treaty of double importance.

Q: Were you involved in the use of weapons of mass destruction when on Earth? If so, when, where and why?

Anunnaki: Over time, we, the Anunnaki, had had recourse to such weapons. There is a large amount of pre-Human history that should not impact Humans, where such weapons were in use. There were turbulent times before Humans that necessitated such weapons. There were some races that were banned from Earth and others restricted. The Anunnaki do not have such weapons within Earth's zones at this time.

Q: Did you assist Zecharia Sitchin in his research? If so, in what ways?

Anunnaki: While the off-Earth Anunnaki did not assist Zecharia Sitchin, there were efforts made to correct some of his work by on-Earth Anunnaki who saw flaws in the work. Sitchin was not aware that these individuals were Anunnaki.

Questions for the Anunnaki – (NG)

General Questions

Q: Are the Anunnaki considered as one group of one species from one home planet?

Anunnaki: Generically, all are Anunnaki. Off-Earth and on-Earth Anunnaki are different in many ways. On-Earth Anunnaki are more organic. There is no home-planet.

Q: Are they complicit in human abductions? If so why?

Anunnaki: As mentioned before, Anunnaki do not abduct Humans. Please return to our original question for more information.

Q: Do the Anunnaki work with any species of the Grays?

Anunnaki: We, the Anunnaki, work with all races. On Earth we interact with all races that visit or co-inhabit the Earth with Humans. Anunnaki do not work with Grays on abductions.

Q: Have the Anunnaki made contact with any Governments of the world? If so which ones and what is the agenda?

Anunnaki: On-Earth Anunnaki are included in staffs and other functions of Human government at many levels. There is also communication between off-Earth Anunnaki and Governments that may shift behavior and actions, from time to time. There is no overt agenda to control government or its employees.

Physiology

Q: What are the average height and weight ranges of the Anunnaki?

Anunnaki: There are three answers to this question. Off-Earth Anunnaki have no defined physiological ranges: it depends on the place, time and function of the entity. Historically, on-Earth Anunnaki were very large, very powerful, very loud, sometimes aggressive when needed, and mainly masculine in appearance. Modern on-Earth Anunnaki are taller than average, very slim, very intelligent, involved in people-based occupations, forward thinkers, yet not in positions of great power.

Q: Is the skin color the same across your species?

Anunnaki: On-Earth Anunnaki blend in with the population it is working with. On-Earth Anunnaki are sometimes hybrids with greater than average Anunnaki constituents.

Q: In what way are the Anunnaki and Nordics biologically different?

Anunnaki: There are several ways that Anunnaki and Nordics differ:

Nordics rarely remain on Earth and, if they do, it is for very short periods, perhaps six months. Anunnaki can remain for long time-periods, sometimes years.

Nordics are mainly blond, have Scandinavian features and coloring. Anunnaki physically blend in with the general population.

Nordics are able to bi-locate into other bodies, when needed. Anunnaki cannot do this.

Nordics are able to communicate telepathically with each other and off-Earth Nordics. Anunnaki do not have the same range of abilities.

Q: Are the Anunnaki telepathic? If so is this technology assisted or has the ability for mind-to-mind communications evolved out of evolutionary processes?

Anunnaki: Anunnaki are telepathic: off-Earth Anunnaki are able to communicate with each other, with on-Earth Anunnaki, and other races. On-Earth Anunnaki not so strongly.

Politics

Q: Please explain the political military and social structures of your society

Anunnaki: These are not the same structures as are Earth-based.

Political: We are subject to Federation rules but also have autonomy in decision-making and activity.

Military: Each Anunnaki can make autonomous decisions about any offensive or defensive action but this is rarely used.

Social Structures: Egalitarian in form and function.

Q: Are there any imperatives associated with genetic manipulation of other intelligent life forms?

Anunnaki: Genetic manipulation is perceived as being of equal benefit to the donor and the recipient. Much like Earth-based practices of donating or receiving a body organ, we, the Anunnaki give our genetic material to others to both serve ourselves and to serve other races.

Q: Are there any planets that the Anunnaki rule over?

Anunnaki: The Anunnaki do not rule over planets. They genetically alter the inhabitants to make it easier to co-inhabit the planet. In doing so, the altered race is also improved.

Q: Do the Anunnaki feel any responsibility for their genetic manipulation of humanity and if so are they waiting for humans to reach a point in their development before official contact is reestablished?

Anunnaki: Anunnaki take full responsibility for the genetic alteration of Humanity. Contact has been ongoing for as long as Humans have been on the Earth. Contact with off-Earth Anunnaki has been sporadic but could be strengthened if needed.

Science & Technology

Q: Do they traverse the universe through wormhole technologies or is their deep space travel based on linear travel? How are your craft powered; what propulsion system?

Anunnaki: Please see the previous question about travel and technology.

Q: Do you use thought-activated technologies to navigate deep space?

Anunnaki: Same response.

Q: Is the use of reptilians or other species employed in operations associated with craft navigation?

Anunnaki: The Anunnaki do not cooperate with Reptilians: Reptilians mainly operate alongside Grays and Nordics.

Spirituality

Q: Are the Anunnaki embedded within the same reality as Earth Humans?

Anunnaki: NR

Q: Do the Anunnaki commune with a/their higher power?

Anunnaki: Anunnaki are egalitarian.

Q: In what ways do their spiritual beliefs manifest socially, politically and universally?

Anunnaki: There is no difference between spiritual beliefs, social, political or universal form or function.

Q: How do they reconcile their spirituality with their genetic interventions?

Anunnaki: Anunnaki and Humans do not share the same beliefs on this matter.

Q: Are the Anunnaki emotions in any way similar to those of humans?

Anunnaki: We, the Anunnaki have a wide range of emotions when we are on-Earth but do not need these when off-Earth. We are flexible in this regard.

Q: Is there a technologically derived afterlife [embedded in an android or other?] in any form or do they have knowledge of an afterlife and, if so, could this be elaborated on?

Anunnaki: Anunnaki do not have a concept, like Humans, for a continuation of life following physical ending. The Nordics transmigrate into another body, we just end. Before we end, we experience a lifetime that is many centuries that of Earth years.

ATS: We thank the Anunnaki for their thoughtful and educational answers. We plan to return to you again with respect and more questions.

Second Round of Questions from NF, CBSJ, NG

Questions for the Anunnaki - CBSJ

Q: We opened this communication by requesting a dialogue with the Anunnaki. You responded. Are you satisfied with us identifying you as the Anunnaki, or do you prefer another name?

Anunnaki: It does not matter. We have been known by many names throughout Earth history and Anunnaki is sufficient for this time. If you wish to call us something else that will be in order. We have a name for ourselves but it is in a language Humans would not comprehend. You can call us Anunnaki. It is satisfactory to us. We do not prefer anything else. There is a consensus among Humans using this name, we will use it.

Q: Will we be communicating with the same individual in these exchanges or will there be different spokespersons?

Anunnaki: If this communication is in one length, there will be one of us communicating but many others attending and commenting through the one. If it is in several lengths, there will be more than one of us communicating. We will tell you it this changes.

ATS: Are we communicating with the same Anunnaki that communicated with us in Round One and with NG's recent questions:

Anunnaki: No, each successive communication was with a different Anunnaki.

Q: Will you please tell us your name? These questions are from CBSJ. The contacting person is ATS.

Anunnaki: Welcome. You would not understand our name in our language and there is no real definition in your language. We do not have individual names: we are the Anunnaki.

ATS: How do you recognize each other and identify who is communicating?

Anunnaki: We read the signatures of that individual and know who they are.

Q: The first round of questions started without exchanging formal introductions. This Earth team is a small private group with no government affiliation. We are planetary citizens. We are slaves to no one. We aspire to be masters of knowledge to be used in service of all. To achieve this we require the following:

(a) Full understanding of the history of our ancient relationship with extraterrestrial cultures, particularly those who were involved with our creation and development;

Anunnaki: We will supplement and correct what is already known, that has been passed down in Human history. There is much that is incorrect. It is richer and more interesting than presently known. We do not know how to do this. Will it be through this level of communication?

ATS: Yes or something similar.

(b) Partnership with ET cultures that are most qualified and willing to answer questions about these ancient relationships;

Anunnaki: We will make introductions to races with knowledge that will assist.

Q: The first round of questions and responses from you has raised our expectations that this will be a fruitful undertaking for all parties. Specifically it appears to us that one important outcome will be to increase the odds for survival of humanity on Earth. The consequences of current levels of violence to each other, and to the natural resources of Earth must be viewed with concern by off-Earth and on-Earth Anunnaki who want Earth humanity to survive and to qualify for an invitation to formally join the Cosmic Community. Our team believes that we can work with you and reach agreements that will facilitate educating Earth's population about our ancient beginning and our future as a responsible member of the Cosmic Community. Do you agree with this? If so, we request you to consider the following action programs, and to comment with advice about how we can work together on them.

Anunnaki: We must first make it clear that we do not consider Human survival on Earth as one of our top priorities. Humans will survive or fail by their own accord. If Humans wish to survive we will assist them. We will consider the action programs and decide. If Humans have the aim of joining the Cosmic Community, we will assist. We also make it clear that not all will be eligible or succeed. The Anunnaki need to see balance among Humans, this makes it easier for us, but our survival does not rest on Human survival.

Q: I believe that the final question that Zecharia Sitchin asks at the end of his book: *The 12th Planet* is most important, and the answer will be critical to how Earth responds to the awakening of whom we really are and who you are. "And if the Nefilim (Anunnaki) were the 'gods' who 'created' Man on Earth.... (who) created the Nefilim?"

Anunnaki: Nobody created the Nefilim (Anunnaki), we also were and always will be. There is no story about our being created. We always have been. Humans like to see a beginning and an end and this is not always so.

Q: We look forward to an increasingly open and productive relationship with you. There is much important work to do together.

Anunnaki: We are in agreement.

Q: Are there very large craft positioned behind the Moon, If so, why and who is responsible for them?

Anunnaki: These are not unusual craft. Craft have been traveling to this moon for longer than Humans have been on the Earth. It is natural for them to be there. Humans could think of it as a haven or harbor. Humans become very excited when unusual events occur. This is unusual in that the craft were perceived in transit. There is nothing dangerous or threatening with the craft behind the moon.

ATS: Could you say this was business as usual?

Anunnaki: Yes.

ATS: Thank you.

Questions from NF

Q: What is the most essential condition the human species must meet for you to make public, definitive, constructive contact and interaction?

Anunnaki: On-Earth Anunnaki can be asked for contact and communication. There are no essential conditions. On-Earth Anunnaki have been communicating and interacting with Humans for a long time. It is more difficult for off-Earth Anunnaki to communicate and interact. It would have to be discussed and arranged but not impossible. We do not expect Humans to change.

Q: In our previous conversation you said that your usual state of being are as light beings and that you could take on a physical human form when you wished. I, we, wish to know the fundamentals of conscious, controlled evolution which prompts me to ask: Did you evolve through a physical human stage of being to the light being stage?

Anunnaki: The Anunnaki have never been Human. Anunnaki can change to a physical stage but we cannot share with you the process. We become Human in form when we need to be. It is similar in process to how an Earth chameleon changes color to match its surroundings. That is the closest we can come to Human understanding.

Q: Had you reached the light being stage before you colonized planet Earth and eventually created us genetically, purposely as a slave species? If so (only), that presents a startling puzzle to me: I assume that the trajectory of evolution of a humanoid species such as you or we is from a mix of primitive competition, violence, aggression, anger, affection, care of children, love. Further assumption is that reaching light being stage is an advanced stage totally beyond those relatively primitive elements. But the ancient records of your history on this planet speak of internecine conflict, heavy competition, violence, even killing and rape. If indeed you had reached the light being stage before that history played out, could you please explain the seeming deep paradox?

Anunnaki: Humans are a contradiction: they are a chaotic mix of primitive and new. The new is the chaotic part. Humans are still evolving although many Humans think they are now evolved. Humans are the least evolved of the inhabitants of Earth. Anunnaki are not immune from this chaotic mix. We have been involved in battles and other chaotic behavior and we are also still evolving. You cannot have the light without the dark.

Achieving light being stage is not an advanced stage, just a different stage. The physical form does not mask the interior form, it remains the same. Anunnaki are the same whether in light or physical form. It is hard to explain more.

Q: I, we, would deeply appreciate your going into detailed teaching about the precise trajectory of humanoid evolution inherent in the universe, how we can self-evolve into a greater and greater self-directed, controlled, consciously evolved state --- if indeed we are correct in assuming that concept is correct. We further assume that that evolutionary trajectory involves expanding dimensional perception and action and development of the paranormal powers. Please fine tune or correct those concepts if necessary.

Anunnaki: It is best to see a picture. A Human, in the beginning of the process was amorphous, a shadow of modern humans. There were many beginnings and many endings and new beginnings. It was not a smooth process from beginning to end. It has not yet ended. It is possible that what was started with current Humans may end, too, and a new beginning made, we do not know. Anunnaki set in place the process and allowed it to self-modulate over time. We are not in charge of the process. Nobody is in charge of the process. Humans cannot control the process. The process controls itself.

Q: How much or how little should we directly manipulate our genetics? Is there a limit or degree of alteration that must be respected to avoid damage?

Anunnaki: Humans should not interfere with the process. The process controls itself.

Team: Thank you for your concern and information.

Round Three – Questions for the Anunnaki – NF, CBSJ, NG
Preliminary Questions from CBSJ and NF

Q: We are entering an action phase, new ground for us. I am obviously unsure if this will be worth the effort, but we need to find out.

Anunnaki: There are some things that we can do: there are some things that Humans can do. Some of these overlap and this is the area in which we can work. It is good to be doubtful because there are things that the Anunnaki cannot do: there are things that Humans cannot do, and these, too, overlap. The Anunnaki can help in the areas where the things that we both can do overlap. That is what we need to find out. Do not be disappointed in the things that Humans and Anunnaki cannot do.

Third Round Main Questions for the Anunnaki
CBSJ

Q: Is it correct to assume that on-Earth Anunnaki are found in most countries of Earth, and that they would have the physical characteristics of citizens of these countries?

Anunnaki: There are on-Earth Anunnaki in every Earth country and yes. Also we refer to Earth as Terra.

ATS: I have an insight and a question. Up to this point I was assuming that I was communicating with off-Earth Anunnaki. Are you on-Earth Anunnaki or off-Earth Anunnaki?

Anunnaki: We are on-Earth Anunnaki.

ATS: Wow, thank you, this is exciting! Have we already met? Have I already met Anunnaki?

Anunnaki: We have not yet met. You have met on-Earth Anunnaki in your lifetime.

Q: Human words are simply utterances; we hope you are able to receive our deepest true intent over our determination to see this project through in order to free up Humanity and assist with the transformation to overt control of the planet by a new Human order capable of handling new technologies for the benefit of the whole.

Anunnaki: Yes, the intent, emotion and energy are perceived. New technologies do not always bring transformation. We agree that the benefit of the whole (Humans, Anunnaki, other races) is paramount. Intent is important and such should be decided before any meeting.

Q: We would like to know if your technologies would afford us with protection throughout this process and whether you would be happy to do so.

Anunnaki: On-Earth Anunnaki only use such protection for its own people and do not offer such protection for Humans.

Earth Team: We thank the Anunnaki for their support, communication, and understanding.

Chapter 9

In Conclusion

C. B. Scott Jones

In an early chapter in this book, the reader was introduced to the Outer Space Security and Development Treaty. Details were given about why Cosmic Cultures are parties to that treaty. Their inclusion is a first in the annals of known diplomatic legal history. You may remember that along with Cosmic Cultures, there was another party identified that in modern time is rarely seen in treaty law. That party is Indigenous Nations. They were specifically included because of their importance to a clearly understood purpose of this Treaty. Indigenous Nations provide a link between Earth and Cosmic Cultures. They also provide a cautionary story of what could happen in the future unless a mature dialogue takes place about expectations of world-wide meetings between Earth and the vastly technologically superior Cosmic Cultures.

It is obvious now that twenty-five years ago I was seeded with this thought in the first formal talk I gave on the UFO/ET subject. What follows is the ending of a presentation I gave at the Ninth UFO Contactee Conference in Laramie, Wyoming. This important conference series has been a needful gift from its founder Dr. Leo Sprinkle. This presentation was first published in the book: *Phoenix in the Labyrinth*. The title of the presentation is: UFO Phenomena: A Profound Learning Opportunity.

"I will end with a statement from a Native American tradition on the nature of gathered wisdom. It has been shared with me by a colleague, Turtle Woman Singing, whose Anglicized name is Paula Underwood Spencer. She is keeper of the Iroquois oral tradition. Please listen carefully. When Turtle Woman sings this, it comes out with great elegance because it is an oral history. It will not be as elegant coming from me. But I would like you to listen carefully because in this she addresses both the problems and the promise of Earthlings as well as the Visiting Others. This is on the nature of gathered wisdom.

No matter how large the circle, the sphere of understanding, it is never large enough until it encompasses the whole of the Universe. At that point you are Universe, and individuation disappears. Short of that, no person, no people, no nation, no planet no mere galaxy contains the wholeness of understanding. And such each individual person, nation, and planet is located around its own center, there is no exact concentricity with any other individuation.

Therefore, the understanding encompassed by any one person, nation, planet will not be simply more or less than any other individual. It will be different, overlapping perhaps, but never identical, never concentric. Given this awareness, we understand that much may be learned from everything. This is not merely a learning about, it is a learning from. Any individuation, person, nation, planet who closes their ears to wisdom from outside their own circle, their own sphere, fails in learning.

This is difficult enough to understand as between members of our group here on Earth, where consensus is a thing we must learn, or perhaps a thing we have forgotten. How much more difficult it must be for any people, who easily think together and who have long been doing so for thousands of years devoid of the acceptance of the wisdom of that which is external. The sphere of understanding begins to seem complete. Their small echo of Universe begins to seem the whole symphony.

So it is, I think, for the Visiting Others. Some completely limited to this thought. Some few not so limited, and so it is that I think they are here to learn from us, but most of them fail to perceive this possibility. If then, we only cooperated or only oppose what will be learned? Some steadfastness to our own nature, some confidence in the wisdom of that nature, some fuller demonstration of who we are: this may be learned from.

So let us remember the wisdom of our own way. The wisdom of every way. Each part of the whole. Let us welcome the learning, however inconvenient, and invite understanding. However rarely the invitation may be accepted, let us be indeed children of the broader Universe, brothers and sisters to all such children. Aware that we bring gifts, as well as to ask them, understanding, being the greatest gift of all."

Appendices

Telepathy

C. B. Scott Jones & Angela T. Smith

Once called "*thought transference*", *telepathy* has a long history of research, it is the paranormal ability most often recognized by conventional science, and the most robust of the paranormal abilities. The term telepathy was coined by the English writer F. W. Myers in 1882 as the "supposed communication between minds by some means other than the normal sensory channels." The term telepathy can be broken down into two parts: *tele (far) and pathein (to experience)*. Telepathy can include images, feelings, ideas, thoughts, and sensations. Telepathy rarely includes words, numbers or left brain analysis.

Telepathy most often refers to information shared between two or more people, other than through the normal means of communication. Related terms such as *clairvoyance and remote viewing* have different definitions. Clairvoyance refers to the perception of distant events by one or more people, rather than a mind-to-mind sharing of information. Remote viewing (RV) is the trained ability to perceive locations, objects, events, and individuals using something other than the known five senses. RV includes elements of both clairvoyance and telepathy. In fact, telepathy is considered to be a complicating factor in remote viewing and ESP experiments. However, it is very difficult to exclude telepathy from any interpersonal interaction.

Telepathy comes under the umbrella term *extrasensory perception* (often referred to as ESP or psi). Charles Tart describes ESP as the understanding that "people can sometimes acquire knowledge about things happening at a distance in space or time, or about other people's thoughts, when there is no possibility of this knowledge having been acquired through the known senses." Other countries also study telepathy, including the UK, China, India, and Russia.

In 1882, researcher Charles Richet first carried out tests of telepathy using playing cards and other researchers soon followed his lead. By 1934, Joseph Rhine at Duke University was carrying out research into telepathy using Zenner cards having special symbols: a square, circle, star, plus sign, and wavy lines.

Rhine collaborated with Behaviorist Prof. William McDougal. Rhine and published Extra Sensory Perception describing their results.

In 1962 Upton and Mary Craig Sinclair carried out a series of telepathy experiments in which they mentally sent and received pencil line drawings. With Mary as subject, Upton Sinclair transmitted simple drawings with good results. They published their results in their book Mental Radio in 1962. This book has since been republished by Hampton Roads Publishing Company.

Several different laboratories have conducted research to show that the human body can perceive telepathic information. That is, an individual's physical system can become activated upon telepathic reception of information from a partner. Researchers at the University of Washington's Conscious Science Laboratory, psi labs in Scotland, Germany, Rhine Research Center in Durham, North Carolina and IONS in CA have replicated this research.

Dean Radin, a researcher and author in the field of parapsychology has been Senior Scientist at the Institute of Noetic Sciences, in Petaluma, California, USA, since 2001. Radin, reporting on years of telepathy research, concluded that "after three decades of such tests, the overall observed hit rate is "astronomically beyond chance expectation.

Think about living and surviving in a telepathic universe. It may well be that the communication norm of the universe is telepathic. The interviews with extraterrestrial races suggest that the telepathic process has an embedded translation capability that NSA and other worldly intelligence agencies would pay big bucks for a smart civilian contractor to come up with. And there are other attributes of telepathy that should be noted. First of all it operates at the speed of thought. There aren't any published figures on how fast that is, but it certainly is faster than the speed of light. The CETI organization might take note of that. It would cut down on their equipment, energy and other expenses. It would also finally get them a rather robust signal, pages of them. Those telepathy attributes are on the plus side of the ledger. There is one, however, that will require some ethical and practical adjustments. If Earth ever qualifies to be formally invited to join the Cosmic Community, It will enter a domain where all thoughts are perceived. That will mean that cooperation rather than competition is the functional ethic in politics and business. Don't think for a minute that the Earth's controlling Corporate States don't recognize this and anguish over what will happen when the serfs of the world awaken from their controlled slumber.

Are there others using this psychological communication tool? Certainly, there are. For example the Mary Barr and Steve Reichmuth's team have recently published *Alien Voices*. This book presents a detailed dialogue with a Zeta Reticuli culture. The following two responses illustrate the potential power of telepathy as a transforming agent.

"The issue: My hope was that a species that has reached your level of knowledge would no longer need military means.

The response: In the network of life, most of our neighbors are aware of each other. We interact peaceable. The capability exists, but it is not needed. Nevertheless, should an unknown force come within our region that does not hold our values, we could collectively develop that capability. At our current level of understanding this need does not exist. The best we understand it, your term 'politics' is a unique human form of orchestrating selfishness. This originates from living on a planet of abundant, but still limited resources and space. We understand this concept from interacting with your world. Advanced intelligence life is connected telepathically within a larger community where understanding and plenty exists, making military forms of interaction unnecessary. (p. 73)

The questions: Does your species have faculties or aspects that would, if they were introduced into the genetics of man, eventually change the outcome of human progression? What might they be?

The response: I feel that our natural telepathic abilities would greatly change the human species. It would change many of the institutions, social structures, and methods in which the humans conduct themselves on this planet. There would be certain losses of individuality, but at the same time, there would be a number of positive things. Certain institutions might diminish or go away. It would entail a new understanding about humans themselves and the way that they look at each other. Whether their morals or values would change as a result is difficult to predict. When telepathy become possible in humans, it is hoped that a new personal threshold of understanding will emerge. The need for police and prisons would diminish or disappear. Communication would be on a level that would create interdependence and understanding to make these institutions less needed." (p. 127).

And so the cosmic dialog continues.

Remote Viewing

Angela T. Smith

The term remote viewing (RV) was coined in the mid-1970s, researched at Stanford Research Institute (SRI) International in Palo Alto, CA, and presented to the public in 1976 in a scientific, peer-reviewed IEEE journal.* Remote viewing is defined as the trained ability to perceive hidden information using something other than the known five senses.

A robust training protocol called Controlled Remote Viewing or CRV was developed by Mr. Ingo Swann for use by the United States military, and developed by U.S. intelligence agencies for research and applications work for 20 years.

Concurrently, The Princeton Engineering Anomalies Research (PEAR) Laboratory at Princeton University, NJ, and the Psychophysics Research Laboratory (PRL), also in NJ, both became the civilian counterparts to the military effort and carried out over 25 years of RV research. They researched a more spontaneous form of "stream of consciousness" remote viewing

In the early 1990s, retired military remote viewers began setting up schools to teach the Controlled Remote Viewing or CRV protocol to civilians and 20 years later there are hundreds of trained remote viewers carrying out humanitarian and paid RV applications work.

In 1999 the first remote viewing professional organization was formed: The International Remote Viewing Association (IRVA). IRVA hosts a yearly conference and supports remote viewing research and education. Dr. Smith was a founding member and director of IRVA.

From 1986 through 1992, I volunteered at PRL, and then worked as a member of staff at PEAR for 5 years. PEAR staff also participated as research subjects and my results were consistently at significant levels.

From 1991 through 2001, graduate-level research work was carried out that replicated the PEAR Random Number Generator (RNG) studies and was presented towards my Ph.D. in Psychology in 2001 from Saybrook University, CA.

Prior to my PEAR employment and onwards, I participated in multiple research projects and in the mid-1990s took remote viewing training with two of the ex-military remote viewing schools: with Paul Smith of Remote Viewing Instructional Services, and Lyn Buchanan of P.S.I.

From the mid 1990s until now I have participated in a wide range of humanitarian, research and paid remote viewing work. Several of my clients have been long-term (16 years, 9 years, and 6 years). One 9-year business client estimated that remote viewing data added an additional 2% to his multi-million-dollar bottom line. During our business collaboration, our group predicted the 2008 decline in the economy and remote viewing assisted a client in selling his business during a difficult financial climate.

*Puthoff, H.E., & Targ, R. (1976). A perceptual channel for information transfer over kilometer distances.: Historical perspective and recent research. Proceedings of the IEEE, 64, 329-354

The Abduction Dilemma

C. B. Scott Jones

This appendix will be the most important discussion in the book for many readers who follow the field of extraterrestrial contact. Some of the pioneer researchers in this field focused on reports of personal contact with ETs that involved individuals being taken aboard ET craft, subjected to a variety of medical-like procedures and returned to where they were taken. These memories were most frequently recovered in hypnotic regression sessions. If you have reached this point in the book after reading the entire book, you know that these events were discussed in many of the ET interviews and dialogues. The personal encounters were miss-labeled by researchers as abductions, and that label has stuck. The legal definition of abduction is:

The act of restraining another through the use or threat of Deadly Force or through fraudulent persuasion. The requisite restraint generally requires that the abductor intend to prevent the liberation of the abductee.

A "taking and returning" event is certainly more accurate than abduction, but that old label will probably remain forever. But the taking and returning was just the process. What happened aboard the ET craft to each person, and why, is what is important.

First of all, the Small Grays deserve to be given a pass. They are just doing their job, and have been doing it for eons. After World War II a small number of German and Japanese Generals and Admirals were indicted and convicted of crimes. If the Allies had lost the war they would have received the same treatment. The point is that no privates or seamen were put on trial. Before we spend any time looking for a high ranking cosmic general or admiral to charge with a crime, let's remember why the medical-like procedures took place aboard the ET craft. The procedures were part of a program to create the Indigo Hybrid from Human, Gray and Nordic genetic material. This program has been going on for thousands of years and the Indigo Hybrids are travelers throughout the universe. The humans who were taken and returned have contributed to a program authorized by someone or some group with a high pay grade.

We suggest that some thoughtful recalibration is needed when we consider the cosmic cost/benefits of what happens aboard ET crafts when human are taken, sampled and returned. Most certainly the recalled memories of the medical-like procedures can be stressful, and by most earth legal systems there is a violation because permission was not asked nor permission consciously given.

Without diminishing the importance of the personal violations involved, there is a much more important issue to surface. The "abduction dilemma" has provided a false foundation for a claim that the ETs present a threat to Earth.

Taxpayers watch your pocketbooks! The Corporate State will spring this canard with equally bogus evidence to support a false flag event. It could look spooky, but it will be homegrown.

E. T. Humor With Meaning

Out in space two alien life forms are talking.

The first alien says, “The dominant life forms on the earth planet have developed satellite-based weapons.”

The second alien, who looks exactly like the first, asks, “Are they an emerging intelligence?”

The first alien says. “I don’t think so. They have aimed at themselves.”

Post Script

The Nature of Disclosure and How It Will Happen

In the previous 200 plus pages the subject of disclosure of the reality of Earth and Extraterrestrial contact had been a major theme. The subject of disclosure is one of the most active and controversial issues in the global exopolitics community. Evidence supporting the reality of contact is a spectrum of views, opinions, expert testimony, speculation (some reasonable, some not so), and some carefully created to confuse and mislead. The core material of this book, the interviews with more than a dozen unique ET races, and dialogue with them is evidence that should be seriously considered. The authors put it in a category of weighted evidence that disclosure has already taken place, and the reader may recall that the dialogue we had with the on-Earth Anunnaki began to focus on what we can do together in service of Earth and the Cosmic Community. We identified a small number of projects that we believe would be important to both groups. Their responses were guardedly positive. Greater understanding of each other and trust building are essential issues that will precede agreements for joint ventures.

Frequently in the interviews and dialogue presented in chapter 8, the ETs made the point strongly that they were on Earth long before the human race developed here. The on-Earth Anunnaki announced that they work and walk among us. That would seem to transform the issue of "contact" to one of acknowledging contact. Smith and Jones have held this view for many years, and the following is a scenario that the reader may want to consider if they are interested in reaching a personal opinion about acknowledging contact. While that step is important, the real challenge is thinking about what the global impact will be of confirmed contact.

There are major and minor players in this game, and qualitative differences in evidence to support acceptance of contact. An important semantic issue is the frequent use of UFO as if it is synonymous with an extraterrestrial craft. As a reminder, UFO means Unidentified Flying Object. As long as it is unidentified and flying, that covers everything from butterflies to awesome creations such as those seen on TV and the silver screen.

Major Players: Countries with technical capabilities to detect and discern flying objects; countries and corporations with space satellites with a variety of sensing capabilities; countries with nuclear weapons and nuclear power plants; the United States for the previous reasons and for unknown reasons the ETs have selected for special attention; select U.S. corporations chosen to engineer craft based upon ET assistance.

Important Players: Private citizens in Italy, and in a number of South American countries, and increasingly in additional countries where unheralded private contact is taking place, and global citizens who have received ET information and acted upon it in a positive way without necessarily recognizing its source; and Indigenous Cultures.

Quality of evidence: Formal announcement by a Head of State. While this is unlikely to happen, confirmation of other high quality information likely will. An obviously deliberate demonstration by ET sources. This is most unlikely to happen. A statement from a recognized professional with a position that gives that person a need to know about what is revealed. This is the first high quality level of evidence that has happened and important to anticipate in the future. The one prime example of this took place over twenty years ago in 1993 when Ben Rich, former Head of the Lockheed Skunk Works in an Alumni Speech at UCLA said: "We already have the means to travel among the stars, but these technologies are locked up in black projects and it would take an Act of God to ever get them out to benefit humanity...Anything you can imagine, we already know how to do." Whether the Rich statement was authorized is unknown, but this brilliant and respected engineer was certainly in a position to know what he claimed.

The Disclosure Squeeze. A key question is who is the gate-keeper on disclosure? ET sources tell us that Earth is not ready for revelation of formal proof of ET/Earth contact, and that such action should be preceded by a rich dialogue on the likely political, economic, religious, and other consequences of disclosure. This book is a modest and sincere effort to promote such a dialogue.

As unsettling as it is, we have concluded some time ago that the gate keepers of this issue are the financial forces that have garnered tremendous power and profit from well-known businesses and technologies, some of which may have an extraterrestrial link, but most do not. Because one of the most significant cash-cows in this line up are carbon-based energy sources, it would be unprofitable to acknowledge to any degree the possibility of energy technologies that could totally and more than effectively replace them.

We will spare the reader the utopian paragraph that details the glories of "free" non-polluting energy that could rapidly be made available to every global village, and what that would mean to the global political and economic web (it would crash). In place of that paragraph we will just repeat what the ETs have told us for years, the world is not ready for disclosure because the reality shockwave would change the orbits of everything that keeps us together.

However, and this is a huge "however," nature always has the last "at bat." The simple reality is that nature rules. Another important reality is that the top one-percent money-makers and holders didn't get there on luck alone. They are very successful, very smart dreamers and schemers, and know very well about ET technologies.

The disclosure squeeze is on the top one-percent. The reader many have a variety of labels for them, but they are not suicidal, and are survivors. They will open the disclosure gate, reinvent a global energy web that cannot now be described, but will provide solutions to health, food and water issues. The one thing that technology will not directly address is world population. The spotlight will be on world religious leaders and what they learn from disclosure that can address that issue.

When will this fully start? That decision is up to the financiers that have used their knowledge and resources to gain and maintain their power. They will make their complex moves when forced to by conditions of Nature they cannot control.

The beginning roll out very likely has been underway for some time, and the game plan is to confirm disclosure rather than to announce disclosure. The psychological difference is important. It is being confirmed by controlled leaking of the reality that the U.S. has a space travel capability that Hollywood has found to be so profitable to market. That puts us in the league (albeit the minor league) with the ETs, and of course we were "given" this capability by the ETs. That identifies the ETs for what they really are, concerned and cooperative. That takes the "threat spin" of disclosure off the table, saves the tax payer money and gives the U.S. Air Force missions they really can be proud of: shepherds of a weapon-free space, and pathfinders of deep space travel.

A very recent report sponsored by NASA's Goddard Space Flight Center sends a warning flare that would be highly hazardous to ignore. This research project is based upon a cross-disciplinary 'Human And Nature Dynamical (HANDY) model. The conclusion is that global industrial civilization could collapse in coming decades due to unsustainable resource exploitation and increasing unequal wealth distribution. Based upon historical record, while the Roman Empire, the advanced Han, Mauryan and Gupta (India) Empires and others, were advanced, sophisticated, complex, and creative civilizations, they became fragile, impermanent and vulnerable because of the interrelated factors of population, climate, water, agriculture and energy. This research speaks directly to modern elites who have an option that elites of previously civilization which failed, either did not have or failed to recognize. Energy is the key to all business and survival. When you make a fundamental change in energy cost and availability, new doors will quickly open for innovation in all sectors of life. If the current financial elite will allow a reasonable distribution of the fruits flowing from a new global energy bonanza, a transformed Earth civilization becomes possible.

We end with a personal request for a member of a most elite U.S. community, only four are alive. President Bill Clinton: You have clearly identified your strong personal interest in extraterrestrial phenomena. We have a proposition of considerable importance. One ET group has assisted us in drafting the Outer Space Security and Development Treaty. This Treaty will ban all space-based weapons. Our principal task now is to present it to Heads of States to get the treaty signed into international and space law. In exchange for your assistance in meeting with global Heads of States, we will share information with you about ET activity that you would not have learned in any official classified briefing. If you are interested, please give us a call.

A Sequel to *Voices from the Cosmos*...

Faces of the Cosmos

C. B. Scott Jones & Angela T. Smith

Scott has written in *Voices from the Cosmos* "There is a huge problem with anthropomorphizing the ET races, when they are very different from us. However, until we have a Universal Decoder Ring, or meet them face-to-face, this is the best we can do." Two popular assumptions about the ET races are that they are either very like us or very unlike us! Perhaps the reality is somewhere in the middle.

What would it be like to meet someone from an ET race? Perhaps one who had been here on Earth for some time and had been interacting with Humans, undetected and concealed in plain sight? Without trivializing or rejecting the face-to-face experiences of people who have been taken and returned by the Grays, there are countless anecdotes of Humans meeting and interacting with ET races, right here on Earth. The current political climate of labeling these meetings as symptoms of mental illness, misinterpreted normal events, or outright fraud, causes them to be kept hidden, rationalized, and even denied.

There is a Biblical quote (Hebrews 13:2) "Be not forgetful to entertain strangers: for thereby some have entertained angels unawares." Just who are these angels? How often do we meet individuals in modern life, who might be very different from us but living among us as humans?

In the Exobiology Interviews we met Earth-resident ET races such as the Nordics, Hybrids, Annunaki, Duvel, and others. They say they were "here before us and will be here after us": indicating that they have been on Earth for a very long time. It is quite possible that we have all encountered them in daily life without even realizing!

Why are they here? They say they are here to learn and understand Humans. Some are only here for short periods, some are born and die here, and others quickly come and go. They say they are not here to invade us, or heal us, or resolve our myriad problems but they can assist if asked. They add that they welcome communication and will physically visit with Humans, if asked.

History is full of stories of Human/ET contact: these anecdotal accounts will be described and examined in *Faces of the Cosmos*, as well as many modern encounters. The main focus of the book will be a description of current attempts, from 2000 onwards, by the authors and others to directly communicate and interact with On-Earth ETs: a complex and unusual task. Naturally, to protect the authors and the ETs, not all details of the encounters will be shared: the ETs have put in place elaborate protections and safety precautions to shield their identities. What is exciting is that we will eventually be able to acknowledge and meet our cosmic neighbors on our own turf. There will be opportunities to interact, plan, and venture with our neighbors in a new future for Humankind!

Index

C. B. SCOTT JONES, Ph.D.

C. B. Scott Jones, Ph.D., is an octogenarian in full karmic payback mode. Thirty-years in the military, half in combat arms and half in intelligence, with high marks in both areas, created an aura of mixed hues. His current rehabilitating work in progress has included teaching international relations at three major universities, six years on Capitol Hill (which ledger does that go in?) as Special Assistant to the Chairman of the Senate Foreign Relations Committee, and currently in his twenty-sixth year of global peace work. The stint on Capitol Hill was the door opener to reality. Visits to research facilities in both the old Soviet Union and China established that they knew that some UFOs were extraterrestrial in origin, and worried that others came from the U.S. This personal disclosure reframed the strategy and hope for global peace, and you are at the right place to get on that journey. As philosopher Jerry Reed sings: "We've got a long way to go and a short time to get there." For those who wonder if Scott is human or not, additional details are in his website: www.peaceroom.com.

ANGELA THOMPSON SMITH, Ph.D.

Dr. Angela Thompson Smith's primary qualifications were in nursing and social work and she worked as a registered nurse and social worker in the UK. She also served a two-year volunteer term working at a Colombian orphanage in South America. Returning to England, she gained her B.S. in Psychology at the University of Wales, in Cardiff, an M.S. at the Faculty of Medicine of Manchester University, England, and later, in the U.S., her Ph.D. in Psychology at Saybrook University, CA.

She describes her life as taking place in three parts: the first part dealt with the Physical: working as a nurse, social worker, and medical researcher in the U.K. and the U.S.; the second part of her life focused on the Mind: when she worked at the PEAR Lab at Princeton University and studied psychology at Saybrook Graduate School; and the third part of her life has focused on Spirit: after decades of study and experience Dr. Smith was recently ordained as a shamanic practitioner.

In the U.S., Dr. Smith has worked as a medical researcher, research coordinator, as a trainer for the University of Nevada, and has worked extensively as a research contractor for individuals, businesses, and organizations around the United States and abroad. She trained as a remote viewer with two of the ex-military remote viewers, and was a founding member and director of the International Remote Viewing Association (IRVA). Dr. Smith has trained hundreds of individuals in remote viewing and other disciplines, as well as being a published author and researcher. Her website can be found at http://www.mindwiseconsulting.com.